THE HOME UNIVERSITY LIBRARY
OF MODERN KNOWLEDGE

27

MODERN
ENGLISH LITERATURE
1450–1959

Modern
English Literature

1450–1959

G. H. MAIR

With additional chapters by
A. C. WARD

Third Edition

LONDON

OXFORD UNIVERSITY PRESS

NEW YORK   TORONTO

Oxford University Press, Amen House, London E.C.4

GLASGOW NEW YORK TORONTO MELBOURNE WELLINGTON
BOMBAY CALCUTTA MADRAS KARACHI KUALA LUMPUR
CAPE TOWN IBADAN NAIROBI ACCRA

First edition 1911
Reprinted (revised) 1914, 1916, 1917, 1918, 1921, 1923, 1924, 1925, 1927,
1929, 1931, 1934, and 1939
Second edition (revised and enlarged) 1944
Reprinted 1944, 1945, 1948, and 1951
Third edition 1960 and reprinted 1961

MC-27

PRINTED IN GREAT BRITAIN

PREFACE TO THIRD EDITION

THE Epilogue I wrote for this book in 1944 appears, with some modifications, as Chapter XI in the present edition, and I have added a further chapter.

Mair's text rightly stands unchanged.

A. C. W.

1960

PREFACE TO SECOND EDITION

I FIRST made the acquaintance of this book (then a shilling flat-backed volume in green and gold) on the day it was published in October 1911. It was exactly the right kind of guide for a young student eager to find his way through the maze of modern literature, for G. H. Mair's style has a friendly intimacy which at once inspires confidence in his liberal and humane outlook and makes the reader receptive to his informative, sane, and stimulating commentary. I have turned back to his pages at intervals during the past thirty years, never without a renewed sense of gratitude and never without wonder that in so brief a compass so much ground could have been covered and so much said that was worth saying. Still more remarkably, in view of the strict limitation of length, the author wrote easily and spaciously, with no suggestion of being cramped or hurried: to read him is to feel that one is given liberty of movement within a capacious mind and made free not of inanimate books but of a living library.

The fact that it has been so often reprinted is evidence that Mair's book is still very much alive, and I trust that the Epilogue[1] (on later writers) added to this edition is in harmony with the rest.

While revising the original text I have not interfered with the opinions expressed. Apart from the correction of typographical errors and some amendment of punctuation, my changes do not go beyond factual ones made necessary by the passage of time and the deaths of authors who were living when the book was written.

1944   A. C. W.

[1] Now Chapter XI

PREFACE TO FIRST EDITION

THE intention of this book is to lay stress on ideas and tendencies that have to be understood and appreciated, rather than on facts that have to be learned by heart. Many authors are not mentioned and others receive scanty treatment, because of the necessities of this method of approach. The book aims at dealing with the matter of authors more than with their lives; consequently it contains few dates. All that the reader need require to help him have been included in a short chronological table at the end.

To have attempted a severely ordered and analytic treatment of the subject would have been, for the author at least, impossible within the limits imposed, and, in any case, would have been foreign to the purpose indicated by the editors of the Home University Library. The book pretends no more than to be a general introduction to a very great subject, and it will have fulfilled all that is intended for it if it stimulates those who read it to set about reading for themselves the books of which it treats.

Its debts are many, its chief creditors two teachers, Professor Grierson at Aberdeen University and Sir Walter Raleigh at Oxford, to the stimulation of whose books and teaching my pleasure in English literature and any understanding I have of it are due. To them and to the other writers (chief of them Professor Herford) whose ideas I have wittingly or unwittingly incorporated in it, as well as to the kindness and patience of Professor Gilbert Murray, I wish here to express my indebtedness.

G. H. M.

MANCHESTER
August 1911

CONTENTS

By A. C. WARD

CHAPTER I

THE RENAISSANCE

(1)

THERE are times in every man's experience when some sudden widening of the boundaries of his knowledge, some vision of hitherto untried and unrealized possibilities, has come and seemed to bring with it new life and the inspiration of fresh and splendid endeavour. It may be some great book read for the first time not as a book, but as a revelation; it may be the first realization of the extent and moment of what physical science has to teach us; it may be, like Carlyle's 'Everlasting Yea', an ethical illumination, or spiritual like Augustine's or John Wesley's. But whatever it is, it brings with it new eyes, new powers of comprehension, and seems to reveal a treasury of latent and unsuspected talents in the mind and heart. The history of mankind has its parallels to these moments of illumination in the life of the individual. There are times when the boundaries of human experience, always narrow, and fluctuating but little between age and age, suddenly widen themselves, and the spirit of man leaps forward to possess and explore its new domain. These are the great ages of the world. They could be counted, perhaps, on one hand. The age of Pericles in Athens; the less defined age when Europe passed, spiritually and artistically, from what we call the Dark to what we call the Middle Ages; the Renaissance; the period of the French Revolution. Two of them, so far as English literature is concerned, fall within the compass of this book, and it is with one of them—the Renaissance—that it begins.

It is as difficult to find a comprehensive formula for

what the Renaissance meant as to tie it down to a date.
The year 1453 A.D., when the Eastern Empire—the last
relic of the continuous spirit of Rome—fell before the
Turks, used to be given as the date, and perhaps the
word 'Renaissance' itself—'a new birth'—is as much as
can be accomplished shortly by way of definition.
Michelet's resonant 'discovery by mankind of himself
and of the world' rather expresses what a man of the
Renaissance himself must have thought it, than what
we in this age can declare it to be. But both endeavours
to date and to define are alike impossible. One cannot
fix a term to day or night, and the theory of the Renaissance as a kind of tropical dawn—a sudden passage to
light from darkness—is not to be considered. The
Renaissance was, and was the result of, a numerous and
various series of events which followed and accompanied one another from the fourteenth to the beginning of the sixteenth centuries. First and most
immediate in its influence on art and literature and
thought, was the rediscovery of the ancient literatures.
In the Middle Ages knowledge of Greek and Latin
literatures had withdrawn itself into monasteries, and
there narrowed till of secular Latin writing scarcely
any knowledge remained save of Vergil (because of his
supposed Messianic prophecy) and Statius; and of
Greek, except Aristotle, none at all. What had been
lost in the Western Empire, however, subsisted in the
East, and the continual advance of the Turk on the
territories of the Emperors of Constantinople drove
westward to the shelter of Italy and the Church, and to
the patronage of the Medicis, a crowd of scholars who
brought with them their manuscripts of Homer and the
dramatists, of Thucydides and Herodotus, and, most
momentous perhaps for the age to come, of Plato and
Demosthenes and of the New Testament in its original

Greek. The quick and vivid intellect of Italy, which had been torpid in the decadence of mediævalism and its mysticism and piety, seized with avidity the revelation of the classical world which the scholars and their manuscripts brought. Human life, which the mediæval Church had taught them to regard but as a threshold and stepping-stone to eternity, acquired suddenly a new momentousness and value; the promises of the Church paled like its lamps at sunrise; and a new paganism, which had Plato for its high priest, and Demosthenes and Pericles for its archetypes and examples, ran like wild-fire through Italy. The Greek spirit seized on art, and produced Raphael, Leonardo, and Michelangelo; on literature and philosophy and gave us Pico della Mirandola: on life and gave us the Medicis and Castiglione and Machiavelli. Then—the invention not of Italy but of Germany—came the art of printing, and made this revival of Greek literature quickly portable into other lands.

Even more momentous was the new knowledge the age brought of the physical world. The brilliant conjectures of Copernicus paved the way for Galileo, and the warped and narrow cosmology which conceived the earth as the centre of the universe, suffered a blow that in shaking it shook also religion. And while the conjectures of the men of science were adding regions undreamt of to the physical universe, the discoverers were enlarging the territories of the earth itself. The Portuguese, with the aid of sailors trained in the great Mediterranean ports of Genoa and Venice, pushed the track of exploration down the western coast of Africa; the Cape was circumnavigated by Vasco da Gama, and India reached for the first time by Western men by way of the sea. Columbus reached Trinidad and discovered the 'New' World; his successors pushed past him and touched the Continent. Spanish colonies grew up along the coasts of North and Central America and in Peru, and the Portuguese reached Brazil. Cabot and the English voyagers reached Newfoundland and Labrador; the French made their way up the St. Lawrence. The discovery of the gold mines brought new and unimagined possibilities of wealth to the Old World, while the imagination of Europe, bounded since the beginning of recorded time by the Western ocean, and with the Mediterranean as its centre, shot out to the romance and mystery of untried seas.

It is difficult for us in these later days to conceive the profound and stirring influence of such an alteration on thought and literature. To men at the end of the fifteenth century scarcely a year but brought another bit of received and recognized thinking to the scrapheap; scarcely a year but some new discovery found itself surpassed and in its turn discarded, or lessened in significance by something still more new. Columbus sailed westward to find a new sea route, and as he imagined, a more expeditious one to 'the Indies'; the name West Indies still survives to show the theory on which the early discoverers worked. The rapidity with which knowledge widened can be gathered by a comparison of the maps of the day. In the earlier of them the mythical Brazil, a relic perhaps of the lost Atlantis, lay a regularly and mystically blue island off the west coast of Ireland; then the Azores were discovered and the name fastened on to one of the islands of that archipelago. Then Amerigo reached South America and the name became finally fixed to the country that we know. There is nothing nowadays that can give us a parallel to the stirring and exaltation of the imagination which intoxicated the men of the

Renaissance, and gave a new birth to thought and art. The great scientific discoveries of the nineteenth century came to men more prepared for the shock of new surprises, and they carried evidence less tangible and indisputable to the senses. Perhaps if the strivings of science should succeed in proving as evident and comprehensible the existences which spiritualist and psychical research is striving to establish, we should know the thrill that the great twin discoverers, Copernicus and Columbus, brought to Europe.

(2)

This rough sketch of the Renaissance has been set down because it is only by realizing the period in its largest and broadest sense that we can understand the beginnings of our own modern literature. The Renaissance reached England late. By the time that the impulse was at its height with Spenser and Shakespeare, it had died out in Italy; and in France, to which in its turn Italy had passed the torch, it was already a waning fire. When it came to England it came in a special form shaped by political and social conditions, and by the accidents of temperament and inclination in the men who began the movement. But the essence of the inspiration remained the same as it had been on the Continent, and the twin threads of its two main impulses, the impulse from the study of the classics, and the impulse given to men's minds by the voyages of discovery, runs through all the texture of our Renaissance literature.

Literature as it developed in the reign of Elizabeth ran counter to the hopes and desires of the men who began the movement; the common usage which extends the term Elizabethan backwards outside the limits of the reign itself, has nothing but its carelessness to recommend it. The men of the early Renaissance in the reigns of Edward VI and Mary, belonged to a graver school than their successors. They were no splendid courtiers, nor daring and hardy adventurers, still less swashbucklers, exquisites, or literary dandies. Their names—Sir John Cheke, Roger Ascham, Nicholas Udall, Thomas Wilson, Walter Haddon, belong rather to the universities and to the coteries of learning than to the court. To the nobility, from whose essays and *belles lettres* Elizabethan poetry was to develop, they stood in the relation of tutors rather than of companions, suspecting the extravagances of their pupils rather than sympathizing with their ideals. They were a band of serious and dignified scholars, men preoccupied with morality and good-citizenship, and holding those as worth more than the lighter interests of learning and style. It is perhaps characteristic of the English temper that the revival of the classical tongues, which in Italy made for paganism and the pursuit of pleasure in life and art, in England brought with it in the first place a new seriousness and gravity of life, and in religion the Reformation. But in a way the scholars fought against tendencies in their age, which were both too fast and too strong for them. At a time when young men were writing poetry modelled on the delicate and extravagant verse of Italy, were reading Italian novels, and affecting Italian fashions in speech and dress, they were fighting for sound education, for good classical scholarship, for the purity of native English, and behind all these for the native strength and worth of the English character, which they felt to be endangered by orgies of reckless assimilation from abroad. The revival of the classics at Oxford and Cambridge could not produce an Erasmus

or a Scaliger; we have no fine critical scholarship of
this age to put beside that of Holland or France. Sir
John Cheke and his followers felt they had a public
and national duty to perform, and their knowledge of
the classics only served them for examples of high
living and morality, on which education, in its sense of
the formation of character, could be based.

The literary influence of the revival of letters in
England, apart from its moral influence, took two
contradictory and opposing forms. In the curricula
of schools, logic, which in the Middle Ages had been
the groundwork of thought and letters, gave place to
rhetoric. The reading of the ancients awakened new
delight in the melody and beauty of language: men
became intoxicated with words. The practice of
rhetoric was universal and it quickly coloured all
literature. It was the habit of the rhetoricians to choose
some subject for declamation and round it to encourage
their pupils to set embellishments and decorations,
which commonly proceeded rather from a delight in
language for language's sake, than from any effect in
enforcing an argument. Their models for these exercises can be traced in their influence on later writers.
One of the most popular of them, Erasmus's *Discourse
Persuading a Young Man to Marriage*, which was
translated in an English text-book of rhetoric, reminds
one of the first part of Shakespeare's sonnets. The
literary affectation called euphuism was directly based
on the precepts of the handbooks on rhetoric; its
author, John Lyly, only elaborated and made more
precise tricks of phrase and writing which had been
used as exercises in the schools of his youth. The prose
of his school, with its fantastic delight in exuberance of
figure and sound, owed its inspiration in its form
ultimately to Cicero, and in the decorations with which

it was embellished to the elder Pliny and later writers of his kind. The long declamatory speeches and the sententiousness of the early drama were directly modelled on Seneca, through whom was faintly reflected the tragedy of Greece, unknown directly or almost unknown to English readers. Latinism, like every new craze, became a passion and ran through the less intelligent kinds of writing in a wild excess. Not much of the literature of this time remains in common knowledge, and for examples of these affectations one must turn over the black-letter pages of forgotten books. There, highsounding and familiar words are handled and bandied about with delight, and you can see in volume after volume these minor and forgotten authors gloating over the new found treasure which placed them in their time in the van of literary success. That they are obsolete now, and indeed were obsolete before they were dead, is a warning to authors who intend similar extravagances. Strangeness and exoticism are not lasting wares. By the time of *Love's Labour's Lost* they had become nothing more than matter for laughter, and it is only through their reflection and distortion in Shakespeare's pages that we know them now.

Had not a restraining influence, anxiously and even acrimoniously urged, broken in on their endeavours the English language to-day might have been almost as completely latinized as Spanish or Italian. That the essential Saxon purity of our tongue has been preserved is to the credit not of sensible unlettered people eschewing new fashions they could not comprehend, but to the scholars themselves. The chief service that Cheke and Ascham and their fellows rendered to English literature was their crusade against the exaggerated latinity that they had themselves helped to make possible, the crusade against what they called 'inkhorn terms'. 'I am of this opinion,' said Cheke in a prefatory letter to a book translated by a friend of his, 'that our own tongue should be written clean and pure, unmixed and unmangled with the borrowing of other tongues, wherein if we take not heed by time, ever borrowing and never paying, she shall be fain to keep her house as bankrupt.' Writings in the Saxon vernacular—like the sermons of Latimer, who was careful to use nothing not familiar to the common people—did much to help the scholars to save our prose from the extravagances which they dreaded. Their attack was directed no less against the revival of really obsolete words. It is a paradox worth noting for its strangeness that the first revival of mediævalism in modern English literature was in the Renaissance itself. Talking in studious archaism seems to have been a fashionable practice in society and court circles. 'The fine courtier,' says Thomas Wilson in his *Art of Rhetoric*, 'will talk nothing but Chaucer.' The scholars of the English Renaissance fought not only against the ignorant adoption of their importations, but against the renewal of forgotten habits of speech.

Their efforts failed, and their ideals had to wait for their acceptance till the age of Dryden, when Shakespeare and Spenser and Milton, all of them authors who consistently violated the standards of Cheke, had done their work. The fine courtier who would talk nothing but Chaucer was in Elizabeth's reign the saving of English verse. The beauty and richness of Spenser is based directly on words he got from *Troilus and Cressida* and *The Canterbury Tales*. Some of the most sonorous and beautiful lines in Shakespeare break every canon laid down by the humanists.

> Th' extravagant and erring spirit hies
> To his confine

B

is a line, three of the chief words of which are Latin importations that come unfamiliarly, bearing their original interpretation with them. Milton is packed with similar things: he will talk of a crowded meeting as 'frequent' and use constructions which are unintelligible to anyone who does not possess a knowledge —and a good knowledge—of Latin syntax. Yet the effect is a good poetic effect. In attacking latinisms in the language borrowed from older poets, Cheke and his companions were attacking the two chief sources of Elizabethan poetic vocabulary. All the sonorousness, beauty and dignity of the poetry and the drama which followed them would have been lost had they succeeded in their object, and their verse would have been constrained into the warped and ugly forms of Sternhold and Hopkins and those with them who composed the first and worst metrical version of the Psalms. When their idea reappeared for its fulfilment phantasy and imagery had temporarily worn themselves out, and the richer language made simplicity possible and adequate for poetry.

There are other directions, that need not detain us here, in which the classical revival influenced writing. The attempt to transplant classical metres into English verse, which was the concern of a little group of authors who called themselves the Areopagus, came to no more success than a similar and contemporary attempt did in France. An earlier and more lasting result of the influence of the classics on new ways of thinking is the *Utopia* of Sir Thomas More, based on Plato's *Republic*, and followed by similar attempts on the part of other authors, of which the most notable are Harrington's *Oceana* and Bacon's *New Atlantis*. In one way or another the rediscovery of Plato proved the most valuable part of the Renaissance's gift from Greece.

The doctrines of the Symposium coloured in Italy the writings of Castiglione and Mirandola. In England they gave us Spenser's *Hymn to Intellectual Beauty*, and they affected, each in his own way, Sir Philip Sidney and others of the circle of Court writers of his time. More's book was written in Latin, though there is an English translation almost contemporary. He combines in himself the two strains that we found working in the Renaissance, for besides its origin in Plato *Utopia* owes not a little to the influence of the voyages of discovery. In 1507 there was published a little book called an *Introduction to Cosmography*, which gave an account of the four voyages of Amerigo. In the story of the fourth voyage it is narrated that twenty-four men were left in a fort near Cape Bahia. More used this detail as a starting-point, and one of the men whom Amerigo left tells the story of this 'Nowhere', a republic partly resembling England but, most of all, the ideal world of Plato. Partly resembling England, because no man can escape from the influences of his own time whatever road he takes, whether the road of imagination or any other. His imagination can only build out of the materials afforded him by his own experience: he can alter, he can rearrange, but he cannot in the strictest sense of the word create, and every city of dreams is only the scheme of things as they are remoulded nearer to the desire of a man's heart. In a way More has less invention than some of his subtler followers, but his book is interesting because it is the first example of a kind of writing which has been attractive to many men since his time, and particularly to writers of our own day.

There remains one circumstance in the revival of the classics which had a marked and continuous influence on the literary age that followed. To get the classics, English scholars had as we have seen to go to Italy. Cheke went there and so did Wilson, and the path of travel across France and through Lombardy to Florence and Rome was worn hard by the feet of their followers for over a hundred years after. On the heels of the men of learning went the men of fashion, eager to learn and copy the new manners of a society whose moral teacher was Machiavelli and whose patterns of splendour were the courts of Florence and Ferrara, and to learn the trick of verse that in the hands of Petrarch and his followers had fashioned the sonnet and other new lyric forms. This could not be without its influence on the manners of the nation, and the scholars who had been the first to show the way were the first to deplore the pell-mell assimilation of Italian manners and vices, which was the unintended result of the inroad on insularity which had already begun. They saw the danger ahead and they laboured to meet it as it came. Ascham in his *Schoolmaster* railed against the translation of Italian books, and the corrupt manners of living and false ideas which they seemed to him to breed. The Italianate Englishman became the chief part of the stock-in-trade of the satirists and moralists of the day. Stubbs, a Puritan chronicler, whose book *The Anatomy of Abuses* is a valuable aid to the study of Tudor social history, and Harrison, whose description of England prefaces Holinshed's *Chronicles*, both deal in detail with the Italian menace, and condemn in good set terms the costliness in dress and the looseness in morals which they laid to its charge. Indeed, the effect on England was profound, and it lasted for more than two generations. The romantic traveller, Coryat, writing well within the seventeenth century in praise of the luxuries of Italy (among which he numbers forks for table use), is as enthusiastic as the authors who began the imitation of Italian metres in *Tottel's Miscellany*; and Donne and Hall in their satires written under James wield the rod of censure as sternly as had Ascham a good half-century before. No doubt there was something in the danger they dreaded, but the evil was not unmixed with good, for insularity will always be an enemy of good literature. The Elizabethans learned much more than their plots from Italian models, and the worst effects dreaded by the patriots never reached our shores. Italian vice stopped short of real life; poisoning and hired ruffianism flourished only on the stage.

(3)

The influence of the spirit of discovery and adventure, though it is less quickly marked, more pervasive, and less easy to define, is perhaps more universal than that of the classics or of the Italian fashions which came in their train. It runs right through the literature of Elizabeth's age and after it, affecting, each in their special way, all the dramatists, the authors who were also adventurers like Ralegh, scholars like Milton, and the philosophers like Hobbes and Locke. It reappears in the Romantic revival with Coleridge, whose *Ancient Mariner* owes much to reminiscences of his favourite reading—*Purchas his Pilgrim*, and other old books of voyages. The matter of this too-little-noticed strain in English literature would suffice to fill a whole book; only a few of the main lines of its influence can be noted here.

For the English Renaissance—for Elizabeth's England—action and imagination went hand in hand; the dramatists and poets held up the mirror to the voyagers. In a sense, the cult of the sea is the oldest note in English literature. There is not a poem in Anglo-Saxon but breathes the saltness and the bitterness of the sea-air. To the old English the sea was something inexpressibly melancholy and desolate, mist-shrouded and lonely, terrible in its grey and shivering spaces; and their tone about it is always elegiac and plaintive, as a place of dreary spiritless wandering and unmarked graves. When the English settled they lost the sense of the sea; they became a little parochial people, tilling fields and tending cattle, wool-gathering and wool-bartering, their shipping confined to cross-Channel merchandise, and coastwise sailing from port to port. Chaucer's shipman, almost the sole representative of the sea in mediæval English literature, plied a coastwise trade. But with the Cabots and their followers, Frobisher and Gilbert and Drake and Hawkins, all this was changed; once more the ocean became the highway of our national progress and adventure, and by virtue of our shipping we became competitors for the dominion of the earth. The rising tide of national enthusiasm and exaltation that this occasioned flooded popular literature. The voyagers themselves wrote down the stories of their adventures; and collections of these—Hakluyt's and Purchas's—were among the most popular books of the age. To them, indeed, we must look for the first beginnings of our modern English prose, and some of its noblest passages. The writers, as often as not, were otherwise utterly unknown—ship's pursers, supercargoes, and the like—men without much literary craft or training, whose style is great because of the greatness of their subject, because they had no literary artifices to stand between them and the plain and direct telling of a stirring tale. But the ferment worked outside the actual doings of the voyagers themselves, and it can be traced beyond

definite allusions to them. Allusions, indeed, are
surprisingly few; Drake is scarcely as much as mentioned among the greater writers of the age. None the
less there is not one of them that is not deeply touched
by his spirit and that of the movement which he led.
New lands had been discovered, new territories opened
up, wonders exposed which were perhaps only the
first-fruits of greater wonders to come. Spenser makes
the voyagers his warrant for his excursion into fairy-
land. Some, he says, have condemned his fairy world
as an idle fiction.

> But let that man with better sense advise,
> That of the world least part to us is red:
> And daily how through hardy enterprise,
> Many great regions are discovered,
> Which to late age were never mentioned.
> Who ever heard of th' Indian *Peru*?
> Or who in venturous vessel measured
> The *Amazons* huge river now found true?
> Or fruitfullest *Virginia* who did ever view?
>
> Yet all these were, when no man did them know;
> Yet have from wisest ages hidden been:
> And later times things more unknown shall show.

It is in the drama that this spirit of adventure caught
from the voyagers gets its full play. 'Without the
voyagers,' says Professor Walter Raleigh,[1] 'Marlowe
is inconceivable.' His imagination in every one of his
plays is preoccupied with the lust of adventure, and
the wealth and power adventure brings. Tamburlaine,
Eastern conqueror though he is, is at heart an Englishman of the school of Hawkins and Drake. Indeed the
comparison must have occurred to his own age, for a
historian of the day, the antiquary Stow, declares Drake
to have been 'as famous in Europe and America as

[1] To whose terminal essay in *Hakluyt's Voyages* (Mac-
lehose) I am indebted for much of the matter in this section.

Tamburlaine was in Asia and Africa'. The high-sounding names and quests which seem to us to give the play an air of unreality and romance were to the Elizabethans real and actual; things as strange and foreign were to be heard any day amongst the motley crowd in the Bankside outside the theatre door. Tamburlaine's speech in the last scene, when he calls for a map and points the way to unrealised conquests, is the very epitome of the age of discovery.

> Lo, here, my sons, are all the golden mines,
> Inestimable drugs and precious stones,
> More worth than Asia and the world beside;
> And from th' Antarctic Pole eastward behold
> As much more land, which never was descried,
> Wherein are rocks of pearl that shine as bright
> As all the lamps that beautify the sky!

It is the same in his other plays. Dr. Faustus assigns to his serviceable spirits tasks that might have been studied from the books of Hakluyt.

> I'll have them fly to India for gold,
> Ransack the ocean for orient pearl,
> And search all corners of the new round world
> For pleasant fruits and princely delicates.

When there is no actual expression of the spirit of adventure, the air of the sea which it carried with it still blows. Shakespeare, save for his scenes in *The Tempest* and in *Pericles*, which seize in all its dramatic poignancy the terror of storm and shipwreck, has nothing dealing directly with the sea or with travel; but it comes out, none the less, in figure and metaphor, and plays like *The Merchant of Venice* and *Othello* testify to his accessibility to its spirit. Milton, a scholar whose mind was occupied by other and more ultimate matters, is full of allusions to it. Satan's journey through Chaos in *Paradise Lost* is the occasion for a whole series of metaphors drawn from seafaring. In *Samson Agonistes* Dalila comes in,

> Like a stately ship . . .
> With all her bravery on, and tackle trim,
> Sails filled, and streamers waving,
> Courted by all the winds that hold them play.

and Samson speaks of himself as one who,

> Like a foolish pilot, have shipwrecked
> My vessel trusted to me from above,
> Gloriously rigged.

The influence of the voyages of discovery persisted long after the first bloom of the Renaissance had flowered and withered. On the reports brought home by the voyagers were founded in part those conceptions of the condition of the 'natural' man which form such a large part of the philosophic discussions of the seventeenth and eighteenth centuries. Hobbes's description of the life of nature as 'nasty, solitary, brutish, and short', Locke's theories of civil government, and eighteenth-century speculators like Monboddo, all took as the basis of their theory the observations of the men of travel. Abroad, this connection of travellers and philosophers was no less intimate. Both Montesquieu and Rousseau owed much to the tales of the Iroquois, the North American Indian allies of France. Locke himself is the best example of the closeness of this alliance. He was a diligent student of the texts of the voyagers, and himself edited out of Hakluyt and Purchas the best collection of them current in his day. The purely literary influence of the age of discovery persisted down to *Robinson Crusoe*; in that book by a refinement of satire a return to travel itself (it must be remembered Defoe posed not as a novelist but as an actual traveller) is used to make play with the deductions founded on it. Crusoe's conversation with the Man Friday will be found to be a satire of Locke's famous controversy with the Bishop of Worcester. With *Robinson Crusoe* the influence of the age of discovery finally perishes. An inspiration hardens into the mere subject matter of books of adventure. We need not follow it further.

CHAPTER II

ELIZABETHAN POETRY AND PROSE

(1)

To understand Elizabethan literature it is necessary to remember that the social status it enjoyed was far different from that of literature in our own day. The splendours of the Medicis in Italy had set up an ideal of courtliness, in which letters formed an integral and indispensable part. For the Renaissance, the man of letters was only one aspect of the gentleman, and the true gentleman, as books so early and late respectively as Castiglione's *Courtier* and Peacham's *Complete Gentleman* show, numbered poetry as a necessary part of his accomplishments. In England special circumstances intensified this tendency of the time. The queen was unmarried: she was the first single woman to wear the English crown, and her vanity made her value the devotion of the men about her as something more intimate than mere loyalty or patriotism. She loved personal homage, particularly the homage of half-amatory eulogy in prose and verse. It followed that the ambition of every courtier was to be an author, and of every author to be a courtier; in fact, outside the drama, which was almost the only popular writing at the time, every author was in a greater or less degree attached to the Court. If they were not enjoying its favours they were pleading for them, mingling high and fantastic compliment with bitter reproaches and a tale of misery. And consequently both the poetry and the prose of the time are restricted in their scope and temper to the artificial and romantic, to high-flown eloquence, to the celebration of love and devotion, or to the inculcation of those courtly virtues and accomplishments which composed the perfect pattern of a gentleman. Not that there was not both poetry and prose written outside this charmed circle. The pamphleteers and chroniclers, Dekker and Nash, Holinshed and Harrison and Stow, were setting down their histories and descriptions, and penning those detailed and realistic indictments of the follies and extravagances of fashion, which together with the comedies have enabled us to picture accurately the England and especially the London of Elizabeth's reign. There was fine poetry written by Marlowe and Chapman as well as by Sidney and Spenser, but the Court was still the main centre of literary endeavour, and the main incitement to literary fame and success.

But whether an author was a courtier or a Londoner living by his wits, writing was never the main business of his life: all the writers of the time were in one way or another men of action and affairs. As late as Milton it is probably true to say that writing was in the case even of the greatest an avocation, something indulged in at leisure outside a man's main business. All the Elizabethan authors had crowded and various careers. Of Sir Philip Sidney his earliest biographer says, 'The truth is his end was not writing, even while he wrote, but both his wit and understanding bent upon his heart to make himself and others not in words or opinion but in life and action good and great.' Ben Jonson was in turn a soldier, a poet, a bricklayer, an actor, and ultimately the first Poet Laureate. Lodge, after leaving Oxford, passed through the various professions of soldiering, medicine, playwriting, and fiction, and he wrote his novel *Rosalynde*, on which Shakespeare based *As You Like It*, while he was sailing on a piratical venture on the Spanish Main.

This connection between life and action affected as we have seen the tone and quality of Elizabethan writing. 'All the distinguished writers of the period,' says Thoreau, 'possess a greater vigour and naturalness than the more modern. . . . You have constantly the warrant of life and experience in what you read. The little that is said is eked out by implication of the much that was done.' In another passage the same writer explains the strength and fineness of the writings of Sir Walter Ralegh by this very test of action, 'The word which is best said came nearest to not being spoken at all, for it is cousin to a deed which the speaker could have better done. Nay almost it must have taken the place of a deed by some urgent necessity, even by some misfortune, so that the truest writer will be some captive knight after all.' This bond between literature and action explains more than the writings of the voyagers or the pamphlets of men who lived in London by what they could make of their fellows. Literature has always a twofold relation to life as it is lived. It is both a mirror and an escape: in recent times the stirring romances of Stevenson, the full-blooded and vigorous life which beats through the pages of Kipling, the conscious brutalism of such writers as Conrad and Maurice Hewlett, the plays of J. M. Synge, occupied with the vigorous and coarse-grained life of tinkers and peasants, are all in their separate ways a reaction against an age in which the overwhelming majority of men and women have sedentary pursuits. Just in the same way the Elizabethan who passed his commonly short and crowded life in an atmosphere of throat-cutting and powder and shot, and in a time when affairs of state were more momentous for the future of the nation than they have ever been since, needed his escape from the things which pressed in upon him every day. So grew the vogue and popularity of pastoral poetry and the pastoral romance.

(2)

It is with two courtiers that modern English poetry begins. The lives of Sir Thomas Wyatt and the Earl of Surrey both ended early and unhappily, and it was not until ten years after the death of the second of them that their poems appeared in print. The book that contained them, *Songs and Sonnets*, known as *Tottel's Miscellany*, is one of the landmarks of English literature. It begins lyrical love poetry in our language. It begins, too, the imitation and adaptation of foreign and chiefly Italian metrical forms, many of which have since become characteristic forms of English verse: so characteristic, that we scarcely think of them as other than native in origin. To Wyatt belongs the honour of introducing the sonnet, and to Surrey the more momentous credit of writing, for the first time in English, blank verse. Wyatt fills the most important place in the *Miscellany*, and his work, experimental in tone and quality, formed the example which Surrey and minor writers in the same volume and all the later poets of the age copied. He tries his hand at everything—songs, madrigals, elegies, complaints, and sonnets—and he takes his models from both ancient Rome and modern Italy. Indeed, there is scarcely anything in the volume for which with some trouble and research one might not find an original in Petrarch, or in the poets of Italy who followed him. But imitation, universal though it is in his work, does not altogether crowd out originality of feeling and poetic-temper. At times he sounds a personal note, his joy on leaving Spain for England, his feelings in the Tower, his life at the Court amongst his books, and as a country gentleman enjoying hunting and other outdoor sports.

> This maketh me at home to hunt and hawk,
> And in foul weather at my book to sit,
> In frost and snow, then with my bow to stalk,
> No man doth mark where so I ride or go:
> In lusty leas at liberty I walk.

It is easy to see that poetry as a melodious and enriched expression of a man's own feelings is in its infancy here. The new poets had to find their own language, to enrich with borrowings from other tongues the stock of words suitable for poetry which the dropping of inflection had left to English. Wyatt was at the beginning of the process, and apart from a gracious and courtly temper, his work has, it must be confessed, hardly more than an antiquarian interest. Surrey, it is possible to say on reading his work, went one step further. He allows himself oftener the luxury of a reference to personal feelings, and his poetry contains from place to place a fairly full record of the vicissitudes of his life. A prisoner at Windsor, he recalls his childhood there:

> The large green courts where we were wont to hove . . .
> The palme-play, where, despoiled for the game,
> With dazed eyes oft we by gleams of love
> Have missed the ball, and got sight of our dame.

Like Wyatt's, his verses are poor stuff, but a sympathetic ear can catch in them something of the accent that distinguishes the verse of Sidney and Spenser. He is greater than Wyatt, not so much for greater skill as for more boldness and experiment. Wyatt in his sonnets had used the Petrarchan or Italian form, the form used later in England by Milton and in the nineteenth century by Rossetti. He built up each poem,

that is, in two parts, the octave, a two-rhymed section
of eight lines at the beginning, followed by the sestet,
a six-line close with three rhymes. The form fits itself
very well to the double mood which commonly inspires
a poet using the sonnet form; the second section as it
were both echoing and answering the first, following
doubt with hope, or sadness with resignation, or resolv-
ing a problem set itself by the heart. Surrey tried
another manner, the manner which by its use in
Shakespeare's sonnets has come to be regarded as the
English form of this kind of lyric. His sonnets are
virtually three stanza poems with a couplet for close,
and he allows himself as many rhymes as he chooses.
The structure is obviously easier, and it gives a better
chance to an inferior workman, but in the hands of a
master its harmonies are no less delicate, and its
capacity to represent changing modes of thought no
less complete than those of the true form of Petrarch.
Blank verse, which was Surrey's other gift to English
poetry, was in a way a compromise between the two
sources from which the English Renaissance drew its
inspiration. Latin and Greek verse is quantitative and
rhymeless; Italian verse, built up on the metres of the
troubadours and the degeneration of Latin which gave
the world the Romance languages, used many elaborate
forms of rhyme. Blank verse took from Latin its
rhymelessness, but it retained accent instead of quantity
as the basis of its line. The line Surrey used is the
five-foot or ten-syllable line of what is called 'heroic
verse'—the line used by Chaucer in his Prologue and
most of his Tales. Like Milton he deplored rhyme as
the invention of a barbarous age, and no doubt he
would have rejoiced to go further and banish accent as
well as rhymed endings. That, however, was not to be,
though in the best blank verse of later time accent and

quantity both have their share in the effect. The instrument he forged passed into the hands of the dramatists: Marlowe perfected its rhythm. Shakespeare broke its monotony and varied its cadences by altering the spacing of the accents, and occasionally by adding an extra unaccented syllable. It came back from the drama to poetry with Milton. His blindness and the necessity under which it laid him of keeping in his head long stretches of verse at one time, because he could not look back to see what he had written, probably helped his naturally quick and delicate sense of cadence to vary the pauses, so that a variety of accent and interval might replace the valuable aid to memory which he put aside in putting aside rhyme. Perhaps it is to two accidents, the accident by which blank verse as the medium of the actor had to be retained easily in the memory, and the accident of Milton's blindness, that must be laid the credit of more than a little of the richness of rhythm of this, the chief and greatest instrument of English verse.

The imitation of Italian and French forms which Wyatt and Surrey began, was continued by a host of younger amateurs of poetry. Laborious research has indeed found a Continental original for almost every great poem of the time, and for very many forgotten ones as well. It is easy for the student engaged in this kind of literary exploration to exaggerate the importance of what he finds, and of late years criticism, written mainly by these explorers, has tended to assume that since it can be found that Sidney, and Daniel, and Watson, and all the other writers of mythological poetry and sonnet sequences took their ideas and their phrases from foreign poetry, their work is therefore to be classed merely as imitative literary exercise, that it is frigid, that it contains or conveys no real feeling, and

C

that except in the secondary and derived sense it is not really lyrical at all. Petrarch, they will tell you, may have felt deeply and sincerely about Laura, but when Sidney uses Petrarch's imagery and even translates his words in order to express his feelings for Stella, he is only a plagiarist and not a lover, and the passion for Lady Rich which is supposed to have inspired his sonnets nothing more than a not too seriously intended trick to add the excitement of a transcript of real emotion to what was really an academic exercise. If that were indeed so, then Elizabethan poetry is a very much lesser and meaner thing than later ages have thought it. But is it so ? Let us look into the matter a little more closely. The unit of all ordinary kinds of writing is the word, and one is not commonly quarrelled with for using words that have belonged to other people. But the unit of the lyric, like the unit of spoken conversation, is not the word but the phrase. Now in daily human intercourse the use, which is universal and habitual, of set forms and phrases of talk is not commonly supposed to detract from or destroy sincerity. In the crises indeed of emotion it must be most people's experience that the natural speech that rises unbidden and easiest to the lips is something quite familiar and commonplace, some form which the accumulated experience of many generations of separate people has found best for such circumstances or such an occasion. The lyric is just in the position of conversation at such a heightened and emotional moment. It is the speech of deep feeling, that must be articulate or choke, and it falls naturally and inevitably into some form which accumulated passionate moments have created and fixed. The course of emotional experiences differs very little from age to age, and from individual to individual, and so the same phrases may be used quite sincerely and naturally as the direct expression of feeling at its highest point by men apart in country, circumstances, or time. This is not to say that there is no such thing as originality; a poet is a poet first and most of all because he discovers truths that have been known for ages as things that are fresh and new and vital for himself. He must speak of them in language that has been used by other men just because they are known truths, but he will use that language in a new way and with a new significance, and it is just in proportion to the freshness and the air of personal conviction and sincerity which he imparts to it that he is great.

The point at issue bears very directly on the work of Sir Philip Sidney. In the course of the history of English letters certain authors disengage themselves who have more than a merely literary position: they are symbolic of the whole age in which they live, its life and action, its thoughts and ideals, as well as its mere modes of writing. There are not many of them and they could be easily numbered: Addison, perhaps, certainly Dr. Johnson, certainly Byron, and in the later age probably Tennyson. But the greatest of them all is Sir Philip Sidney: his symbolical relation to the time in which he lived was realized by his contemporaries, and it has been a commonplace of history and criticism ever since. Elizabeth called him one of the jewels of her crown, and at the age of twenty-three, so fast did genius ripen in that summer time of the Renaissance, William the Silent could speak of him as 'one of the ripest statesmen of the age'. He travelled widely in Europe, knew many languages, and dreamed of adventure in America and on the high seas. In a court of brilliant figures, his was the most dazzling, and his death at Zutphen only served to intensify the halo of romance which had gathered round his name. His literary exercises were various: in prose he wrote the *Arcadia* and the *Apologie for Poetrie*, the one the beginning of a new kind of imaginative writing, and the other the first of the series of those rare and precious commentaries on their own art which some of our English poets have left us. To the *Arcadia* we shall have to return later in this chapter. It is his other great work, the sequence of sonnets entitled *Astrophel and Stella*, which concerns us here. They celebrate the history of his love for Penelope Devereux, sister of the Earl of Essex, a love brought to disaster by the intervention of Queen Elizabeth with whom he had quarrelled. As poetry they mark an epoch. They are the first direct expression in English literature of an intimate and personal experience, struck off in the white heat of passion, and though they are coloured at times with that over-fantastic imagery which is at once a characteristic fault and excellence of the writings of the time, they never lose the one merit above all others of lyric poetry, the merit of sincerity. The note is struck with certainty and power in the first sonnet of the series:—

Loving in truth, and fain in verse my love to show,
That she, dear she, might take some pleasure of my pain,
Pleasure might cause her read, reading might make her know,
Knowledge might pity win, and pity grace obtain,
I sought fit words to paint the blackest face of woe,
Studying inventions fine, her wits to entertain;
Oft turning others' leaves to see if thence would flow
Some fresh and fruitful showers upon my sun-burned brain.
But words came halting forth . . .
Biting my truant pen, beating myself for spite,
'Fool,' said my Muse to me, 'look in thy heart and write.'

And though he turned others' leaves it was quite literally looking in his heart that he wrote. He analyses the sequence of his feelings with a vividness and minuteness which assure us of their truth. All that he tells is the fruit of experience, dearly bought:

> Desire! desire! I have too dearly bought
> With price of mangled mind thy worthless ware.
> Too long, too long, asleep thou hast me brought,
> Who should my mind to higher things prepare.

and earlier in the sequence—

> I now have learned love right, and learn'd even so
> As they that being poisoned, poison know.

In the last two sonnets, with crowning truth and pathos he renounces earthly love which reaches but to dust, and which because it fades brings but fading pleasure:

> Then farewell, world! thy uttermost I see.
> Eternal Love, maintain thy life in me.

The sonnets were published after Sidney's death, and it is certain that like Shakespeare's they were never intended for publication at all. The point is important because it helps to vindicate Sidney's sincerity, but were any vindication needed another more certain might be found. The *Arcadia* is strewn with love songs and sonnets, the exercises solely of the literary imagination. Let any one who wishes to gauge the sincerity of the impulse of the Stella sequence compare any of the poems in it with those in the romance.

With Sir Philip Sidney literature was an avocation, constantly indulged in, but outside the main business of his life; with Edmund Spenser public life and affairs were subservient to an overmastering poetic impulse. He did his best to carve out a career for himself like other young men of his time, followed the fortunes of the Earl of Leicester, sought desperately and unavailingly the favour of the Queen, and ultimately accepted a place in her service in Ireland, which meant banishment as virtually as a place in India would to-day. Henceforward his visits to London and the Court were few;

sometimes a lover of travel would visit him in his house in Ireland as Ralegh did, but for the most he was left alone. It was in this atmosphere of loneliness and separation, hostile tribes pinning him in on every side, murder lurking in the woods and marshes round him, that he composed his greatest work. In it at last he died, on the heels of a sudden rising in which his house was burnt and his lands over-run by the wild Irish whom the tyranny of the English planters had driven to vengeance. Spenser was not without interest in his public duties; his *View of the State of Ireland* shows that. But it shows, too, that he brought to them singularly little sympathy or imagination. Throughout, his tone is that of the worst kind of English officialdom; rigid subjection and in the last resort massacre are the remedies he would apply to Irish discontent. He would be a fine text—which might be enforced by modern examples—for a discourse on the evil effects of immersion in the government of a subject race upon men of letters. No man of action can be so consistently and cynically an advocate of brutalism as your man of letters. Spenser, of course, had his excuses: the problem of Ireland was new and it was something remote and difficult; in all but the mere distance for travel, Dublin was as far from London as Bombay is to-day. But to him and his like we must lay down partly the fact that the Irish problem persisted down to the present century.

But though fate and the necessity of a livelihood drove him to Ireland and the life of a colonist, poetry was his main business. He had been the centre of a brilliant set at Cambridge, one of those coteries whose fame, if they are brilliant and vivacious enough and have enough self-confidence, penetrates to the outer world before they leave the University. The thing has continued to happen, as the case of Oscar Wilde is witness; it happened in the case of Spenser; and when he and his friends Gabriel Harvey and Edward Kirke came 'down' it was to immediate fame amongst amateurs of the arts. They corresponded with each other about literary matters, and Harvey published his part of the correspondence; like Du Bellay in France, they played with the idea of writing English verse in the quantitative measures of classical poetry; Spenser had a love affair in Yorkshire and wrote poetry about it, letting just enough be known to stimulate the imagination of the public. They tried their hands at everything, imitated everything, and in all were brilliant, sparkling, and decorative; they got a kind of entrance to the circle of the Court. Then Spenser published *The Shepheard's Calender*, a series of pastoral eclogues for every month of the year, after a manner taken from French and Italian pastoral writers, but coming ultimately from Vergil, and Edward Kirke furnished it with an elaborate prose commentary. Spenser took the same liberties with the pastoral form as did Vergil himself; that is to say he used it as a vehicle for satire and allegory, made it carry political and social allusions, and planted in it references to his friends. By its publication Spenser became the first poet of the day. It was followed by some of his finest and most beautiful things—by the Platonic *Hymns*, by the *Amoretti*, a series of sonnets inspired by his love for his wife; by the *Epithalamium*, on the occasion of his marriage to her; by *Mother Hubbard's Tale*, a satire written when despair at the coldness of the Queen and the enmity of Burleigh was beginning to take hold on the poet and endowed with a plainness and vigour foreign to most of his other work—and then by *The Faerie Queene*.

The poets of the Renaissance were not afraid of big things; every one of them had in his mind as the goal of poetic endeavour the idea of the heroic poem, aimed at doing for his own country what Vergil had intended to do for Rome in the *Æneid*, to celebrate it—its origin, its prowess, its greatness, and the causes of it—in epic verse. Milton, three-quarters of a century later, turned over in his mind the plan of an English epic on the wars of Arthur, and when he left it it was only to forsake the singing of English origins for the ultimate theme of the origins of mankind. Spenser designed to celebrate the character, the qualities and the training of the English gentleman. And because poetry, unlike philosophy, cannot deal with abstractions but must be vivid and concrete, he was forced to embody his virtues and foes to virtue and to use the way of allegory. His outward plan, with its knights and dragons and desperate adventures, he procured from Ariosto. As for the use of allegory, it was one of the discoveries of the Middle Ages which the Renaissance condescended to retain. Spenser elaborated it beyond the wildest dreams of those students of Holy Writ who had first conceived it. His stories were to be interesting in themselves as tales of adventure, but within them they were to conceal an intricate treatment of the conflict of truth and falsehood in morals and religion. A character might typify at once Protestantism and England and Elizabeth and chastity and half the cardinal virtues, and it would have all the while the objective interest attaching to it as part of a story of adventure. All this must have made the poem difficult enough. Spenser's manner of writing it made it worse still. One is familiar with the type of novel which only explains itself when the last chapter is reached— Stevenson's *The Wrecker* is an example. *The Faerie*

Queene was designed on somewhat the same plan. The last section was to relate and explain the unrelated and unexplained books which made up the poem, and at the court to which the separate knights of the separate books—the Red Cross Knight and the rest—were to bring the fruit of their adventures, everything was to be made clear. Spenser did not live to finish his work; *The Faerie Queene*, like the *Æneid*, is an uncompleted poem, and it is only from a prefatory letter to Sir Walter Ralegh issued with the second published section that we know what the poem was intended to be. Had Spenser not published this explanation, it is impossible that anybody, even the acutest minded German professor, could have guessed.

The poem, as we have seen, was composed in Ireland, in the solitude of a colonists' plantation, and the author was shut off from his fellows while he wrote. The influence of his surroundings is visible in the writing. The elaboration of the theme would have been impossible or at least very unlikely if its author had not been thrown in on himself during its composition. Its intricacy and involution is the product of an over-concentration born of empty surroundings. It lacks vigour and rapidity; it winds itself into itself. The influence of Ireland, too, is visible in its landscapes, in its description of bogs and desolation, of dark forests in which lurk savages ready to spring out on those who are rash enough to wander within their confines. All the scenery in it which is not imaginary is Irish and not English scenery.

Its reception in England and at the Court was enthusiastic. Men and women read it eagerly and longed for the next section as a later generation longed for the next section of *Pickwick*. They really liked it, really loved the intricacy and luxuriousness of it, the heavy exotic language, the thickly painted descriptions, the languorous melody of the verse. Mainly, perhaps, that was so because they were all either in wish or in deed poets themselves. Spenser has always been 'the poets' poet'. Milton loved him; so did Dryden, who said that Milton confessed to him that Spenser was 'his original', a statement which has been pronounced incredible, but is, in truth, perfectly comprehensible, and most likely true. Pope admired him; Keats learned from him the best part of his music. We can trace echoes of him in W. B. Yeats. What is it that gives him this hold on his peers? Well, in the first place his defects do not detract from his purely poetic qualities. The story is impossibly told, but that will only worry those who are looking for a story. The allegory is hopelessly difficult; but as Hazlitt said 'the allegory will not bite you'; you can let it alone. The crudeness and bigotry of Spenser's dealings with Catholicism, which are ridiculous when he pictures the monster Error vomiting books and pamphlets, and disgusting when he draws Mary Queen of Scots, do not hinder the pleasure of those who read him for his language and his art. He is great for other reasons than these. First because of the extraordinary smoothness and melody of his verse and the richness of his language— a golden diction which he drew from every source—new words, old words, obsolete words—such a mixture that the purist Ben Jonson remarked acidly that he wrote no language at all. Second because of the profusion of his imagery and the extraordinarily keen sense for beauty and sweetness that went to its making. In an age of golden language and gallant imagery his was the most golden and the most gallant. And the language of poetry in England is richer and more varied than that in any other country in Europe to-day, because of what he did.

(3)

Elizabethan prose brings us face to face with a difficulty which has to be met by every student of literature. Does the word 'literature' cover every kind of writing? Ought we to include in it writing that aims merely at instruction or is merely journey-work, as well as writing that has an artistic intention, or writing that, whether its author knew it or not, is artistic in its result? Of course such a question causes us no sort of difficulty when it concerns itself only with what is being published to-day. We know very well that some things are literature and some merely journalism; that of novels, for instance, some deliberately intend to be works of art and others only to meet a passing desire for amusement or mental occupation. We know that most books serve or attempt to serve only a useful and not a literary purpose. But in reading the books of three centuries ago, unconsciously one's point of view shifts. Antiquity gilds journey-work; remoteness and quaintness of phrasing lend a kind of distinction to what are simply pamphlets or text-books that have been preserved by accident from the ephemeralness which was the common lot of hundreds of their fellows. One comes to regard as literature things that had no kind of literary value for their first audiences; to apply the same seriousness of judgement and the same tests to the pamphlets of Nash and Dekker as to the prose of Sidney and Bacon. One loses, in fact, that power to distinguish the important from the trivial which is one of the functions of a sound literary taste. Now a study of the minor writings of the past is, of course, well worth a reader's pains. Pamphlets, chronicle histories, text-books and the like have an historical importance; they give us glimpses of the manners and habits and modes of thought of the day. They tell us more about the outward show of life than do the greater books. If you are interested in social history, they are the very thing. But the student of literature ought to beware of them, nor ought he to touch them till he is familiar with the big and lasting things. A man does not possess English literature if he knows what Dekker tells of the seven deadly sins of London and does not know *The Faerie Queene*. Though the wide and curious interest of the Romantic critics of the nineteenth century found and illumined the byways of Elizabethan writing, the safest method of approach is the method of their predecessors—to keep hold on common sense, to look at literature, not historically as through the wrong end of a telescope, but closely and without a sense of intervening time, to know the best—the 'classic'—and study it before the minor things.

In Elizabeth's reign, prose became for the first time, with cheapened printing, the common vehicle of amusement and information, and the books that remain to us cover many departments of writing. There are the historians who set down for us for the first time what they knew of the earlier history of England. There are the writers, like Harrison and Stubbs, who described the England of their own day, and there are many authors, mainly anonymous, who wrote down the accounts of the voyages of the discoverers in the Western Seas. There are the novelists who translated stories mainly from Italian sources. But of authors as conscious of a literary intention as the poets were, there are only two, Sidney and Lyly, and of authors who, though their first aim was hardly an artistic one, achieved an artistic result, only Hooker and the translators of the Bible. The Authorized Version of the Bible belongs strictly not to the reign **of** Elizabeth but to that of James, and we shall have to look at it when we come to discuss the seventeenth century. Hooker, in his book on Ecclesiastical Polity (an endeavour to set forth the grounds of orthodox Anglicanism) employed a generous, flowing, melodious style which has influenced many writers since and is familiar to us to-day in the copy of it used by Ruskin in his earlier works. Lyly and Sidney are worth looking at more closely.

The age was intoxicated with language. It went mad of a mere delight in words. Its writers were using a new tongue, for English was enriched beyond all recognition with borrowings from the ancient authors; and like all artists who become possessed of a new medium, they used it to excess. The early Elizabethans' use of the new prose was very like the use some educated Indians make of English. It is not that these write it incorrectly, but only that they write too richly. And just as fuller use and knowledge teaches them spareness and economy and gives their writing simplicity and vigour, so seventeenth-century practice taught Englishmen to write a more direct and undecorated style and gave us the smooth, simple, and vigorous writing of Dryden—the first really modern English prose. But the Elizabethans loved gaudier methods; they liked highly decorative modes of expression, in prose no less than in verse. The first author to give them these things was John Lyly, whose *Euphues* was for the five or six years following its publication a fashionable craze that infected all society and gave its name to a peculiar and highly artificial style of writing that coloured the work of hosts of obscure and forgotten followers. Lyly wrote other things; his comedies may have taught Shakespeare the trick of *Love's Labour's Lost*; he attempted a sequel to his most famous work with better success than commonly attends sequels, but for us and for his own generation he is the author of one book. Everybody read it, everybody copied it. The maxims and sentences of advice for gentlemen which it contained were quoted and admired in the Court, where the author, though he never attained the lucrative position he hoped for, did what flattery could do to make a name for himself. The word 'Euphuism' became a current description of an artificial way of using words that overflowed out of writing into speech and was in the mouths, while the vogue lasted, of everybody who was anybody in the circle that fluttered round the Queen.

The style of *Euphues* was parodied by Shakespeare and many attempts have been made to imitate it since. Most of them are inaccurate—Sir Walter Scott's wild attempt the most inaccurate of all. They fail because their authors have imagined that 'Euphuism' is simply a highly artificial and 'flowery' way of talking. As a matter of fact it is made up of very exact and very definite series of parts. The writing is done on a plan which has three main characteristics. First, the structure of the sentence is based on antithesis and alliteration; that is to say, it falls into equal parts similar in sound but with a different sense; for example, Euphues is described as a young gallant 'of more wit than wealth, yet of more wealth than wisdom'. All the characters in the book, which is roughly in the form of a novel, speak in this way, sometimes in sentences long drawn out which are oppressively monotonous and tedious, and sometimes shortly with a certain approach to epigram. The second characteristic of the style is the reference of every stated fact to some classical authority, that is to say, the author cannot mention friendship without quoting David and Jonathan, nor can lovers in his book accuse each other of faithlessness without quoting the instance of Cressida or Æneas. This appeal to classical authority and wealth of classical allusion is used to decorate pages which deal with matters of everyday experience. Seneca, for instance, is quoted as reporting 'that too much bending breaketh the bow', a fact which might reasonably have been supposed to be known to the author himself. This particular form of writing perhaps influenced those who copied Lyly more than anything else in his book. It is a fashion of the more artificial kind of Elizabethan writing in all schools to employ a wealth of classical allusion. Even the simple narratives in *Hakluyt's Voyages* are not free from it, and one may hardly hope to read an account of a voyage to the Indies without stumbling on a preliminary reference to the opinions of Aristotle and Plato. Lastly, *Euphues* is characterized by an extraordinary wealth of allusion to natural history, mostly of a fabulous kind. 'I have read that the bull being tied to the fig tree loseth his tail; that the whole herd of deer stand at gaze if they smell a sweet apple; that the dolphin after the sound of music is brought to the shore', and so on. His book is full of these things, and the style weakens and loses its force because of them.

Of course there is much more in his book than this outward decoration. He wrote with the avowed purpose of instructing courtiers and gentlemen how to live. *Euphues* is full of grave reflections and weighty morals, and is indeed a collection of essays on education, on friendship, on religion and philosophy, and on the favourite occupation and curriculum of Elizabethan youth—foreign travel. The fashions and customs of his countrymen which he condemns in the course of his teaching are the same as those inveighed against by Stubbs and other contemporaries. He disliked manners and fashions copied from Italy; particularly he disliked the extravagant fashions of women. One woman only escapes his censure, and she, of course, is the Queen, whom Euphues and his companion in the book come to England to see. In the main the teaching of Euphues inculcates a humane and liberal if not very profound creed, and the book shares with *The Faerie Queene* the honour of the earlier Puritanism—the Puritanism that besides the New Testament had the *Republic*.

But Euphues, though he was in his time the popular idol, was not long in finding a successful rival. Seven years before his death Sir Philip Sidney in a period of retirement from the Court wrote *The Countess of Pembroke's Arcadia*; it was published ten years after it had been composed. The *Arcadia* is the first English example of the prose pastoral romance, as *The Shepheardes Calender* is of our pastoral verse. Imitative essays in its style kept appearing for two hundred years after it, till Wordsworth and other poets who knew the country drove its unrealities out of literature. The aim of it and of the school to which it belonged abroad was to find a setting for a story which should leave the author perfectly free to plant in it any improbability he liked, and to do what he liked with the relations of his characters. In the shade of beech trees, the coils of elaborated and intricate love-making wind and unravel themselves through an endless afternoon. In that art nothing is too far-fetched, nothing too sentimental, no sorrow too unreal. The pastoral romance was used, too, to cover other things besides a sentimental and decorative treatment of love. Authors wrapped up as shepherds their political friends and enemies, and the pastoral eclogues in verse which

Spenser and others composed are full of personal and political allusion. Sidney's story carries no politics and depends for its interest solely on the wealth of differing episodes and the stories and arguments of love which it contains. The story would furnish plot enough for twenty ordinary novels, but probably those who read it when it was published were attracted by other things than the march of its incidents. Certainly no one could read it for the plot now. Its attraction is mainly one of style. It goes, we feel, one degree beyond *Euphues* in the direction of freedom and poetry. And just because of this greater freedom its characteristics are much less easy to fix than those of *Euphues*. Perhaps its chief quality is best described as that of exhaustiveness. Sidney will take a word and toss it to and fro on a page till its meaning is sucked dry and more than sucked dry. On page after page the same trick is employed, often in some new and charming way, but with the inevitable effect of wearying the reader, who tries to do the unwisest of all things with a book of this kind—to read on. This trick of bandying words is, of course, common in Shakespeare. Other marks of Sidney's style belong similarly to poetry rather than to prose. Chief of them is what Ruskin christened the 'pathetic fallacy'—the assumption (not common in his day) which connects the appearance of nature with the moods of the artist who looks at it, or demands such a connection. In its day the *Arcadia* was hailed as a reformation by men nauseated by the rhythmical patterns of Lyly. A modern reader finds himself confronting it in something of the spirit that he would confront, say, the prose romances of William Morris, finding it charming as a poet's essay in prose but no more; not to be ranked with the highest.

D

CHAPTER III

THE DRAMA

(1)

BIOLOGISTS tell us that the hybrid—the product of a
variety of ancestral stocks—is more fertile than an
organism with a direct and unmixed ancestry; perhaps
the analogy is not too fanciful as the starting-point of a
study of Elizabethan drama, which owed its strength
and vitality, more than to anything else, to the variety
of the discordant and contradictory elements of which
it was made up. The drama was the form into which
were moulded the thoughts and desires of the best
spirits of the time. It was the flower of the age. To
appreciate its many-sided significances and achievements it is necessary to disentangle carefully its roots,
in religion, in the revival of the classics, in popular
entertainments, in imports from abroad, in the air of
enterprise and adventure which belonged to the time.

As in Greece, drama in England was in its beginning
a religious thing. Its oldest continuous tradition was
from the mediæval Church. Early in the Middle Ages
the clergy and their parishioners began the habit, at
Christmas, Easter and other holy days, of playing some
part of the story of Christ's life suitable to the festival
of the day. These plays were liturgical, and originally,
no doubt, overshadowed by a choral element. But
gradually the inherent human capacity for mimicry
and drama took the upper hand; from ceremonies they
developed into performances; they passed from the
stage in the church porch to the stage in the street.
A waggon, the natural human platform for mimicry
or oratory, became in England as it was in Greece,

the cradle of the drama. This momentous change in the history of the miracle play, which made it in all but its occasion and its subject a secular thing, took place about the end of the twelfth century. The rise of the town guilds gave the plays a new character; the friendly rivalry of leagued craftsmen elaborated their production; and at length elaborate cycles were founded which were performed at Whitsuntide, beginning at sunrise and lasting all through the day right on to dusk. Each town had its own cycle, and of these the cycles of York, Wakefield, Chester and Coventry still remain. So too, does an eye-witness's account of a Chester performance where the plays took place yearly on three days, beginning with Whit Monday. 'The manner of these plays were, every company had his pageant or part, a high scaffold with two rooms, a higher and a lower, upon four wheels. In the lower they apparelled themselves and in the higher room they played, being all open on the top that all beholders might hear and see them. They began first at the abbey gates, and when the first pageant was played, it was wheeled to the high cross before the mayor and so to every street. So every street had a pageant playing upon it at one time, till all the pageants for the day appointed were played.' The 'companies' were the town guilds and the several 'pageants' different scenes in Old or New Testament story. As far as was possible each company took for its pageant some Bible story fitting to its trade; in York the goldsmiths played the three Kings of the East bringing precious gifts, the fishmongers the flood, and the shipwrights the building of Noah's ark. The tone of these plays was not reverent; reverence after all implies near at hand its opposite in unbelief. But they were realistic and they contained within them the seeds of later drama in the aptitude with which they grafted on to the sacred story pastoral and city manners taken straight from life. The shepherds who watched by night at Bethlehem were real English shepherds furnished with boisterous and realistic comic relief. Noah was a real shipwright.

> It shall be clinched ever-ilka deal
> With nails that are both noble and new.
> Thus shall I fest it fast to feele,
> Take here a rivet and there a rewe,
> With there bow there now, work I well,
> This work I warrant, both good and true.

Cain and Abel were English farmers just as truly as Bottom and his fellows were English craftsmen. But then Julius Cæsar has a doublet and in Dutch pictures the apostles wear broad-brimmed hats. Squeamishness about historical accuracy is of a later date, and when it came we gained in correctness less than we lost in art.

The miracle plays, then, are the oldest antecedent of Elizabethan drama, but it must not be supposed they were over and done with before the great age began. The description of the Chester performances, part of which has been quoted, was written in 1594. Shakespeare must, one would think, have seen the Coventry cycle; at any rate he was familiar, as everyone of the time must have been, with the performances: 'Out-heroding Herod' bears witness to that. One must conceive the development of the Elizabethan age as something so rapid in its accessibility to new impressions and new manners and learning and modes of thought that for years the old and new subsisted side by side. Think of modern Japan, a welter of old faiths and crafts and ideals and inrushing Western civilization all mixed up and side by side in the strangest contrasts and you will understand what it was. The miracle plays stayed on beside Marlowe and Shakespeare till

Puritanism frowned upon them. But when the end came it came quickly. The last recorded performance took place in London when King James entertained Gondomar, the Spanish ambassador. And perhaps we should regard that as a 'command' performance reviving, as command performances commonly do, something dead for a generation—in this case, purely out of compliment to the faith and inclination of a distinguished guest.

Next in order of development after the miracle or mystery plays, though contemporary in their popularity, came what we called 'moralities' or 'moral interludes'—pieces designed to enforce a religious or ethical lesson and perhaps to get back into drama something of the edification which realism had ousted from the miracles. They dealt in allegorical and figurative personages, expounded wise saws and moral lessons, and squared rather with the careful self-concern of the newly established Protestantism than with the frank and joyous zest in life which was more characteristic of the time. *Everyman*, the oftenest revived and best known of them, if not the best, is very typical of the class. They had their influences, less profound than that of the miracle plays, on the full drama. It is said the 'Vice'—unregeneracy commonly degenerated into comic relief—is the ancestor of the fool in Shakespeare, but more likely both are successive creations of a dynasty of actors who practised the unchanging and immemorial art of the clown. The general structure of *Everyman* and some of its fellows, heightened and made more dramatic, gave us Marlowe's *Faustus*. There perhaps the influence ends.

The rise of a professional class of actors brought one step nearer the full growth of drama. Companies of strolling players formed themselves and passed from town to town seeking, like the industrious amateurs of the guilds, civic patronage, and performing in town-halls, market-place booths, or inn yards, whichever served them best. The structure of the Elizabethan inn-yard (some survive still, and there are the pictures in *Pickwick*) was very favourable for their purpose. The galleries round it made seats like our boxes and circle for the more privileged spectators; in the centre on the floor of the yard the crowd stood or, if they had stools with them, sat. The stage was a platform set on this floor space with its back against one side of the yard, where perhaps one of the inn-rooms served as a dressing room. So suitable was this 'fit-up', as actors call it, that when theatres came to be built in London they were built on the inn-yard pattern. All the play-houses of the Bankside from the 'Curtain' to the 'Globe' were square or circular places with galleries rising above one another three parts round, a floor space of beaten earth open to the sky in the middle, and jutting out on to it a platform stage with a tiring room capped by a gallery behind it.

The entertainment given by these companies of players (who usually got the patronage and took the title of some lord) was various. They played moralities and interludes, they played formless chronicle history plays like the *Troublesome Raigne of King John*, on which Shakespeare worked for his *King John*; but above and before all they were each a company of specialists, every one of whom had his own talent and performance for which he was admired. The Eliza-bethan stage was the ancestor of the modern music-hall, and to it rather than to the theatre it bears affinity. The quality of the audience is a point of agreement. The Globe was frequented by young 'bloods' and by the more disreputable portions of the community, racing men (or their equivalents of that day), 'coney catchers' and the like; commonly the only women present were women of the town. The similarity extends from the auditorium to the stage. The Elizabethan playgoer delighted in virtuosity; in exhibitions of strength or skill from his actors; the broad-sword combat in *Macbeth*, and the wrestling in *As You Like It*, were real trials of skill. The bear in *A Winter's Tale* was no doubt a real bear got from a bear pit near by on Bankside. The comic actors especially were the very grandfathers of modern music-hall stars; Tarleton and Kemp and Cowley, the chief of them, were as much popular favourites and esteemed as separate from what they played in as was Harry Lauder. Their songs and tunes were printed and sold in hundreds as broadsheets, just as pirated music-hall songs were later on. This is to be noted because it explains a great deal in the subsequent evolution of the drama. It explains the delight in having everything represented actually on the stage, all murders, battles, duels. It explains the magnificent largesse given by Shakespeare to the professional fool. Work had to be found for him, and Shakespeare, whose difficulties were stepping-stones to his triumphs, gave him Touchstone and Feste, the Porter in *Macbeth* and the Fool in *Lear*. Others met the problem in an attitude of frank despair. Not all great tragic writers can easily or gracefully wield the pen of comedy, and Marlowe in *Dr. Faustus* took the course of leaving to an inferior collaborator the low comedy which the audience loved and a high salaried actor demanded.

Alongside this drama of street platforms and inn-yards and public theatres, there grew another which, blending with it, produced the Elizabethan drama which we know. The public theatres were not the only places at which plays were produced. At the University, at the Inns of Court (which then more than now were, besides centres of study, rather exclusive and expensive clubs), and at the Court they were an important part of almost every festival. At these places were produced academic compositions, either allegorical like the masques, copies of which we find in Shakespeare and by Ben Jonson, or comedies modelled on Plautus or Terence, or tragedies modelled on Seneca. The last were incomparably the most important. The Elizabethan age, which always thought of literature as a guide or handmaid to life, was naturally attracted to a poet who dealt in maxims and 'sentences'; his rhetoric appealed to men for whom words and great passages of verse were an intoxication that only a few to-day can understand or sympathize with; his bloodthirstiness and gloom to an age so full-blooded as not to shrink from horrors. Tragedies early began to be written on the strictly Senecan model, and generally, like Seneca's, with some ulterior intention. Norton and Sackville's *Gorboduc*, the first tragedy in English, produced at a great festival at the Inner Temple, aimed at inducing Elizabeth to marry and save the miseries of a disputed succession. To be put to such a use argues the importance and dignity of this classical tragedy of the learned societies and the Court. None of the pieces composed in this style was written for the popular theatre, and indeed could not have been a success in it. The Elizabethan audience, as we have seen, loved action, and in these Senecan tragedies the action took place 'off'. But they had a strong and abiding influence on the popular stage: they gave it its ghosts, its supernatural warnings, its conception of nemesis and revenge; they gave it its love of introspection and the long passages in which introspection, description or reflection, either in soliloquy or dialogue, holds up the action; contradictorily enough they gave it something at least of its melodrama. Perhaps they helped to enforce the lesson of the miracle plays that a dramatist's proper business was elaboration rather than invention. None of the Elizabethan dramatists except Ben Jonson habitually constructed their own plots. Their method was to take something ready at hand and overlay it with realism or poetry or romance. The stories of their plays, like that of Hamlet's Mousetrap, were 'extant and writ in choice Italian', and very often their methods of preparation were very like his.

Something of the way in which the spirit of adventure of the time affected and finished the drama we have already seen. It is time now to turn to the dramatists themselves.

(2)

Of Marlowe, Kyd, Greene, and Peele—the 'University Wits' who fused the academic and the popular drama, and by giving the latter a sense of literature and learning to mould it to finer issues gave us Shakespeare—only Marlowe can be treated here. Greene and Peele, the former by his comedies, the latter by his historical plays, and Kyd by his tragedies, have their places in the text-books, but they belong to a secondary order of dramatic talent. Marlowe ranks amongst the greatest. It is not merely that historically he is the head and fount of the whole movement, that he changed blank verse, which had been a lumbering instrument before him, into something rich and ringing and rapid and made it the vehicle for the greatest English poetry after him. Historical relations apart, he is great in himself. More than any other English writer of any age, except Byron, he symbolizes the youth of his time; its hot-bloodedness, its lust after knowledge and power and life inspires all his pages. The teaching of Machiavelli, misunderstood for their own purposes by would-be imitators, furnished the reign of Elizabeth with the only political ideals it possessed. The simple brutalism of the creed, with means justified by ends and the unbridled self-regarding pursuit of power, attracted men for whom the Spanish monarchy and the struggle to overthrow it were the main factors and politics. Marlowe took it and turned it to his own uses. There is in his writings a lust of power, 'a hunger and thirst after unrighteousness', a glow of the imagination unhallowed by anything but its own energy, which is in the spirit of the time. In *Tamburlaine* it is the power of conquest, stirred by and reflecting, as we have seen, the great deeds of his day. In *Dr. Faustus* it is the pride of will and eagerness of curiosity. Faustus is devoured by a tormenting desire to enlarge his knowledge to the utmost bounds of nature and art and to extend his power with his knowledge. His is the spirit of Renaissance scholarship heightened to a passionate excess. The play gleams with the pride of learning and the knowledge which learning brings, and with the nemesis that comes after it. 'Ah, gentlemen, hear me with patience, and tremble not at my speeches. Though my heart pants and quivers to remember that I have been a student here these thirty years, oh, would I had never seen Wittemburg, never read book!' And after the agonizing struggle in which Faustus's soul is torn from him to hell, learning comes in at the quiet close.

Yet, for he was a scholar, admired once
For wondrous knowledge in our German schools,
We'll give his mangled limbs due burial;
And all the students, clothed in mourning black,
Shall wait upon his heavy funeral.

Some one character is a centre of overmastering
pride and ambition in every play. In the *Jew of Malta*
it is the hero Barabbas. In *Edward II*, it is Piers
Gaveston. In *Edward II.* indeed, two elements are
mixed—the element of Machiavelli and Tamburlaine
in Gaveston, and the purely tragic element which
evolves from within itself the style in which it shall
be treated, in the king. 'The reluctant pangs of abdi-
cating Royalty,' wrote Charles Lamb in a famous
passage, 'furnished hints which Shakespeare scarcely
improved in his *Richard II.*; and the death scene of
Marlowe's King moves pity and terror beyond any
scene, ancient or modern, with which I am acquainted.'
Perhaps the play gives the hint of what Marlowe might
have become had not an assailant's dagger in a Deptford
tavern cut short at thirty his burning career.

Even in that time of romance and daring speculation
he went further than his fellows. He was said to have
been tainted with atheism, to have denied God and
the Trinity; had he lived he might have had trouble
with the Star Chamber. The free-voyaging intellect
of the age found this one outlet, but if literary evidences
are to be trusted sixteenth and seventeenth century
atheism was a very crude business. *The Atheist's
Tragedie* of Tourneur (a dramatist who need not
otherwise detain us) gives some measure of its intelligence and depth. Says the villain to the heroine,

No? Nay then, invoke
Your great supposed Protector. I will do't.

to which she:

> Supposed Protector! Are you an atheist? then
> I know my prayers and tears are spent in vain.

Marlowe's very faults and extravagances, and they
are many, are only the obverse of his greatness. Magnitude and splendour of language when the thought is
too shrunken to fill it out becomes mere inflation. He
was a butt of the parodists of the day. And Shakespeare, though he honoured him 'on this side idolatry',
did his share of ridicule. Ancient Pistol is fed and
stuffed with relics and rags of Marlowesque affectation—

> Holla, ye pampered jades of Asia!
> What, can ye draw but twenty miles a day.

is a quotation taken straight from *Tamburlaine*.

(3)

A study of Shakespeare, who refuses to be crushed
within the limits of a general essay, is no part of the
plan of this book. We must take up the story of the
drama with the reign of James and with the contemporaries of his later period, though, of course, a
treatment which is conditioned by the order of development is not strictly chronological, and some of the
plays we shall have to refer to belong to the close of the
sixteenth century. We are apt to forget that alongside
Shakespeare and at his heels other dramatists were
supplying material for the theatre. The influence of
Marlowe and particularly of Kyd, whose *Spanish
Tragedy* with its crude mechanism of ghosts and
madness and revenge caught the popular taste, worked
itself out in a score of journeymen dramatists, mere hack
writers, who turned their hand to plays as the hacks
of to-day turn their hand to novels, and with no more

literary merit than that caught as an echo from better
men than themselves. One of the worst of these—he
is also one of the most typical—was John Marston, a
purveyor of tragic gloom and sardonic satire, and an
impostor in both, whose tragedy *Antonio and Mellida*
was published in the same year as Shakespeare's
Hamlet. Both plays owed their style and plot to the
same tradition—the tradition created by Kyd's *Spanish
Tragedy*—in which ghostly promptings to revenge,
terrible crime, and a feigned madman waiting his
opportunity are the elements of tragedy. Nothing
could be more fruitful in an understanding of the
relations of Shakespeare to his age than a comparison
of the two. The style of *Antonio and Mellida* is the
style of *The Murder of Gonzago*. There is no subtlety
nor introspection, the pale cast of thought falls with no
shadow over its scenes. And it is typical of a score of
plays of the kind we have, and beyond doubt of hundreds that have perished. Shakespeare stands alone.

Beside this journey-work tragedy of revenge and
murder which had its root through Kyd and Marlowe
in Seneca and in Italian romance, there was a journey-
work comedy of low life made up of loosely constructed
strings of incidents, buffoonery and romance, that had
its roots in a joyous and fantastic study of the common
people. These plays are happy and high-spirited and,
compared with the ordinary run of the tragedies, of
better workmanship. They deal in the familiar situations of low comedy—the clown, the thrifty citizen
and his frivolous wife, the gallant, the bawd, the good
apprentice and the bad portrayed vigorously and
tersely and with a careless kindly gaiety that still charms
in the reading. The best writers in this kind were
Middleton and Dekker—and the best play to read as a
sample of it *Eastward Ho!* in which Marston put off

his affectation of sardonical melancholy and joined with Jonson and Dekker to produce what is the masterpiece of the non-Shakespearean comedy of the time.

For all our habit of grouping their works together it is a far cry in spirit and temperament from the dramatists whose heyday was under Elizabeth and those who reached their prime under her successor. Quickly though insensibly the temper of the nation suffered eclipse. The high hopes and the ardency of the reign of Elizabeth saddened into a profound pessimism and gloom in that of James. This apparition of unsought melancholy has been widely noted and generally assumed to be inexplicable. In broad outline its causes are clear enough. 'To travel hopefully is a better thing than to arrive.' The Elizabethans were, if ever any were, hopeful travellers. The winds blew them to the four quarters of the world; they navigated all seas; they sacked rich cities. They beat off the great Armada, and harried the very coasts of Spain. They pushed discovery to the ends of the world and amassed great wealth. Under James all these things were over. Peace was made with Spain: national pride was wounded by the solicitous anxiety of the king for a Spanish marriage for the heir to the throne. Sir Walter Ralegh, a romantic adventurer lingering beyond his time, was beheaded out of hand by the ungenerous timidity of the monarch to whom had been transferred devotion and loyalty he was unfitted to receive. The Court which had been a centre of flashing and gleaming brilliance degenerated into a knot of sycophants humouring the pragmatic and self-important folly of a king in whom had implanted themselves all the vices of the Scots and none of their virtues. Nothing seemed left remarkable beneath the visiting moon. The bright day was done and they were for the dark.   The

uprising of Puritanism and the shadow of impending
religious strife darkened the temper of the time.

The change affected all literature and particularly
the drama, which, because it appeals to what all men
have in common, commonly reflects soonest a change
in the outlook or spirit of a people. The onslaughts of
the dramatists on the Puritans, always implacable
enemies of the theatre, became more virulent and
envenomed. What a difference between the sunny
satire of Sir Andrew Aguecheek and the dark animosity
of *The Atheist's Tragedie* with its Languebeau Snuffe
ready to carry out any villainy proposed to him! 'I
speak, sir,' says a lady in the same play to a courtier
who played with her in an attempt to carry on a quick-
witted, 'conceited' love passage in the vein of *Much
Ado*, 'I speak, sir, as the fashion now is, in earnest.'
The quick-witted, light-hearted age was gone. It is
natural that tragedy reflected this melancholy in its
deepest form. Gloom deepened and had no light to
relieve it, men supped full of horrors—there was no
slackening of the tension, no concession to overwrought
nerves, no resting-place for the overwrought soul. It
is in the dramatist John Webster that this new spirit
has its most powerful exponent.

The influence of Machiavelli, which had given
Marlowe tragic figures that were bright and splendid
and burning, smouldered in Webster into a duskier
and intenser heat. His fame rests on two tragedies,
The White Devil and *The Duchess of Malfi*. Both are
stories of lust and crime, full of hate and hideous
vengeances, and through each runs a vein of bitter and
ironical comment on men and women. In them chance
plays the part of fate. 'Blind accident and blundering
mishap—"such a mistake", says one of the criminals,
"as I have often seen in a play" are the steersmen of

their fortunes and the doomsmen of their deeds.' His characters are gloomy; meditative and philosophic murderers, cynical informers, sad and loving women, and they are all themselves in every phrase that they utter. But they are studied in earnestness and sincerity. Unquestionably he is the greatest of Shakespeare's successors in the romantic drama, perhaps his only direct imitator. He has single lines worthy to set beside those in *Othello* or *King Lear*. His dirge in the *Duchess of Malfi*, Charles Lamb thought worthy to be set beside the ditty in *The Tempest*, which reminds Ferdinand of his drowned father. 'As that is of the water, watery, so this is of the earth, earthy.' He has earned his place among the greatest of our dramatists by his two plays, the theme of which matched his sombre genius and the sombreness of the season in which it flowered.

But the drama could not survive long the altered times, and the voluminous plays of Beaumont and Fletcher mark the beginning of the end. They are the decadence of Elizabethan drama. Decadence is a term often used loosely and therefore hard to define, but we may say broadly that an art is decadent when any particular one of the elements which go to its making occurs in excess and disturbs the balance of forces which keeps the work a coherent and intact whole. Poetry is decadent when the sound is allowed to outrun the sense or when the suggestions, say, of colour which it contains are allowed to crowd out its deeper implications. Thus we can call such a poem as this of O'Shaughnessy's,

> We are the music-makers,
> We are the dreamers of dreams,

decadent because it conveys nothing but the mere

delight in an obvious rhythm of words, or such a poem as Morris's 'Two red roses across the moon', because a meaningless refrain, merely pleasing in its word texture, breaks in at intervals on the reader. The drama of Beaumont and Fletcher is decadent in two ways. In the first place those variations and licences with which Shakespeare in his later plays diversified the blank verse handed on to him by Marlowe, are used by them without restraint or measure. 'Weak' endings and 'double' endings—i.e. lines which end either on a conjunction or proposition or some other unstressed word, or lines in which there is a syllable too many—abound in their plays. They destroyed blank verse as a musical and resonant poetic instrument by letting this element of variety outrun the sparing and skilful use which alone could justify it. But they were decadent in other and deeper ways than that. Sentiment in their plays usurps the place of character. Eloquent and moving speeches and fine figures are no longer subservient to the presentation of character in action, but are set down for their own sake. 'What strange self-trumpeters and tongue-bullies all the brave soldiers of Beaumont and Fletcher are', said Coleridge. When they die they die to the music of their own virtue. When dreadful deeds are done they are described not with that authentic and lurid vividness which throws light on the working of the human heart in Shakespeare or Webster but in tedious rhetoric. Resignation, not fortitude, is the authors' forte and they play upon it amazingly. The sterner tones of their predecessors melt into the long-drawn broken accent of pathos and woe. This delight not in action or in emotion arising from action but a passivity of suffering is only one aspect of a certain mental flaccidity in grain. Shakespeare may be free and even coarse. Beaumont and

E

Fletcher cultivate indecency. They made their subject not their master but their plaything, or an occasion for the convenient exercise of their own powers of figure and rhetoric.

Of their followers, Massinger, Ford, and Shirley, no more need be said than that they carried one step further the faults of their masters. Emotion and tragic passion give way to wire-drawn sentiment. Tragedy takes on the air of a masquerade. With them romantic drama died a natural death and the Puritans' closing of the theatres only gave it a *coup de grâce*. In England it has had no second birth.

(4)

Outside the direct romantic succession there worked another author whose lack of sympathy with it, as well as his close connection with the age which followed, justifies his separate treatment. Ben Jonson shows a marked contrast to Shakespeare in his character, his accomplishments, and his attitude to letters, while his career was more varied than Shakespeare's own. The first 'classic' in English writing, he was a 'romantic' in action. In his adventurous youth he was by turns scholar, soldier, bricklayer, actor. He trailed a pike with Leicester in the Low Countries; on his return to England he fought a duel and killed his man, only escaping hanging by benefit of clergy; at the end of his life he was Poet Laureate. Such a career is sufficiently diversified, and it forms a striking contrast to the plainness and severity of his work. But it must not lead us to forget or under-estimate his learning and knowledge. Not Gray nor Tennyson nor Swinburne—perhaps not even Milton—was a better scholar. He is one of the earliest of English writers to hold and express different theories about literature. He con-

sciously appointed himself a teacher; was a missionary
of literature with a definite creed.

But though in a general way his dramatic principles
are opposed to the romantic tendencies of his age, he
is by no means blindly classical. He never consented
to be bound by the 'Unities'—that conception of
dramatic construction evolved out of Aristotle and
Horace and elaborated in the Renaissance till, in its
strictest form, it laid down that the whole scene of a
play should be in one place, its whole action deal with
one single series of events, and the time it represented
as elapsing be no greater than the time it took in
playing. He was always pre-eminently an Englishman
of his own day with a scholar's rather than a poet's
temper, hating extravagance, hating bombast and cant,
and only limited because in ruling out these things he
ruled out much else that was essential to the spirit of
the time. As a craftsman he was uncompromising; he
never bowed to the tastes of the public and never
veiled his scorn of those—Shakespeare among them—
whom he conceived to do so; but he knew and valued
his own work, as his famous last word to an audience
who might be unsympathetic stands to witness,

> By God 'tis good, and if you like 't you may.

Compare the temper it reveals with the titles of the
two contemporary comedies of his gentler and greater
brother, the one *As You Like It*, the other *What You
Will*. Of the two attitudes towards the public, and
they might stand as typical of two kinds of artists,
neither perhaps can claim complete sincerity. A
truculent and noisy disclaimer of their favours is not
a bad tone to assume towards an audience; in the end
it is apt to succeed as well as the sub-ironical com-
pliance which is its opposite.

Jonson's theory of comedy and the consciousness with which he set it against the practice of his contemporaries, and particularly of Shakespeare, receive explicit statement in the prologue to *Every Man Out of His Humour*—one of his earlier plays. 'I travail with another objection, Signior, which I fear will be enforced against the author ere I can be delivered of it', says Mitis. 'What's that, sir?' replies Cordatus. Mitis: 'That the argument of his comedy might have been of some other nature, as of a duke to be in love with a countess, and that countess to be in love with the duke's son, and the son to love the lady's waiting maid; some such cross-wooing, with a clown to their servingman, better than to be thus near and familiarly allied to the time.' Cordatus: 'You say well, but I would fain hear one of these autumn-judgments define once, *Quin sit comœdia?* If he cannot, let him content himself with Cicero's definition, till he have strength to propose to himself a better, who would have a comedy to be *imitatio vitæ, speculum consuetudinis, imago veritatis*; a thing throughout pleasant and ridiculous and accommodated to the correction of manners.' That was what he meant his comedy to be, and so he conceived the popular comedy of the day, *Twelfth Night* and *Much Ado*. Shakespeare might play with dukes and countesses, serving-women and pages, clowns and disguises; he would come down more near and ally himself familiarly with the times. So comedy was to be medicinal, to purge contemporary London of its follies and its sins; and it was to be constructed with regularity and elaboration, respectful to the Unities if not ruled by them, and built up of characters each the embodiment of some 'humour' or eccentricity, and each, when his eccentricity is displaying itself at its fullest, outwitted and exposed. This conception of 'humours', based on a physiology which was already obsolescent, takes heavily from the realism of Jonson's methods, nor does his use of a careful vocabulary of contemporary colloquialism and slang save him from a certain dryness and tediousness to modern readers. The truth is he was less a satirist of contemporary manners than a satirist in the abstract who followed the models of classical writers in this style, and he found the vices and follies of his own day hardly adequate to the intricacy and elaborateness of the plots which he constructed for their exposure. At the first glance his people are contemporary types, at the second they betray themselves for what they are really—cock-shies set up by the new comedy of Greece that every 'classical' satirist in Rome or France or England has had his shot at since. One wonders whether Ben Jonson, for all his satirical intention, had as much observation—as much of an eye for contemporary types—as Shakespeare's rustics and roysterers prove him to have had. It follows that all but one or two of his plays, when they are put on the stage to-day are apt to have a sense of remoteness and other-worldliness which we hardly feel with Shakespeare or Molière. Jonson's muse moves along the high-road of comedy which is the Roman road, and carries in her train types that have done service to many since the ancients fashioned them. Jealous husbands, foolish pragmatic fathers, a dissolute son, a boastful soldier, a cunning slave—they all are merely counters by which the game of comedy used to be played. In England, since Shakespeare took his hold on the stage, that road has been stopped for us, that game has ceased to amuse.

Ben Jonson, then, in a certain degree failed in his intention. Had he kept closer to contemporary life, instead of merely grafting on to it types he had learned

from books, he might have made himself an English
Molière—without Molière's breadth and clarity, but
with a corresponding vigour and strength which would
have kept his work sweet. And he might have founded
a school of comedy that would have got its roots
deeper into our national life than the trivial and
licentious Restoration comedy ever succeeded in doing.
As it is, his importance is mostly historical. One must
credit him with being the first of the English classics—
of the age which gave us Dryden and Swift and Pope.
Perhaps that is enough in his praise.

CHAPTER IV

THE SEVENTEENTH CENTURY

(1)

WITH the seventeenth century the great school of imaginative writers that made glorious the last years of Elizabeth's reign had passed away. Spenser was dead before 1600, Sir Philip Sidney a dozen years earlier, and though Shakespeare and Drayton and many other men whom we class roughly as Elizabethan lived on to work under James, their temper and their ideals belong to the earlier day. The seventeenth century, not in England only but in Europe, brought a new way of thinking with it, and gave a new direction to human interest and to human affairs. It is not perhaps easy to define nor is it visible in the greater writers of the time. Milton, for instance, and Sir Thomas Browne are both of them too big, and in their genius too far separated from their fellows to give us much clue to altered conditions. It is commonly in the work of lesser and forgotten writers that the spirit of an age has its fullest expression. Genius is a law to itself; it moves in another dimension; it is out of time. To define this seventeenth-century spirit, then, one must look at the literature of the age as a whole. What is there that one finds in it which marks a change in temperament and outlook from the Renaissance, and the time which immediately followed it?

Putting it very broadly one may say that literature in the seventeenth century becomes for the first time essentially modern in spirit. We began our survey of modern English literature at the Renaissance because the discovery of the New World, and the widening of human experience and knowledge, which that and the revival of classical learning implied, mark a definite break from a way of thought which had been continuous since the break-up of the Roman Empire. The men of the Renaissance felt themselves to be modern. They started afresh, owing nothing to their immediate forbears, and when they talked, say, of Chaucer, they did so in very much the same accent as we do to-day. He was mediæval and obsolete; the interest which he possessed was a purely literary interest; his readers did not meet him easily on the same plane of thought, or forget the lapse of time which separated him from them. And in another way too, the Renaissance began modern writing. Inflections had been dropped. The revival of the classics had enriched our vocabulary, and the English language, after a gradual impoverishment which followed the obsolescence one after another of the local dialects, attained a fairly fixed form. There is more difference between the language of the English writings of Sir Thomas More and that of the prose of Chaucer than there is between that of More and of Ruskin. But it is not till the seventeenth century that the modern spirit, in the fullest sense of the word, comes into being. Defined it means a spirit of observation, of preoccupation with detail, of stress laid on matter of fact, of analysis of feelings and mental processes, of free argument upon institutions and government. In relation to knowledge, it is the spirit of science; and the study of science, which is the essential intellectual fact in modern history, dates from just this time, from Bacon and Newton and Descartes. In relation to literature, it is the spirit of criticism, and criticism in England is the creation of the seventeenth century. The positive temper, the attitude of realism, is everywhere in the ascendant. The sixteenth century made voyages of discovery; the seventeenth sat down to take stock of the riches it had gathered. For the first time in English literature writing becomes a vehicle for storing and conveying facts.

It would be easy to give instances: one must suffice here. Biography, which is one of the most characteristic kinds of English writing, was unknown to the moderns as late as the sixteenth century. Partly the awakened interest in the careers of the ancient statesmen and soldiers which the study of Plutarch had excited, and partly the general interest in and craving for facts, set men writing down the lives of their fellows. The earliest English biographies date from this time. In the beginning they were concerned, like Plutarch, with men of action, and when Sir Fulke Greville wrote a brief account of his friend Sir Philip Sidney it was the courtier and the soldier, and not the author, that he designed to celebrate. But soon men of letters came within their scope, and though the interest in the lives of authors came too late to give us the contemporary life of Shakespeare we so much long for, it was early enough to make possible those masterpieces of condensed biography in which Izaak Walton celebrates Herbert and Donne. Fuller and Aubrey, to name only two authors, spent lives of laborious industry in hunting down and chronicling the smallest facts about the worthies of their day and the time immediately before them. Autobiography followed where biography led. Lord Herbert of Cherbury and Margaret Duchess of Newcastle, as well as less reputable persons, followed the new mode. By the time of the Restoration Pepys and Evelyn were keeping their diaries, and Fox his journal. Just as in poetry the lyric, which is the expression of personal feeling, became more widely practised, more subtle and more sincere, in prose the letter, the journal, and the autobiography formed themselves to meet the new and growing demand for analysis of the feelings and the intimate thoughts and sensations of real men and women. A minor form of literature which had a brief but popular vogue ministered less directly to the same need. The 'Character', a brief descriptive essay on a contemporary type—a tobacco seller, an old college butler or the like—was popular because in its own way it matched the newly awakened taste for realism and fact. The drama which in the hands of Ben Jonson had attacked folly and wickedness proper to no place or time, descended to the drawing-rooms of the day, and Congreve occupied himself with the portrayal of the social frauds and foolishnesses perpetrated by actual living men and women of fashion in contemporary London. Satire ceased to be a mere expression of a vague discontent, and became a weapon against opposing men and policies. Readers in the new generation were nothing if not critical. They were for testing directly institutions whether they were literary, social, or political. They wanted facts, and they wanted to take a side.

In the distinct and separate realm of poetry a revolution no less remarkable took place. Spenser had been both a poet and a Puritan: he had designed to show by his great poem the training and fashioning of a Puritan English gentleman. But the alliance between poetry and Puritanism which he typified failed to survive his death. The essentially pagan spirit of the Renaissance which caused him no doubts nor difficulties proved too strong for his readers and his followers, and the emancipated artistic enthusiasm in which it worked alienated from secular poetry men with deep and strong religious convictions. Religion and morality and poetry, which in Sidney and Spenser had gone hand in hand, separated from each other. Poems like *Venus and Adonis* or like Shakespeare's sonnets could hardly be squared with the sterner temper which persecution began to breed. Even within orthodox Anglicanism poetry and religion began to be deemed no fit company for each other. When George Herbert left off courtier and took orders he burnt his earlier love poetry, and only the persuasion of his friends prevented Donne from following the same course. Pure poetry became more and more an exotic. All Milton's belongs to his earlier youth; his middle age was occupied with controversy and propaganda in prose; when he returned to poetry in blindness and old age it was 'to justify the ways of God to man'—to use poetry, that is, for a spiritual and moral rather than an artistic end.

Though the age was curious and inquiring, though poetry and prose tended more and more to be enlisted in the service of non-artistic enthusiasms and to be made the vehicle of deeper emotions and interests than perhaps a northern people could ever find in art pure and simple, it was not like the time that followed it, a 'prosaic' age. Enthusiasm burned fierce and clear, displaying itself in the passionate polemic of Milton, in the fanaticism of Bunyan and Fox, hardly more than in the gentle, steadfast search for knowledge in Burton, and the wide and vigilant curiousness of Bacon. Its eager experimentalism tried the impossible; wrote poems and then gave them a weight of meaning they could not carry, as when Fletcher in *The Purple Island* designed to allegorize all that the physiology of his day knew of the human body, or when Donne sought to convey abstruse scientific fact in a lyric. It gave men a passion for pure learning, set Jonson to turn himself from a bricklayer into the best equipped scholar of his day, and Fuller and Camden grubbing among English records and gathering for the first time materials of scientific value for English history. Enthusiasm gave us poetry that was at once full of learning and of imagination, poetry that was harsh and brutal in its roughness and at the same time impassioned. And it set up a school of prose that combined colloquial readiness and fluency, pregnancy and high sentiment, with a cumbrous pedantry of learning which was the fruit of its own excess.

The form in which enthusiasm manifested itself most fiercely was as we have seen not favourable to literature. Puritanism drove itself like a wedge into the art of the time, broadening as it went. Had there been no more in it than the moral earnestness and religiousness of Sidney and Spenser, Cavalier would not have differed from Roundhead, and there might have been no civil war; each party was endowed deeply with the religious sense and Charles I. was a sincerely pious man. But while Spenser and Sidney held that life as a preparation for eternity must be ordered and strenuous and devout but that care for the hereafter was not incompatible with a frank and full enjoyment of life as it is lived, Puritanism as it developed in the middle classes became a sterner and darker creed. The doctrine of original sin, face to face with the fact that art, like other pleasures, was naturally and readily entered into and enjoyed, forced them to the plain conclusion that art was an evil thing. As early as Shakespeare's youth they had been strong enough to keep the theatres outside London walls; at the time of the Civil War they closed them altogether, and the feud which had lasted for over a generation between them and the dramatists ended in the destruction of the literary drama. In the brief years of their ascendancy they produced no literature, for Milton is much too large to be tied down to their negative creed, and, indeed, in many of his qualities, his love of music and his sensuousness, for instance, he is antagonistic to the temper of his day. With the Restoration their earnest and strenuous spirit fled to America. It is noteworthy that it had no literary manifestation there till two centuries after the time of its passage. Hawthorne's novels are the fruit—the one ripe fruit in art—of the Puritan imagination.

(2)

If the reader adopts the seventeenth-century habit himself and takes stock of what the Elizabethans accomplished in poetry, he will recognize speedily that their work reached various stages of completeness. They perfected the poetic drama and its instrument, blank verse; they perfected, though not in the severer Italian form, the sonnet; they wrote with extraordinary delicacy and finish short lyrics in which a simple and freer manner drawn from the classics took the place of the mediæval intricacies of the ballad and the rondeau. And in the forms which they failed to bring to perfection they did beautiful and noble work. The splendour of *The Faerie Queene* is in separate passages; as a whole it is over-tortuous and slow; its affectations, its sensuousness, the mere difficulty of reading it, make us feel it a collection of great passages, strung it is true on a large conception, rather than a great work. The Elizabethans, that is, had not discovered the secret of the long poem; the abstract idea of the 'heroic' epic which was in all their minds had to wait for embodiment till *Paradise Lost*. In a way their treatment of the pastoral or eclogue form was imperfect too. They used it well but not so well as their models, Vergil and

Theocritus; they had not quite mastered the convention on which it is built.

The seventeenth century, taking stock in some such fashion of its artistic possessions, found some things it were vain to try to do. It could add nothing to the accomplishment of the English sonnet, so it hardly tried; with the exception of a few sonnets in the Italian form of Milton, the century can show us nothing in this mode of verse. The literary drama was brought to perfection in the early years of it by the surviving Elizabethans; later decades could add nothing to it but licence, and, as we saw, the licences they added hastened its destruction. But in other forms the poets of the new time experimented eagerly, and, in the stress of experiment, poetry which under Elizabeth had been integral and coherent split into different schools. As the period of the Renaissance was also that of the Reformation it was only natural a determined effort should sooner or later be made to use poetry for religious purposes. The earliest English hymn-writing, our first devotional verse in the vernacular, belongs to this time, and a Catholic and religious school of lyricism grew and flourished beside the pagan neo-classical writers. From the tumult of experiment three schools disengage themselves, the school of Spenser, the school of Jonson, and the school of Donne.

At the outset of the century Spenser's influence was triumphant and predominant; his was the main stream with which the other poetic influences of the time merely mingled. His popularity is referable to qualities other than those which belonged peculiarly to his talent as a poet. Puritans loved his religious ardour, and in those Puritan households where the stricter conception of the diabolical nature of all poetry had not penetrated, his works were read—standing on a shelf, may be, between the new translation of the Bible and Sylvester's translation of the French poet Du Bartas' work on the creation, that had a large popularity at that time as family reading. Probably the Puritans were as blind to the sensuousness of Spenser's language and imagery as they were (and are) to the same qualities in the Bible itself. *The Faerie Queene* would easily achieve innocuousness amongst those who can find nothing but an allegory of the Church in the 'Song of Songs'. His followers made their allegory a great deal plainer than he had done his. In his poem called *The Purple Island*, Phineas Fletcher, a Puritan imitator of Spenser in Cambridge, essayed to set forth the struggle of the soul at grips with evil, a battle in which the body —the 'Purple Island'—is the field. To a modern reader it is a desolating and at times a mildly amusing book, in which everything from the liver to the seven deadly sins is personified; in which after four books of allegorized contemporary anatomy and physiology, the will (Voletta) engages in a struggle with Satan and conquers by the help of Christ and King James! The allegory is clever—too clever—and the author can paint a pleasant picture, but on the whole he was happier in his pastoral work. His brother Giles made a better attempt at the Spenserian manner. His long poem *Christ's Victory and Death* shows, for all its carefully Protestant tone, high qualities of mysticism; across it Spenser and Milton join hands.

It was, however, in pastoral poetry that Spenser's influence found its pleasantest outlet. One might hesitate to advise a reader to embark on either of the Fletchers. There is no reason why any modern should not read and enjoy Browne or Wither, in whose softly flowing verse the sweetness and contentment of the countryside, that 'merry England' which was the background of all sectarian and intellectual strife and labour, finds as in a placid stream a calm reflection and picture of itself. The seventeenth century gave birth to many things that only came to maturity in the nineteenth; if you care for that kind of literary study which searches out origins and digs for hints and models of accepted styles, you will find in Browne that which influenced more than any other single thing the early work of Keats. Browne has another claim to immortality; if it be true as is now thought that he was the author of the epitaph on the Countess of Pembroke:

> Underneath this sable hearse
> Lies the subject of all verse:
> Sidney's sister, Pembroke's mother;
> Death, ere thou hast slain another
> Fair and learn'd and good as she,
> Time shall throw a dart at thee.

then he achieved the miracle of a quintessential statement of the spirit of the English Renaissance. For the breath of it stirs in these slow quiet-moving lines, and its few and simple words implicate the soul of a period.

By the end of the first quarter of the century the influence of Spenser and the school which worked under it had died out. Its place was taken by the twin schools of Jonson and Donne. Jonson's poetic method is something like his dramatic; he formed himself as exactly as possible on classical models. Horace had written satires and elegies, and epistles and complimentary verses, and Jonson quite consciously and deliberately followed where Horace led. He wrote elegies on the great, letters and courtly compliments and love-lyrics to his friends, satires with an air of general censure. But though he was classical, his style was never latinized. In all of them he strove to pour into an ancient form language that was as intense and vigorous and as purely English as the earliest trumpeters of the Renaissance in England could have wished. The result is not entirely successful. He seldom fails to reproduce classic dignity and good sense; on the other hand he seldom succeeds in achieving classic grace and ease. Occasionally, as in his best known lyric, he is perfect and achieves an air of spontaneity little short of marvellous, when we know that his images and even his words in the song are all plagiarized from other men. His expression is always clear and vigorous and his sense good and noble. The native earnestness and sincerity of the man shines through as it does in his dramas and his prose. In an age of fantastic and meaningless eulogy—eulogy so amazing in its unexpectedness and abstruseness that the wonder is not so much that it should have been written as that it could have been thought of—Jonson maintains his personal dignity and his good sense. You feel his compliments are such as the best should be, not necessarily understood and properly valued by the public, but of a discriminating sort that by their very comprehending sincerity would be most warmly appreciated by the people to whom they were addressed. His verses to Shakespeare and his prose commentaries on him too, are models of what self-respecting admiration should be, generous in its praise of excellence, candid in its statement of defects. They are the kind of compliments that Shakespeare himself, if he had grace enough, must have loved to receive.

Very different from his direct and dignified manner is the closely packed style of Donne, who, Milton apart, is the greatest English writer of the century, though his obscurity has kept him out of general reading. No poetry in English, not even Browning, is more difficult to understand. The obscurity of Donne

F

and Browning proceed from such similar causes that they are worth examining together. In both, as in the obscure passages in Shakespeare's later plays, obscurity arises not because the poet says too little but because he attempts to say too much. He huddles a new thought on the one before it, before the first has had time to express itself; he sees things or analyses emotions so swiftly and subtly himself that he forgets the slower comprehensions of his readers; he is for analysing things far deeper than the ordinary mind commonly can. His wide and curious knowledge finds terms and likenesses unknown to us to express his meaning; he sees things from a dozen points of view at once and tumbles in a heap on to the page a hint of each separate vision; his restless intellect finds new and subtler shades of emotion and thought invisible to other pairs of eyes, and cannot, because speech is modelled on the average of our intelligences, find words to express them; he is always trembling on the brink of the inarticulate. All this applies to both Donne and Browning, and the comparison could be pushed further still. Both draw the knowledge which is the main cause of their obscurity from the same source, the bypaths of mediævalism. Browning's *Sordello* is obscure because he knows too much about mediæval Italian history; Donne's *Anniversary* because he is too deeply read in mediæval scholasticism and speculation. Both make themselves more difficult to the reader who is familiar with the poetry of their contemporaries by the disconcerting freshness of their point of view. Seventeenth-century love poetry was idyllic and idealist; Donne's is passionate and realistic to the point of cynicism. To read him after reading Browne or Jonson is to have the same shock as reading Browning after Tennyson. Both poets are salutary in the strong and biting antidote they bring to sentimentalism in thought and melodious facility in writing. They are the corrective of lazy thinking and lazy composition.

Elizabethan love poetry was written on a convention which, though it was used with manliness and entire sincerity by Sidney, did not escape the fate of its kind. Dante's love for Beatrice, Petrarch's for Laura, the gallant and passionate adoration of Sidney for his Stella, became the models for a dismal succession of imaginary woes. They were all figments of the mind, perhaps hardly that; they all use the same terms and write in fixed strains, epicurean and sensuous like Ronsard, ideal and intellectualized like Dante, sentimental and adoring like Petrarch. Into this enclosed garden of sentiment and illusion Donne burst passionately and rudely, pulling up the gay-coloured tangled weeds that choked thoughts, planting, as one of his followers said, the seeds of fresh invention. Where his forerunners had been idealist, epicurean, or adoring, he was brutal, cynical and immitigably realist. He could begin a poem, 'For God sake hold your tongue, and let me love'; he could be as resolutely free from illusion as Shakespeare when he addressed his Dark Lady:

> Hope not for mind in women; at their best
> Sweetness and wit, they're but mummy, possest.

And where the sonneteers pretended to a sincerity which was none of theirs, he was, like Browning, unaffectedly a dramatic lyrist. 'I did best', he said, 'when I had least truth for my subject.'

His love poetry was written in his turbulent and brilliant youth, and the poetic talent which made it turned in his later years to express itself in hymns and religious poetry. But there is no essential distinction between the two halves of his work. It is all of a piece. The same swift and subtle spirit which analyses experiences of passion, analyses, in his later poetry, those of religion. His devotional poems, though they probe and question, are none the less never sermons, but rather confessions or prayers. His intense individualism, eager always, as his best critic has said, 'to find a North-West passage of his own',[1] pressed its curious and sceptical questioning into every corner of love and life and religion, explored unsuspected depths, exploited new discovered paradoxes, and turned its discoveries always into poetry of the closely-packed artificial style which was all its own. Simplicity indeed would have been for him an affectation; his elaborateness is not like that of his followers, constructed painfully in a vicious desire to compass the unexpected, but the natural overflow of an amazingly fertile and ingenious mind. The curiosity, the desire for truth, the search after minute and detailed knowledge of his age is all in his verse. He bears the spirit of his time not less markedly than Bacon does, or Newton, or Descartes.

The work of the followers of Donne and Jonson leads straight to the new school, Jonson's by giving that school a model on which to work, Donne's by producing an era of extravagance and absurdity which made a literary revolution imperative. The school of Donne —the 'fantastics' as they have been called (Dr. Johnson called them the metaphysical poets), produced in Herbert and Vaughan, our two noblest writers of religious verse, the flower of a mode of writing which ended in the somewhat exotic religiousness of Crashaw. In the hands of Cowley the use of far-sought and intricate imagery became a trick, and the fantastic school, the soul of sincerity gone out of it, died when he

[1] Prof. Grierson in *Cambridge History of English Literature*.

died. To the followers of Jonson we owe that delightful and simple lyric poetry which fills our anthologies, their courtly lyricism receiving a new impulse in the intenser loyalty of troubled times. The most finished of them is perhaps Carew; the best, because of the freshness and varity of his subject-matter and his easy grace, Herrick. At the end of them came Waller and gave to the five-accented rhymed verse (the heroic couplet) that trick of regularity and balance which marked the classical school.

(3)

The prose literature of the seventeenth century is extraordinarily rich and varied, and a study of it would cover a wide field of human knowledge. The new and unsuspected harmonies discovered by the Elizabethans were applied indeed to all the tasks of which prose is capable, from telling stories to setting down the results of speculation which was revolutionizing science and philosophy. For the first time the vernacular and not Latin became the language of scientific research, and though Bacon in his *Novum Organum* adhered to the older mode its disappearance was rapid. English was proving itself too flexible an instrument for conveying ideas for it to be longer neglected. It was applied, too, to preaching of a more formal and grandiose kind than the plain and homely Latimer ever dreamed of. The preachers—though their golden-mouthed oratory, which blended in its combination of vigour and cadence the euphuistic and colloquial styles of the Elizabethans, is in itself a glory of English literature—belong by their matter too exclusively to the province of Church history to be dealt with here. The men of science and philosophy, Newton, Hobbes, and Locke, are in a like way outside our province. For the purpose of the literary student the achievement of the seventeenth century can be judged in four separate men or books—in the Bible, in Francis Bacon, and in Burton and Browne.

In a way the Bible, like the preachers, lies outside the domain of literary study in the narrow sense; but its sheer literary magnitude, and the abiding significance of it in our subsequent history, social, political, and artistic as well as religious, compel us to turn aside to examine the causes that have produced such great results. The Authorized Version is not, of course, a purely seventeenth-century work. Though the scholars [1] who wrote and compiled it had before them all the previous vernacular texts and chose the best readings where they found them or devised new ones in accordance with the original, the basis is undoubtedly the Tudor version of Tindall. It has, none the less, the qualities of the time of its publication. It could hardly have been done earlier; had it been so, it would not have been done half so well. In it English has lost both its roughness and its affectation and retained its strength; the Bible is the supreme example of early English prose style. The reason is not far to seek. Of all recipes for good or noble writing that which enjoins the writer to be careful about the matter and never mind the manner, is the most sure. The translators had the handling of matter of the gravest dignity and momentousness, and their sense of reverence kept them right in their treatment of it. They cared passionately for the truth; they were virtually anonymous and not ambitious of originality or literary fame; they had no desire to stand between the book and its readers. It followed that they cultivated that naked plainness and spareness which makes their work

[1] There is a graphic little pen-picture of their method in Selden's *Table Talk*.

supreme. The Authorized Version is the last and greatest of those English translations which were the fruit of Renaissance scholarship and pioneering. It is the first and greatest piece of English prose.

Its influence is one of those things on which it is profitless to comment or enlarge simply because they are an understood part of every man's experience. In its own time it helped to weld England, for whereas, before, one Bible was read at home and another in churches, all now read the new version. Its supremacy was instantaneous and unchallenged, and it quickly coloured speech and literature; it could produce a Bunyan in the century of its birth. To it belongs the native dignity and eloquence of peasant speech. It runs like a golden thread through all our writing subsequent to its coming: men so diverse as Huxley and Carlyle have paid their tribute to its power; Ruskin counted it the one essential part of his education. It will be a bad day for the mere quality of our language when it ceases to be read.

At the time the translators were sitting, Francis Bacon was at the height of his fame. By profession a lawyer—time-serving and over compliant to wealth and influence—he gives singularly little evidence of it in the style of his books. Lawyers, from the necessity they are under of exerting persuasion, of planting an unfamiliar argument in the minds of hearers of whose favour they are doubtful, but whose sympathy they must gain, are usually of purpose diffuse. They cultivate the gift, possessed by Edmund Burke above all other English authors, of putting the same thing freshly and in different forms a great many times in succession. They value copiousness and fertility of illustration. Nothing could be more unlike this normal legal manner than the style of Bacon. 'No man,' says Ben Jonson, speaking in one of those vivid little notes of his, of his oratorical method, ' no man ever coughed or turned aside from him without loss.' He is a master of the aphoristic style. He compresses his wisdom into the quintessential form of an epigram; so complete and concentrated is his form of statement, so shortly is everything put, that the mere transition from one thought to another gives his prose a curious air of disjointedness as if he flitted arbitrarily from one thing to another, and jotted down anything that came into his head. His writing has clarity and lucidity; it abounds in terseness of expression and in exact and discriminating phraseology; and in the minor arts of composition —in the use of quotations for instance—it can be extraordinarily felicitous. But it lacks spaciousness and ease and rhythm; it makes too inexorable a demand on the attention, and the harassed reader soon finds himself longing for those breathing spaces which consideration or perhaps looseness of thought has implanted in the prose of other writers.

His *Essays*, the work by which he is best known, were in their origin merely jottings gradually cohered and enlarged into the series we know. In them he had the advantage of a subject which he had studied closely through life. He counted himself a master in the art of managing men, and 'Human Nature and how to manage it' would be a good title for his book. Men are studied in the spirit of Machiavelli, whose philosophy of government appealed so powerfully to the Elizabethan mind. Taken together the essays which deal with public matters are in effect a kind of manual for statesmen and princes, instructing them how to acquire power and how to keep it, deliberating how far they may go safely in the direction of self-interest, and to what degree the principle of self-interest must be subordinated to the wider interests of the people who are ruled. Democracy, which in England was to make its splendid beginnings in the seventeenth century, finds little to foretell it in the works of Bacon. Though he never advocates cruelty or oppression and is wise enough to see that no statesman can entirely set aside moral considerations, his ethical tone is hardly elevating; the moral obliquity of his public life is to a certain extent explained, in all but its grosser elements, in his published writings. The essays, of course, contain much more than this: the spirit of curious and restless inquiry which animated Bacon finds expression in those on 'Health', 'Gardens', and 'Plantations' and others of the kind; and a deeper vein of earnestness runs through some of them—those for instance on 'Friendship', 'Truth', and 'Death'.

The *Essays* sum up in a condensed form the intellectual interests which find larger treatment in his other works. His *Henry VII.*, the first piece of scientific history in the English language (indeed in the modern world) is concerned with a king whose practice was the outcome of a political theory identical with Bacon's own. *The Advancement of Learning* is a brilliant popular exposition of the cause of scientific inquiry and of the inductive or investigatory method of research. *The New Atlantis* is the picture of an ideal community whose common purpose is scientific investigation. Bacon's name is not upon the roll of those who have enlarged by brilliant conjectures or discoveries the store of human knowledge; his own investigations so far as they are recorded are all of a trivial nature. The truth about him is that he was a brilliantly clever popularizer of the cause of science, a kind of seventeenth-century Huxley, concerned rather to lay down large general principles for the guidance of the work of others, than to be a serious worker himself. The superstition of later times, acting on and refracting his amazing intellectual gifts, has raised him to a godlike eminence which is by right none of his; it has even credited him with the authorship of Shakespeare, and in its wilder moments with the composition of all that is of supreme worth in Elizabethan literature. It is not necessary to take these delusions seriously. The ignorance of mediævalism was in the habit of crediting Vergil with the construction of the Roman aqueducts and temples whose ruins are scattered over Europe. The modern Baconians reach much the same intellectual level.

A similar enthusiasm for knowledge and at any rate a pretence to science belong to the author of *The Anatomy of Melancholy*, Robert Burton. His one book is surely the most amazing in English prose. Its professed object was simple and comprehensive; it was to analyse human melancholy, to describe its effects, and prescribe for its removal. But as his task grew, melancholy came to mean to Burton all the ills that flesh is heir to. He tracked it in obscure and unsuspected forms; drew illustrations from a range of authors so much wider than the compass of the reading of even the most learned since, that he is generally credited with the invention of a large part of his quotations. Ancients and moderns, poets and prose writers, schoolmen and dramatists are all drawn upon for the copious store of his examples; they are always cited with an air of quietly humorous shrewdness in the comments and enclosed in a prose that is straightforward, simple and vigorous, and can on occasion command both rhythm and beauty of phrase. It is a mistake to regard Burton from the point of view (due largely to Charles Lamb) of tolerant or loving delight in quaintness for quaintness' sake. His book is anything but scientific in form, but it is far from being the work of a recluse or a fool. Behind his lack of system he takes a broad and psychologically an essentially just view of human ills, and modern medicine has gone far in its admiration of what is at bottom a most comprehensive and subtle treatise in diagnosis.

A writer of a very different quality is Sir Thomas Browne. Of all the men of his time he is the only one of whom one can say for certain that he held the manner of saying a thing more important than the thing said. He is our first deliberate and conscious stylist, the forerunner of Charles Lamb, of Stevenson (whose *Virginibus Puerisque* is modelled on his method of treatment) and of the stylistic school of the 1890s and 1900s. His eloquence is too studied to rise to the greatest heights, and his speculation, though curious and discursive, never really results in deep thinking. He is content to embroider his pattern out of the stray fancies of an imaginative nature. His best known work, the *Religio Medici*, is a random confession of belief and thoughts, full of the inconsequent speculations of a man with some knowledge of science but not deeply or earnestly interested about it, content rather to follow the wayward imaginations of a mind naturally gifted with a certain poetic quality, than to engage in serious intellectual exercise. Such work could never maintain its hold on taste if it were not carefully finished and constructed with elaborate care. Browne, if he was not a great writer, was a literary artist of a high quality. He exploits a quaint and lovable egoism with extraordinary skill; and though his delicately figured and latinized sentences commonly sound platitudinous and trivial when they are translated into rough Saxon prose, as they stand they are rich and melodious enough.

(4)

In a century of surpassing richness in prose and poetry, one author stands by himself. John Milton refuses to be classed with any of the schools. Though Dryden tells us Milton confessed to him that Spenser was his 'original', he has no connection—other than a general similarity of purpose, moral and religious—with Spenser's followers. To the fantastics he paid in his youth the doubtful compliment of one or two half-contemptuous imitations and never touched them again. He had no turn for the love lyrics or the court-liness of the school of Jonson. In everything he did he was himself and his own master; he devised his own subjects and wrote his own style. He stands alone and must be judged alone.

No author, however, can ever escape from the influences of his time, and, just as much as his lesser contemporaries, Milton has his place in literary history and derives from the great original impulse which set in motion all the enterprises of the century. He is the last and greatest figure in the English Renaissance. The new passion for art and letters which in its earnest fumbling beginnings gave us the prose of Cheke and Ascham and the poetry of Surrey and Sackville, comes to a full and splendid and perfect end in his work. In it the Renaissance and the Reformation, imperfectly fused by Sidney and Spenser, blend in their just proportions. The transplantation into English of classical forms which had been the aim of Sidney and the endeavour of Jonson he finally accomplished; in his work the dream of all the poets of the Renaissance— the heroic poem—finds its fulfilment. There was no poet of the time but wanted to do for his country what Vergil had planned to do for Rome, to sing its origins, and to celebrate its morality and its citizenship in the epic form. Spenser had tried it in *The Faerie Queene* and failed splendidly. Where he failed, Milton succeeded, though his poem is not on the origins of England but on the ultimate subject of the origins of mankind. We know from his notebooks that he turned over in his mind a national subject and that the Arthurian legend for a while appealed to him. But to Milton's earnest temper nothing that was not true was a fit subject for poetry. It was inevitable he should lay it aside. The Arthurian story he knew to be a myth and a myth was a lie; the story of the Fall, on the other hand, he accepted in common with his time for literal fact. It is to be noted as characteristic of his confident and assured egotism that he accepted no less sincerely and literally the imaginative structure which he himself reared on it. However that may be, the solid fact about him is that in this 'adventurous song' with its pursuit of

Things unattempted yet in prose or rhyme,

he succeeded in his attempt, that alone among the moderns he contrived to write an epic which stands on the same eminence as the ancient writings of the kind, and that he found time in a life which hardly extended to old age as we know it, to write, besides noble lyrics and a series of fiercely argumentative prose treatises, two other masterpieces in the grand style, a tragedy modelled on the Greeks and a second epic in the 'compact' style of the Book of Job. No English poet can compare with him in majesty or completeness.

An adequate study of his achievement is impossible within the limits of the few pages that are all a book like this can spare to a single author. All that can be done here is to call attention to some of his most striking qualities. Foremost, of course, is the temper of the man. From the beginning he was sure of himself and sure of his mission; he had his purpose plain and clear. Hardly any mental development is visible in his work, only training, undertaken anxiously and prayerfully and with a clearly conceived end. He designed to write a masterpiece and he would not start till he was ready. The first twenty years of his life were spent in assiduous reading; for twenty more he was immersed in the dust and toil of political conflict, using his pen and his extraordinary equipment of learning and eloquence to defend the cause of liberty, civil and religious, and to attack its enemies; not till he was past middle age had he reached the leisure and the preparedness necessary to accomplish his self-imposed work. But all the time, as we know, he had it in his mind. In *Lycidas*, written in his Cambridge days, he apologizes to his readers for plucking the fruit of his poetry before it is ripe. In passage after passage in his prose works he begs for his reader's patience a little while longer till his preparation be complete. When the time came at last for beginning he was in no doubt; in his very opening lines he intends, he says, to soar no 'middle flight'. This self-assured unrelenting certainty of his, carried into his prose essays in argument, produces sometimes strange results. One has been peculiarly interesting in view of modern controversy. He was unhappily married, and because he was unhappy the law of divorce must be changed. A modern —George Eliot for instance—would have pleaded the artistic temperament and been content to remain outside the law. Milton always argued from himself to mankind at large.

In everything he did, he put forth all his strength. Each of his poems, long or short, is by itself a perfect whole, wrought complete. The reader always must feel that the planning of each is the work of conscious, deliberate, and selecting art. Milton never digresses; he never violates harmony of sound or sense; his poems have all their regular movement from quiet beginning through a rising and breaking wave of passion and splendour to quiet close. His art is nowhere better seen than in his endings.

Is it *Lycidas*? After the thunder of approaching vengeance on the hireling shepherds of the Church, comes sunset and quiet:

> And now the sun had stretch'd out all the hills,
> And now was dropt into the western bay;
> At last he rose, and twitched his mantle blue:
> To-morrow to fresh woods, and pastures new.

Is it *Paradise Lost*? After the agonies of expulsion and the flaming sword:

> Some natural tears they drop'd, but wip'd them soon;
> The world was all before them, where to choose
> Their place of rest, and Providence their guide:
> They, hand in hand, with wandering steps and slow,
> Through Eden took their solitary way.

Is it, finally, *Samson Agonistes*?

> His servants he, with new acquist
> Of true experience from this great event,
> With peace and consolation hath dismist,
> And calm of mind, all passion spent.

'Calm of mind, all passion spent', it is the essence of Milton's art.

He worked in large ideas and painted splendid canvases; it was necessary for him to invent a style which should be capable of sustained and lofty dignity, which should be ornate enough to maintain the interest of the reader and charm him, and at the same time not so ornate as to give an air of meretricious decoration to what was largely and simply conceived.

Particularly it was necessary for him to avoid those incursions of vulgar associations which words carelessly used will bring in their train. He succeeded brilliantly in this difficult task. The unit of the Miltonic style is not the phrase but the word, each word fastidiously chosen, commonly with some air of an original and lost meaning about it, and all set in a verse in which he contrived by an artful variation of pause and stress to give the variety which other writers had from rhyme. In this as in his structure he accomplished what the Renaissance had only dreamed. Though he had imitators (the poetic diction of the age following is modelled on him) he had no followers. No one has been big enough to find his secret since.

CHAPTER V

THE AGE OF GOOD SENSE

(1)

THE student of literature, when he passes in his reading from the age of Shakespeare and Milton to that of Dryden and Pope, will be conscious of certain sharply defined differences between the temper and styles of the writers of the two periods. If besides being a student of literature he is also (for this is a different thing) a student of literary criticism he will find that these differences have led to the affixing of certain labels—that the school to which writers of the former period belong is called 'Romantic' and that of the latter 'Classic', this 'Classic' school being again overthrown towards the end of the eighteenth century by a set of writers who, unlike the Elizabethans, gave the name 'Romantic' to themselves. What is he to understand by these two labels: what are the characteristics of 'Classicism' and how far is it opposite to and conflicting with 'Romanticism'? The question is difficult because the names are used vaguely and they do not adequately cover everything that is commonly put under them. It would be difficult, for instance, to find anything in Ben Jonson which proclaims him as belonging to a different school from Dryden, and perhaps the same could be said in the second and self-styled period of Romanticism of the work of Crabbe. But in the main the differences are real and easily visible, even though they hardly convince us that the names chosen are the happiest that could be found by way of description.

This period of Dryden and Pope on which we are now entering sometimes styled itself the Augustan Age of English poetry. It grounded its claim to classicism

G

on a fancied resemblance to the Roman poets of the golden age of Latin poetry, the reign of the Emperor Augustus. Its authors saw themselves each as a second Vergil, a second Ovid, most of all a second Horace, and they believed that their relation to the big world, their assured position in society, heightened the resemblances. They endeavoured to form their poetry on the lines laid down in the critical writings of the original Augustan age as elaborated and interpreted in Renaissance criticism. It was tacitly assumed—some of them openly asserted it—that the kinds, modes of treatment —and all the minor details of literature—figures of speech, use of epithets and the rest—had been settled by the ancients once and for all. What the Greeks began the critics and authors of the time of Augustus had settled in its completed form, and the scholars of the Renaissance had only interpreted their findings for modern use. There was the tragedy, which had certain proper parts and a certain fixed order of treatment laid down for it; there was the heroic poem, which had a story or 'fable', which must be treated in a certain fixed manner, and so on. The authors of the 'Classic' period so christened themselves because they observed these rules. And they fancied that they had the temper of the Augustan time—the temper displayed in the works of Horace more than in those of anyone else—its urbanity, its love of good sense and moderation, its instinctive distrust of emotion, and its invincible good breeding. If you had asked them to state as simply and broadly as possible their purpose they would have said it was to follow nature, and if you had inquired what they meant by nature it would turn out that they thought of it mainly as the opposite of art and the negation of what was fantastic, tortured, or far sought in thinking or writing. The later 'Romantic' Revival, when it called itself a return to nature, was only claiming the intention which the classical school itself had proclaimed as its main endeavour. The explanation of that paradox we shall see presently; in the meantime it is worth looking at some of the characteristics of classicism as they appear in the work of the 'Classic' authors.

In the first place the 'Classic' writers aimed at simplicity of style, at a normal standard of writing. They were intolerant of individual eccentricities; they endeavoured, and with success, to infuse into English letters something of the academic spirit that was already controlling their fellow-craftsmen in France. For this end, amongst others, they and the men of science founded the Royal Society, an academic committee which has been restricted since to the physical and natural sciences and been supplemented by similar bodies representing literature and learning only in our own day. Clearness, plainness, conversational ease and directness were the aims the society set before its members where their writing was concerned. 'The Royal Society', wrote the Bishop of Rochester, its first historian, 'have exacted from all their members a close, naked, natural way of speaking; positive expressions, clear sense, a native easiness, bringing all things as near the mathematical plainness as they can; and preferring the language of artisans, countrymen, and merchants before that of wits and scholars.' Artisans, countrymen, and merchants—the ideal had been already accepted in France, Malesherbes striving to use no word that was not in the vocabulary of the day labourers of Paris, Molière making his washerwoman first critic of his comedies. It meant for England the disuse of the turgidities and involutions which had marked the prose of the preachers and moralists of the

times of James and Charles I.; scholars and men of
letters were arising who would have taken John
Bunyan, the unlettered tinker of Bedford, for their
model rather than the learned physician Sir Thomas
Browne.

But genius like Bunyan's apart, there is nothing in
the world more difficult than to write with the easy and
forthright simplicity of talk, as anyone may see who
tries for himself—or even compares the letter-writing
with the conversation of his friends. So that this
desire of simplicity, of clarity, of lucidity led at once to
a more deliberate art. Dryden and Swift and Addison
were assiduous in their labour with the file; they excel
all their predecessors in polish as much as the writers
of the first Augustan age excelled theirs in the same
quality. Not that it was all the result of deliberate art;
in a way it was in the air, and quite unlearned people—
journalists and pamphleteers and the like who wrote
unconsciously and hurriedly to buy their supper—
partook of it as well as leisured people and conscious
artists. Defoe is as plain and easy and polished as
Swift, yet it is certain his amazing activity and pro-
ductiveness never permitted him to look back over a
sentence he had written. Something had happened,
that is, to the English language. The assimilation of
latinisms and the revival of obsolete terms of speech
had ceased; it had become finally a more or less fixed
form, shedding so much of its imports as it had failed
to make part of itself and acquiring a grammatical and
syntactical fixity which it had not possessed in Elizabethan times. When Shakespeare wrote

What cares these roarers for the name of king,

he was using, as students of his language never tire of
pointing out to us, a perfectly correct local grammatical

form. Fifty years after that line was written, at the Restoration, local forms had dropped out of written English. We had acquired a normal standard of language, and either genius or labour was polishing it for literary uses.

What they did for prose these 'Classic' writers did even more exactly—and less happily—for verse. Fashions often become exaggerated before their disappearance, and the decadence of Elizabethan romanticism had produced poetry the wildness and extravagance of whose images was well-nigh unbounded. The passion for intricate and far-sought metaphor which had possessed Donne was accompanied in his work and even more in that of his followers with a passion for what was elusive and recondite in thought and emotion and with an increasing habit of rudeness and wilful difficultness in language and versification. Against these ultimate licences of a great artistic period, the classical writers invoked the qualities of smoothness and lucidity, in the same way, so they fancied, as Vergil might have invoked them against Lucretius. In the treatment of thought and feeling they wanted clearness, they wanted ideas which the mass of men would readily apprehend and assent to, and they wanted not hints or half-spoken suggestions but complete statement. In the place of the logical subtleties which Donne and his school had sought in the scholastic writers of the Middle Ages, they brought back the typically Renaissance study of rhetoric; the characteristic of all the poetry of the period is that it has a rhetorical quality. It is never intimate and never profound, but it has point and wit, and it appeals with confidence to the balanced judgement which men who distrust emotion and have no patience with subtleties—intellectual, emotional, or merely verbal—have in

common. Alongside this lucidity, this air of complete
statement in substance, they strove for and achieved
smoothness in form. To the poet Waller, the immediate predecessor of Dryden, the classical writers themselves ascribed the honour of the innovation. In fact
Waller was only carrying out the ideals counselled and
followed by Ben Jonson. It was in the school of Waller
and Dryden and not in that of the minor writers who
called themselves his followers that he came to his own.

What then are the main differences between Classicism of the best period—the Classicism whose
characteristics we have been describing—and the
Romanticism which came before and after? In the
first place we must put the quality we have described
as that of complete statement. Classical poetry is, so
to speak, 'all there'. Its meaning is all of it on the
surface; it conveys nothing but what it says, and what
it says, it says completely. It is always vigorous and
direct, often pointed and aphoristic, never merely
suggestive, never given to half-statement, and never
obscure. You feel that as an instrument of expression
it is sharp and polished and shining; it is always bright
and defined in detail. The great Romantics go to work
in other ways. Their poetry is a thing of half-lights
and half-spoken suggestions, of hints that imagination
will piece together, of words that are charged with an
added meaning of sound over sense, a thing that stirs
the vague and impalpable restlessness of memory or
terror or desire that lies down beneath in the minds of
men. It rouses what a philosopher has called the
'Transcendental feeling', the solemn sense of the
immediate presence of 'that which was and is and ever
shall be', to induce which is the property of the
highest poetry. You will find nothing in classical
poetry so poignant or highly wrought as Webster's

Cover her face; mine eyes dazzle; she died young,

and the answer,

> I think not so: her infelicity
> Seemed to have years too many,

or so subtle in its suggestion, sense echoing back to primeval terrors and despairs, as this from *Macbeth*:

> Stones have been known to move and trees to speak;
> Augurs and understood relations have
> By magot-pies, and choughs, and rooks brought forth
> The secret'st man of blood,

or so intoxicating to the imagination and the senses as an ode of Keats or a sonnet by Rossetti. But you will find eloquent and pointed statements of thoughts and feelings that are common to most of us—the expression of ordinary human nature—

> What oft was thought but ne'er so well exprest.

'Wit and fine writing' consist, as Addison put it in a review of Pope's first published poem, not so much 'in advancing things that are new, as in giving things that are known an agreeable turn'.

Though in this largest sense the 'classic' writers eschewed the vagueness of romanticism, in another and more restricted way they cultivated it. They were not realists as all good romanticists have to be. They had no love for oddities or idiosyncrasies or exceptions. They loved uniformity, they had no use for truth in detail. They liked the broad generalized, descriptive style of Milton, for instance, better than the closely packed style of Shakespeare, which gets its effects from a series of minute observations huddled one after the other and giving the reader, so to speak, the materials for his own impression, rather than rendering, as Milton does, the expression itself.

Every literary discovery hardens ultimately into a

convention; it has its day and then its work is done, and it has to be destroyed so that the ascending spirit of humanity can find a better means of self-expression. Out of the writing which aimed at simplicity and truth to nature grew 'Poetic Diction', a special treasury of words and phrases deemed suitable for poetry, providing poets with a common stock of imagery, removing from them the necessity of seeing life and nature each one for himself. The poetry which Dryden and Pope wrought out of their mental vigour, their followers wrote to pattern. Poetry became reduced, as it never was before and has never been since, to a formula. The Elizabethan sonneteers, as we saw, used a vocabulary and phraseology in common with their fellows in Italy and France, and none the less produced fine poetry. But they used it to express things they really felt. The truth is it is not the fact of a poetic diction which matters so much as its quality—whether it squares with sincerity, whether it is capable of expressing powerfully and directly one's deepest feelings. The history of literature can show poetic dictions—special vocabularies and forms for poetry—that have these qualities; the diction, for instance, of the Greek choruses, or of the Scottish poets who followed Chaucer, or of the troubadours. That of the classic writers of an Augustan age was not of such a kind. Words clothe thought; poetic diction had the artifice of the crinoline; it would stand by itself. The Romantics in their return to nature had necessarily to abolish it.

But when all is said in criticism the poetry of the earlier half of the eighteenth century excels all other English poetry in two respects. Two qualities belong to it by virtue of the metre in which it is most of it written—rapidity and antithesis. Its antithesis made it an incomparable vehicle for satire, its rapidity for narrative. Outside its limits we have hardly any even passable satirical verse; within them there are half-a-dozen works of the highest excellence in this kind. And if we except Chaucer, there is no one else in the whole range of English poetry who has the narrative gift so completely as the classic poets. Bentleys will always exist who will assure us with civility that Pope's *Homer*, though 'very pretty', bears little relation to the Greek, and that Dryden's *Vergil*, though vigorous and virile, is a poor representation of its original. The truth remains that for a reader who knows no ancient languages either of those translations will probably give a better idea of their originals than any other rendering in English that we possess. The foundation of their method has been vindicated in the best modern translations from the Greek.

(2)

The term 'eighteenth century' in the vocabulary of the literary historian is commonly as vaguely used as the term 'Elizabethan'. It borrows as much as forty years from the seventeenth and gives away ten to the nineteenth. The whole of the work of Dryden, whom we must count as the first of the 'classic' school, was accomplished before chronologically it had begun. As a man and as an author he was very intimately related to his changing times; he adapted himself to them with a versatility as remarkable as that of the Vicar of Bray, and, it may be added, as simple-minded. He mourned in verse the death of Cromwell and the death of his successor, successively defended the theological positions of the Church of England and the Church of Rome, changed his religion and became Poet Laureate to James II., and acquiesced with perfect equanimity in the Revolution which brought in his successor. This instability of conviction, though it gave a handle to his opponents in controversy, does not appear to have caused any serious scandal or disgust among his contemporaries, and it has certainly had little effect on the judgement of later times. It has raised none of the reproaches which have been cast at the suspected apostasy of Wordsworth. Dryden had little interest in political or religious questions; his instinct, one must conceive, was to conform to the prevailing mode and to trouble himself no further about the matter. Defoe told the truth about him when he wrote that 'Dryden might have been told his fate that, having his extraordinary genius slung and pitched upon a swivel, it would certainly turn round as fast as the times, and instruct him how to write elegies to Oliver Cromwell and King Charles the Second with all the coherence imaginable; how to write *Religio Laici* and *The Hind and the Panther* and yet be the same man; every day to change his principle, change his religion, change his coat, change his master, and yet never change his nature.' He never changed his nature; he was as free from cynicism as a barrister who represents successively opposing parties in suits or politics; and when he wrote polemics in prose or verse he lent his talents as a barrister lends his for a fee. His one intellectual interest was in his art, and it is in his comments on his art—the essays and prefaces in the composition of which he amused the leisure left in the busy life of a dramatist and a poet of officialdom—that his most charming and delicate work is to be found. In a way they begin modern English prose; earlier writing furnishes no equal to their colloquial ease and the grace of their expression. And they contain some of the most acute criticism in our language—'classical' in its tone (*i.e.* with a preference for conformity) but with its respect for order and tradition always tempered by good sense and wit, and informed and guided throughout by a taste whose catholicity and sureness was unmatched in the England of his time. The preface to his *Fables* contains some excellent notes on Chaucer. They may be read as a sample of the breadth and perspicuity of his critical perceptions.

His chief poetical works were most of them occasional—designed either to celebrate some remarkable event or to take a side and interpret a policy in the conflict, political or religious, of the time. *Absalom and Achitophel* and *The Medal* were levelled at the Shaftesbury-Monmouth intrigues in the closing years of Charles II. *Religio Laici* celebrated the excellence of the Church of England in its character of *via media* between the opposite extravagances of Papacy and Presbyterianism. *The Hind and the Panther* found this perfection spotted. The Church of England has become the Panther, whose coat is a varied pattern of heresy and truth beside the spotless purity of the Hind, the Church of Rome. *Astrea Redux* welcomed the returning Charles; *Annus Mirabilis* commemorated a year of fire and victories. Besides these he wrote many dramas in verse, a number of translations, and some shorter poems, of which the odes are the most remarkable.

His qualities as a poet fitted very exactly the work he set himself to do. His work is always plain and easily understood; he had a fine faculty for narration, and the vigorous rapidity and point of his style enabled him to sketch a character or sum up a dialectical position very surely and effectively. His writing has a kind of spare and masculine force about it. It is this vigour and the impression he gives of intellectual strength and of a logical grasp of his subject, that beyond question has kept alive work which, if ever poetry was, was ephemeral in its origin. The careers of the unscrupulous Caroline peers would have been closed for us were they not visible in the reflected light of his denunciation of them. Though Buckingham is forgotten and Shaftesbury's name swallowed up in that of his more philanthropic descendant, we can read of Achitophel and Zimri still, and feel something of the strength and heat which he caught from a fiercely fought conflict and transmitted with his own gravity and purposefulness into verse. The Thirty-nine Articles are not a proper subject for poetry, but the sustained and serious allegory which Dryden weaves round theological discussion preserves his treatment of them from the fate of the controversialists who opposed him. His work has wit and vitality enough to keep it sweet.

Strength and wit enter in different proportions into the work of his successor, Alexander Pope—a poet whom admirers in his own age held to be the greatest in our language. No one would think of making such a claim now, but the detraction which he suffered at the hands of Wordsworth and the Romantics ought not to make us forget that Pope, though not our greatest, not even perhaps a great, poet is incomparably our most brilliant versifier. Dryden's strength turns in Pope's work into something more fragile and delicate, polished with infinite care like lacquer, and wrought like filigree work to the last point of conscious and perfected art. He was not a great thinker; the thoughts which he embodies in his philosophical poems—the *Essay on Man* and the rest, are almost ludicrously out of proportion to the solemnity of the titles which introduce them, and only very rarely does he get beyond the conceptions common to the average man when he attempts introspection or meditates on his own destiny. The reader in search of philosophy will find little to stimulate him and in the facile Deism of the time probably something to smile at: Pope has no 'message' now. But he will find views current in Pope's time or borrowed from other authors put with perfect felicity and wit, and he will recognize the justice of Addison's comment that Pope's wit and fine writing consist 'not so much in advancing things that are new, as in giving things that are known an agreeable turn'. And he will not fall into the error of dubbing the author a minor poet because he is neither subtle or imaginative nor profound. A great poet would not have written like Pope—one must grant it; but a minor poet could not.

It is characteristic of Pope's type of mind and kind of art that there is no development visible in his work. Other poets, Shakespeare, for instance, and Keats, have written work of the highest quality when they were young, but they have had crudenesses to shed—things to get rid of as their strength and perceptions grew. But Pope, like Minerva, was full grown and full armed from the beginning. If we did not know that his *Essay on Criticism* was his first poem it would be impossible to place it in the canon of his work; it might come in anywhere and so might everything else that he wrote. From the beginning his craftsmanship was perfect; from the beginning he took his subject-matter from others as he found it and worked it up into aphorism and epigram till each line shone like a cut jewel and the essential commonplaceness and poverty of his material was obscured by the glitter the craftsmanship lent to it. Subject apart, however, he was quite sure of his medium from the beginning; it was not long before he found the way to use it to most brilliant purpose.

The Rape of the Lock and the satirical poems come later in his career.

As a satirist Pope, though he did not hit so hard as Dryden, struck more deftly and probed deeper. He wielded a rapier where the other used a broadsword, and though both used their weapons with the highest skill and the metaphor must not be imagined to impute clumsiness to Dryden, the rapier made the cleaner cut. Both employed a method in satire which their successors (a poor set) in England have not been intelligent enough to use. They allow every possible good point to the object of their attack. They appear to deal him an even and regretful justice. His good points, they put it in effect, being so many, how much blacker and more deplorable his meannesses and faults. They do not do this out of charity; there was very little of the milk of human kindness in Pope. Deformity in his case, as in so many in truth and fiction, seemed to bring envy, hatred, malice and all uncharitableness in its train. The method is employed simply because it gives the maximum satirical effect. That is why Pope's epistle to Arbuthnot, with its characterization of Addison, is the most damning piece of invective in our language.

The Rape of the Lock is an exquisite piece of workmanship, breathing the very spirit of the time. You can fancy it like some clock made by one of the Louis XIV. craftsmen, encrusted with a heap of ormulu mock-heroics and impertinences and set perfectly to the time of day. From no other poem could you gather so fully and perfectly the temper of the society in which our 'classic' poetry was brought to perfection, its elegant assiduity in trifles, its brilliant artifice, its paint and powder and patches and high-heeled shoes, its measured strutting walk in life as well as in verse.

The Rape of the Lock is a mock-heroic poem; that is to say it applies the form and treatment which the 'classic' critics of the seventeenth century had laid down as belonging to the 'heroic' or 'epic' style to a trifling circumstance—the loss by a young lady of fashion of a lock of hair. And it is the one instance in which this 'recipe' for an heroic poem which the French critics handed on to Dryden, and Dryden left to his descendants, has been used well-enough to keep the work done with it in memory. In a way it condemns the poetical theory of the time; when forms are fixed, new writing is less likely to be creative and more likely to exhaust itself in the ingenious but trifling exercises of parody and burlesque. *The Rape of the Lock* is brilliant but it is only play.

The accepted theory which assumed that the forms of poetry had been settled in the past and existed to be applied, though it concerned itself mainly with the ancient writers, included also two moderns in its scope. You were orthodox if you wrote tragedy and epic as Horace told you and satire as he had shown you; you were also orthodox if you wrote in the styles of Spenser or Milton. Spenser, though his predecessors were counted barbaric and his followers tortured and obscure, never fell out of admiration; indeed in every age of English poetry after him the greatest poet in it is always to be found copying him or expressing love for him—Milton declaring to Dryden that Spenser was his 'original', Pope reading and praising him, Keats writing his earliest work in close imitation. His characteristic style and stanza were recognized by the classic school as a distinct 'kind' of poetry which might be used where the theme fitted instead of the heroic manner, and Spenserian imitations abound. Sometimes they are serious; sometimes, like Shenstone's

Schoolmistress, they are mocking and another illustration of the dangerous ease with which a conscious and sustained effort to write in a fixed and acquired style runs to seed in burlesque. Milton's fame never passed through the period of obscurity that sometimes has been imagined for him. He had the discerning admiration of Dryden and others before his death. But to Addison belongs the credit of introducing him to the writers of this time; his papers in the *Spectator* on *Paradise Lost*, with their eulogy of its author's sublimity, spurred the interest of the poets among his readers. From Milton the eighteenth century got the chief and most ponderous part of its poetic diction, high-sounding periphrases and borrowings from Latin used without the gravity and sincerity and fullness of thought of the master who brought them in. When they wrote blank verse, the classic poets wrote it in the Milton manner.

The use of these two styles may be studied in the writings of one man, James Thomson. For besides acquiring a kind of anonymous immortality with patriots as the author of *Rule, Britannia*, Thomson wrote two poems in, respectively, the Spenserian and the Miltonic manner, the former *The Castle of Indolence*, the latter *The Seasons*. The Spenserian manner is caught very effectively, but the adoption of the style of *Paradise Lost*, with its allusiveness, circumlocution and weight, removes any freshness *The Seasons* might have had, had the circumstances in it been put down as they were observed. As it is, hardly anything is directly named; birds are always the 'feathered tribe' and everything else has a similar polite generality for its title. Thomson was a simple-minded man, with a faculty for watching and enjoying nature which belonged to few in his sophisticated age; it is unfortunate

he should have spent his working hours in rendering
the fruit of country rambles freshly observed into a
cold and stilted diction. It suited the eighteenth-
century reader well, for not understanding nature
herself he was naturally obliged to read her in translations.

(3)

The chief merits of 'classic' poetry—its clearness,
its vigour, its direct statement—are such as belong
theoretically rather to prose than to poetry. In fact,
it was in prose that the most vigorous intellect of the
time found itself. We have seen how Dryden, reversing
the habit of other poets, succeeded in expressing his
personality not in poetry which was his vocation, but
in prose which was the amusement of his leisure hours.
Spenser had put his politics into prose and his ideals
into verse; Dryden wrote his politics—to order—in
verse, and in prose set down the thoughts and fancies
which were the deepest part of him because they were
about his art. The metaphor of parentage, though
honoured by use, fits badly on to literary history; none
the less the tradition which describes him as the father
of modern English prose is very near the truth. He
puts into practice for the first time the ideals, described
in the first chapter of this book, which were set up by
the scholars who let into English the light of the
Renaissance. With the exception of the dialogue on
Dramatic Poesy, his work is almost all of it occasional,
the fruit of the mood of a moment, and written rather
in the form of a *causerie*, a kind of informal talk, than
of a considered essay. And it is all couched in clear,
flowing, rather loosely jointed English, carefully
avoiding rhetoric and eloquence and striving always to
reproduce the ease and flow of cultured conversation,

rather than the tighter, more closely knit style of consciously 'literary' prose. His methods were the methods of the four great prose-writers who followed him—Defoe, Addison, Steele, and Swift.

Of these Defoe was the eldest and in some ways the most remarkable. He has been called the earliest professional author in our language, and if that is not strictly true, he is at any rate the earliest literary journalist. His output of work was enormous; he wrote on any and every subject; there was no event whether in politics or letters or discovery but he was ready with something pat on it before the public interest faded. It followed that at a time when imprisonment, mutilation, and the pillory took the place of our modern libel actions he had an adventurous career. In politics he followed the Whig cause and served the Government with his pen, notably by his writings in support of the union with Scotland, in which he won over the Scots by his description of the commercial advantage which would follow the abolition of the border. This line of argument, taken at a time when the governing of political tendencies by commercial interests was by no means the accepted commonplace it is now, proves him a man of an active and original mind. His originality, indeed, sometimes over-reached the comprehension both of the public and his superiors; he was imprisoned for an attack on the Hanoverian succession which was intended ironically; apparently he was ignorant of what every journalist ought to know, that irony is at once the most dangerous and the most ineffectual weapon in the whole armoury of the press. The fertility and ingenuity of his intellect may be best gauged by the number of modern enterprises and contrivances that are foreshadowed in his work. Here are a few, all utterly unknown in his own day, collected by a student of his works: a Board of Trade register for seamen; factories for goods; agricultural credit banks; a commission of inquiry into bankruptcy; and a system of national poor relief. They show him to have been an independent and courageous thinker where social questions were concerned.

He was nearly sixty before he published his first novel, *Robinson Crusoe*, the book by which he is universally known, and on which with the seven other novels which followed it the foundation of his literary fame rests. But his earlier works—they are reputed to number over two hundred—possess no less remarkable literary qualities. It is not too much to say that all the gifts which are habitually recommended for cultivation by those who aspire to journalistic success are to be found in his prose. He has in the first place the gift of perfect lucidity no matter how complicated the subject he is expounding; such a book as his *Complete English Tradesman* is full of passages in which complex and difficult subject-matter is set forth so plainly and clearly that the least literate of his readers could have no doubt of his understanding it. He has also an amazingly exact acquaintance with the technicalities of all kinds of trades and professions; none of our writers, not even Shakespeare, shows half such a knowledge of the circumstances of life among different ranks and conditions of men; none of them has realized with such fidelity how so many different persons lived and moved. His gift of narrative and description is masterly, as readers of his novels know (we shall have to come back to it in discussing the growth of the English novel); several of his works show him to have been endowed with a fine faculty of psychological observation. Without the least consciousness of the value of what he was writing, nor indeed with any

deliberate artistic intention, he made himself one of
the masters of English prose.

Defoe had been the champion of the Whigs; on the
Tory side the ablest pen was that of Jonathan Swift.
His works proclaim him to have had an intellect less
wide in its range than that of his antagonist but more
vigorous and powerful. He wrote, too, more carefully.
In his youth he had been private secretary to Sir
William Temple, a writer now as good as forgotten
because of the triviality of his matter, but in his day
esteemed because of the easy urbanity and polish of his
prose. From him Swift learned the labour of the file,
and he declared in later life that it was 'generally
believed that this author has advanced our English
tongue to as great a perfection as it can well bear'. In
fact he added to the ease and cadences he had learned
from Temple qualities of vigour and directness of his
own which put his work far above his master's. And
he dealt with more important subject-matter than the
academic exercises on which Temple exercised his
fastidious and meticulous powers of revision.

In temperament he is opposed to all the writers of
his time. There is no doubt there was some radical
disorder in his system; brain disease clouded his
intellect in his old age, and his last years were death in
life; right through his life he was a savagely irritable,
sardonic, dark and violent man, impatient of the
slightest contradiction or thwarting, and given to
explosive and instantaneous rage. He delighted in
flouting convention, gloried in outraging decency. The
rage, which, as he said himself, tore his heart out,
carried him to strange excesses. There is something
ironical (he would himself have appreciated it) in the
popularity of *Gulliver's Travels* as a children's book—
that ascending wave of savagery and satire which over-

whelms policy and learning to break against the ultimate citadel of humanity itself. In none of his contempories (except perhaps in the sentimentalities of Steele) can one detect the traces of emotion; to read Swift is to be conscious of intense feeling on almost every page. The surface of his style may be smooth and equable but the central fires of passion are never far beneath, and through cracks and fissures come intermittent bursts of flame. Defoe's irony is so measured and studiously commonplace that perhaps those who imprisoned him because they believed him to be serious are hardly to be blamed; Swift's quivers and reddens with anger in every line.

But his pen seldom slips from the strong grasp of his controlling art. The extraordinary skill and closeness of his allegorical writings—unmatched in their kind—is witness to the care and sustained labour which went to their making. He is content with no general correspondences; his allegory does not fade away into a story in which only the main characters have a secondary significance; the minutest circumstances have a bearing in the satire and the moral. In *The Tale of a Tub* and in *Gulliver's Travels*—particularly in the former—the multitude as well as the aptness of the parallels between the imaginary narrative and the facts it is meant to represent is unrivalled in works of the kind. Only the highest mental powers, working with intense fervour and concentration, could have achieved the sustained brilliancy of the result. 'What a genius I had when I wrote that book!' Swift is said to have exclaimed in his old age when he re-read *The Tale of a Tub*, and certainly the book is a marvel of constructive skill, all the more striking because it makes allegory out of history and consequently is denied that freedom of narrative so brilliantly employed in the *Travels*.

Informing all his writings too, besides intense feeling and an omnipresent and controlling art, is strong common sense. His aphorisms, both those collected under the heading of *Thoughts on Various Subjects*, and countless others scattered up and down his pages, are a treasury of sound, if a little sardonic, practical wisdom. His most insistent prejudices foreshadow in their essential sanity and justness those of that great master of life, Dr. Johnson. He could not endure over-politeness, a vice which must have been very oppressive in society of his day. He savagely resented and condemned a display of affection—particularly marital affection—in public. In an age when it was the normal social system of settling quarrels, he condemned duelling; and he said some very wise things—things that might still be said—on modern education. In economics he was as right-hearted as Ruskin and as wrong-headed. Carlyle, who was in so many respects an echo of him, found in a passage in his works a 'dim anticipation' of his philosophy of clothes.

The leading literary invention of the period—after that of the heroic couplet for verse—was the prose periodical essay. Defoe, it is hardly necessary to say, began it; it was his nature to be first with any new thing: but its establishment as a prevailing literary mode is due to two authors, Joseph Addison and Richard Steele. Of the two famous series—the *Tatler* and the *Spectator*—for which they were both responsible, Steele must take the first credit; he began them, and though Addison came in and by the deftness and lightness of his writing took the lion's share of their popularity, both the plan and the characters round whom the bulk of the essays in the *Spectator* came to revolve were the creation of his collaborator. Steele we know very intimately from his own writings and from

Thackeray's portrait of him. He was an emotional, full-blooded kind of man, reckless and dissipated but fundamentally honest and good-hearted—a type very common in his day as the novels show, but not otherwise to be found in the ranks of its writers. What there is of pathos and sentiment, and most of what there is of humour in the *Tatler* and the *Spectator* are his. And he created the *dramatis personæ* out of whose adventures the slender thread of continuity which binds the essays together is woven. Addison, though less open to the onslaughts of the conventional moralist, was a less lovable personality. Constitutionally endowed with little vitality, he suffered mentally as well as bodily from languor and lassitude. His lack of enthusiasm, his cold-blooded formalism, caused comment even in an age which prided itself on self-command and decorum.

His very malevolence proceeded from a flaccidity which meanly envied the activities and enthusiasms of other men. As a writer he was superficial; he had not the requisite energy for forming a clear or profound judgement on any question of difficulty; Johnson's comment, 'He thinks justly but he thinks faintly' sums up the truth about him. His good qualities were of a slighter kind than Swift's; he was a quiet and accurate observer of manners and fashions in life and conversation, and he had the gift of a style—what Johnson calls 'The Middle Style'—very exactly suited to the kind of work on which he was habitually engaged, 'always equable, always easy, without glowing words or pointed sentences' but polished, lucid, and urbane.

Steele and Addison were conscious moralists as well as literary men. They desired to purge society from Restoration licence; to their efforts we must credit the alteration in morality which *The School for Scandal* shows over *The Way of the World* Their professed object as they stated themselves was 'to banish vice and ignorance out of the territories of Great Britain' (nothing less!) and 'to bring philosophy out of closets and libraries, schools and colleges, to dwell in clubs and assemblies, at tea-tables and coffee-houses'. In fact their satires were politically nearer home, and the chief objects of their aversion were the Tory squires whom it was their business as Whigs to deride. On the Coverley papers in the *Spectator* rests the chief part of their literary fame; these belong rather to the special history of the novel than to that of the periodical essay.

CHAPTER VI

DR. JOHNSON AND HIS TIME

(1)

By 1730 the authors whose work made the 'classic' school in England were dead or had ceased writing; by the same date Samuel Johnson had begun his career as a man of letters. The difference between the period of his maturity and the period we have been examining is not perhaps easy to define; but it exists and it can be felt unmistakably in reading. For one thing 'Classicism' had become completely naturalized; it had ceased to regard the French as arbiters of elegance and literary taste; indeed Johnson himself never spoke of them without disdain and hated them as much as he hated Scotsmen. Writing, like dress and the common way of life, became plainer and graver and thought stronger and deeper. In manners and speech something of the brutalism which was at the root of the English character at the time began to colour the refinement of the preceding age. Dilettantism gave way to learning and speculation; in the place of Bolingbroke came Adam Smith; in the place of Addison, Johnson. In a way it is the solidest and sanest time in English letters. Yet in the midst of its urbanity and order forces were gathering for its destruction. The ballad-mongers were busy; Blake was drawing and rhyming; Burns was giving songs and lays to his country-side. In the distance—Johnson could not hear them—sounded, like the horns of elf-land faintly blowing, the trumpet calls of romance.

If the whole story of Dr. Johnson's life were the story of his published books it would be very difficult to understand his pre-eminent and symbolic position in literary history. His best known work—it long remained so—was his dictionary, and dictionaries, for all the licence they give and Johnson took for the expression of a personality, are the business of purely mechanical talents. A lesser man than he might have cheated us of such delights as the definitions of 'oats' or 'net' or 'pension', but his book would certainly have been no worse as a book. In his early years he wrote two satires in verse in imitation of Juvenal; they were followed later by two series of periodical essays on the model of the *Spectator*; neither of them—the *Rambler* nor the *Idler*—was at all successful. *Rasselas*, a tale with a purpose, is melancholy reading; the *Journey to the Western Hebrides* has been utterly eclipsed by Boswell's livelier and more human chronicle of the same events. The *Lives of the Poets*, his greatest work, was composed with pain and difficulty when he was seventy years old; even it is but a quarry from which a reader may dig the ore of a sound critical judgement summing up a life's reflection, out of the grit and dust of perfunctory biographical compilations. There was hardly one of the literary coterie over which he presided that was not doing better and more lasting work. Nothing that Johnson wrote is to be compared, for excellence in its own manner, with *Tom Jones* or *The Vicar of Wakefield* or *The Citizen of the World*. He produced nothing in writing approaching the magnitude of Gibbon's *Decline and Fall of the Roman Empire*, or the profundity of Burke's philosophy of politics. Even Sir Joshua Reynolds, whose main business was painting and not the pen, was almost as good an author as he; his *Discourses* have little to fear when they are set beside Johnson's essays. Yet all these men recognized him as their guide and leader; the spontaneous selection of such a democratic assembly as men of genius in a

tavern fixed upon him as chairman, and we in these
later days, who are safe from the overpowering force
of personality and presence—or at least can only know
of it reflected in books—instinctively recognize him as
the greatest man of his age. What is the reason?

Johnson's pre-eminence is the pre-eminence of
character. He was a great moralist; he summed up in
himself the tendencies of thought and literature of his
time and excelled all others in his grasp of them; and
he was perhaps more completely than anyone else in
the whole history of English literature, the typical
Englishman. He was one of those to whom is applic-
able the commonplace that he was greater than his
books. It became the fashion among certain critics to
speak of his biographer Boswell as if he were a novelist
or a playwright and to classify the Johnson we know
with Hamlet and Don Quixote as the product of
creative or imaginative art, working on a 'lost original'.
No exercise of critical ingenuity could be more futile
or impertinent. The impression of the solidity and
magnitude of Johnson's character which is to be
gathered from Boswell is enforced from other sources:
from his essays and his prayers and meditations, from
the half-dozen or so lives and reminiscences which
were published in the years following his death (their
very number establishing the reverence with which he
was regarded), from the homage of other men whose
genius their books leave indisputable. Indeed the
Johnson we know from Boswell, though it is the
broadest and most masterly portrait in the whole range
of biography, gives less than the whole magnitude of
the man. When Boswell first met him at the age of
twenty-two, Johnson was fifty-four. His long period of
poverty and struggle was past. His *Dictionary* and all
his works except the *Lives of the Poets* were behind

him; a pension from the Crown had established him in security for his remaining years; his position was universally acknowledged. So that though the portrait in the *Life* is a full-length study of Johnson the conversationalist and literary dictator, the proportion it preserves is faulty and its study of the early years—the years of poverty, of *The Vanity of Human Wishes* and *London*, of *Rasselas*, which he wrote to pay the expenses of his mother's funeral—is slight.

It was, however, out of the bitterness and struggle of those early years that the strength and sincerity of character which carried Johnson surely and tranquilly through the time of his triumph were derived. From the beginning he made no compromise with the world and no concession to fashion. The world had to take him at his own valuation or not at all. He never deviated one hair's breadth from the way he had chosen. Judged by the standards of journalistic success, the *Rambler* could not well be worse than he made it. Compared with the lightness and gaiety and the mere lip-service to morality of Addison its edification is ponderous. Both authors state the commonplaces of conduct, but Addison achieves lightness in the doing of it, and his manner, by means of which platitudes are stated lightly and pointedly and with an air of novelty, is the classic manner of journalism. Johnson goes heavily and directly to the point, handling well-worn moral themes in general and dogmatic language without any attempt to enliven them with an air of discovery or surprise. Yet they were, in a sense, discoveries to him; not one of them but was deeply and sincerely felt; not one but is a direct and to us a pathetically dispassionate statement of the reflection of thirty years of grinding poverty and a soul's anguish. Viewed in the light of his life, the *Rambler* is one of the most moving of books. If its literary value is slight it is yet a document in character.

So that when he came to his own, when gradually the public whom he despised and neglected raised him into a pontifical position matched by none before him in England and none since save Carlyle, he was sure of himself; success did not spoil him. His judgement was unwarped by flattery. The almost passionate tenderness and humanity which lay beneath his gruffness was undimmed. His personality triumphed in all the fullness and richness which had carried it in integrity through his years of struggle. For over twenty years from his chair in taverns in the Strand and Fleet Street he ruled literary London, imposed his critical principles on the great body of English letters, and by his talk and his friendships became the embodiment of the literary temperament of his age.

His talk as it is set down by Boswell is his best monument. It was the happiest possible fate that threw those two men together; for Boswell, besides being an admirer and reporter sedulously chronicling all his master said and did, fortunately influenced both the saying and the doing. Most of us have someone in whose company we shine best, who puts our wits on their mettle and spurs us to our greatest readiness and vivacity. There is no doubt that Boswell, for all his assumed humility and for all Johnson's affected disdain, was just such a companion for Johnson. Johnson was at his best when Boswell was present, and Boswell not only drew Johnson out on subjects on which his robust common sense and readiness of judgement were fitted to shine but actually suggested and conducted that tour in Scotland which gave Johnson an opportunity for displaying himself at his best. The recorded talk is extraordinarily varied and entertaining. It is a mistake to conceive Johnson as a monster of bear-like rudeness, shouting down opposition, hectoring his companions, and habitually a blustering verbal bully. We are too easily hypnotized by Macaulay's flashy caricature. He could be merciless in argument and often wrong-headed, and he was always acute, uncomfortably acute, in his perception of a fallacy, and a little disconcerting in his unmasking of pretence. But he could be gay and tender too, and in his heart he was a shrinking and sensitive man.

As a critic (his criticism is the only side of his literary work that need be considered) Johnson must be allowed a high place. His natural indolence in production prevented him from exhausting his faculties in the more exacting labours of creative work, and left him time for omnivorous if desultory reading, the fruits of which he stored in a wonderfully retentive memory against an occasion for their use. To a very fully equipped mind he brought the service of a robust and acute judgement. Moreover, when he applied his mind to a subject he had a faculty of intense, if fitful, concentration; he could seize with great force on the heart of a matter; he had the power in a wonderfully short time of extracting the kernel and leaving the husk. His judgements in writing are like those recorded by Boswell from his conversation; that is to say he does not, as a critic whose medium was normally the pen rather than the tongue would tend to do, search for fine shades of distinction, subdivide subtleties, or take care to admit *caveats* or exceptions; he passes, on the contrary, rapid and forcible verdicts, not seldom in their assertions untenably sweeping, and always decided and dogmatic. He never affects diffidence or defers to the judgement of others. His power of concentration, of seizing on essentials, has given us his best critical work—nothing could be better, for instance, than his characterization of the poets whom he calls the metaphysical school (Donne, Crashaw, and the rest) which is the most valuable part of his life of Cowley. Even where he is most prejudiced—for instance in his attack on Milton's *Lycidas*—there is usually something to be said for his point of view. And after this concentration, his excellence depends on his basic common sense. His classicism is always tempered, like Dryden's, by a humane and sensible dislike of pedantry; he sets no store by the Unities; in his preface to Shakespeare he allows more than a 'classic' could have been expected to admit, writing in it, in truth, some of the manliest and wisest things in Shakespearian literature. Of course, he had his failings—the greatest of them what Lamb called imperfect sympathy. He could see no good in republicans or agnostics, and none in Scotland or France. Not that the phrase 'imperfect sympathy', which expresses by implication the romantic critic's point of view, would have appealed to him. When Dr. Johnson did not like people the fault was in them, not in him; a ruthless objectivity is part of the classic equipment. He failed, too, because he could neither understand nor appreciate poetry which concerned itself with the sensations that come from external nature. Nature was to him a closed book, very likely for a purely physical reason. He was short-sighted to the point of myopia, and a landscape meant nothing to him; when he tried to describe one as he did in the chapter on the 'happy valley' in *Rasselas* he failed. What he did not see he could not appreciate; perhaps it is too much to ask of his self-contained and unbending intellect that he should appreciate the report of it by other men.

(2)

As we have seen, Johnson was not only great in himself, he was great in his friends. Round him meeting him as an equal, gathered the greatest and most prolific writers of the time. There is no better way to study the central and accepted men of letters of the period than to take some full evening at the club from Boswell, read a page or two, watch what the talkers said, and then trace each back to his own works for a complete picture of his personality. The lie of the literary landscape in this wonderful time becomes apparent as we read. We find Johnson enthroned, Boswell at his ear, round him men like Reynolds and Burke, Richardson and Fielding and Goldsmith, Robertson and Gibbon, and, occasionally drawn to the circle, minnows like Beattie and a genius like Adam Smith. Gray, studious in his college at Cambridge, is exercising his fastidious talent; Collins' sequestered, carefully nurtured muse is silent; a host of minor poets are riding to death Pope's poetic diction and heroic couplet. Outside, scattered about, is the van of Romance—Percy collecting his ballads; Burns making songs and verses in Scotland; the 'mad' people, Smart and Chatterton, and above all Blake, obscurely beginning the work that was to finish in Wordsworth and Coleridge and Keats.

Of Johnson's set the most remarkable figure was Edmund Burke—'the supreme writer of his century', as De Quincey called him. His writings belong more to the history of politics than to that of literature, and a close examination of them would be out of place here. His political theory strikes a middle course which offends—and in his own day offended—both parties in the common strife of political thinking. He believed

the best government to consist in a patriotic aristoc-
racy, ruling for the good of the people. By birth an
Irishman, he had the innate practicality which commonly lies beneath the flash and colour of Irish
forcefulness and rhetoric. That, and his historical
training, which influenced him in the direction of
conceiving every institution as the culmination of an
evolutionary development, sent him directly counter
to the newest and most enthusiastically urged political
philosophy of his day—the philosophy stated by
Rousseau, and put in action by the French Revolution.
He disliked and distrusted 'metaphysical theories',
when they left the field of speculation for that of
practice, had no patience with 'natural rights' (which
as an Irishman he conceived as the product of sentimentalism) and applied what would nowadays be
called a 'pragmatic' test to political affairs. Practice
was the touchstone; a theory was useless unless you
could prove that it had worked. It followed that he
was not a democrat, opposed parliamentary reform, and
held that the true remedy for corruption and venality
was not to increase the size of the electorate, but to
reduce it so as to obtain electors of greater weight and
independence. For him a member of Parliament was
a representative and not a delegate, and must act not
on his electors' wishes but on his own judgement.
These opinions are little in fashion in our own day, but
it is well to remember that in Burke's case they were
the outcome not of prejudice but of thought, and that
even democracy may admit they present a case that
must be met and answered.

Burke's reputation as a thinker has suffered somewhat unjustly as a result of his refusal to square his
tenets either with democracy or with its opposite. It
has been said that ideas were only of use to him so far

I

as they were of polemical service, that the amazing fertility and acuteness of his mind worked only in a not too scrupulous determination to overwhelm his antagonists in the several arguments—on India, or America, on Ireland or on France—which made up his political career. He was, said Carlyle, 'vehement rather than earnest; a resplendent far-sighted rhetorician, rather than a deep and earnest thinker'. The words as they stand would be a good description of a certain type of politician; they would fit, for instance, very well on Mr. Gladstone; but they do Burke less than justice. He was an innovator in modern political thought, and his application of the historical method to the study of institutions is in its way a not less epoch-making achievement than Bacon's application of the inductive method to science. At a time when current political thought, led by Rousseau, was drawing its theories from the abstract conception of 'natural rights' Burke was laying down that sounder and deeper notion of politics which has governed thinking in that department of knowledge since. Besides this he had, face to face with the affairs of his own day, a far-sightedness and sagacity which kept him right where other men went wrong. In a nation of the blind he saw the truth about the American colonies; he predicted with exactitude the culmination of the revolution in Napoleon. Mere rhetorical vehemence cannot explain the earnestness with which in a day of diplomatic cynicism he preached the doctrine of an international morality as strict and as binding as the morality which exists between man and man. Surest of all, we have the testimony, uninfluenced by the magic of language, of the men he met. You could not, said Dr. Johnson, shelter with him in a shed for a few moments from the rain without saying, 'This is an extraordinary man.'

His literary position depends chiefly on his amazing gift of expression, on a command of language unapproached by any writer of his time. His eloquence (in writing not in speaking; he is said to have had a monotonous delivery) was no doubt at bottom a matter of race, but to his Irish readiness and flash and colour he added the strength of a full mind, fortified by a wonderful store of reading which a retentive and exact memory enabled him to bring instantly to bear on the subject in hand. No writer before him, except Defoe, had such a wide knowledge of the technicalities of different men's occupations, and of all sorts of processes of daily business, nor could enlighten an abstract matter with such a wealth of luminous analogy. It is this characteristic of his style which has led to the common comparison of his writing with Shakespeare's; both seem to be preternaturally endowed with more information, to have a wider sweep of interest, than ordinary men. Both were not only, as Matthew Arnold said of Burke, 'saturated with ideas', but saturated too in the details of the business and desire of ordinary men's lives; nothing human was alien from them. Burke's language is, therefore, always interesting and always appropriate to his thought; it is also on occasion very beautiful. He had a wonderful command of clear and ringing utterance and could appeal when he liked very powerfully to the sensibilities of his readers. Rhetoricians are seldom free from occasional extravagance, and Burke fell under the common danger of his kind. He had his moments of falsity, could heap coarse and outrageous abuse on Warren Hastings, illustrate the horrors of the Revolution by casting a dagger on the floor of the House of Commons, and nourish hatred beyond the bounds of justice or measure. But these things do not affect his

position, nor take from the solid greatness of his
work.

Boswell we have seen; after Burke and Boswell,
Goldsmith was the most brilliant member of the
Johnson circle. If part of Burke's genius is referable
to his nationality, Goldsmith's is wholly so. The
beginning and the end of him was Irish; every quality
he possessed as a man and as a writer belongs to his
race. He had the Irish carelessness, the Irish generosity, the Irish quick temper, the Irish humour. This
latter gift, displayed constantly in a company which
had little knowledge of the peculiar quality of Irish wit
and no faculty of sympathy or imagination, is at the
bottom of the constant depreciation of him on the part
of Boswell and others of his set. His mock self-
importance they thought ill-breeding; his humorous
self-depreciation and keen sense of his own ridiculous-
ness, mere lack of dignity and folly. It is curious to
read Boswell and watch how often Goldsmith, without
Boswell's knowing it, got the best of the joke. In
writing he had what we can now recognize as peculiarly
Irish gifts. All our modern writers of light half-
farcical comedy are Irish. Goldsmith's *She Stoops to
Conquer* is only the first of a series which includes
The School for Scandal, *The Importance of Being Earnest*,
and *You Never Can Tell*. And his essays—particularly
those of *The Citizen of the World* with its Chinese vision
of England and English life—are the first fruit of that
Irish detachment, that ability to see 'normally' English
habits and institutions and foibles which reappeared
later in the prefaces of Bernard Shaw. As a writer
Goldsmith has a lightness and delicate ease which
belongs rather to the school of the earlier eighteenth
century than to his own day; the enthusiasm of Addison for French literature which he retained gave him

a more graceful model than the 'Johnsonian' school, to which he professed himself to belong, could afford.

(3)

The eighteenth-century novel demands separate treatment, and of the other prose authors the most eminent, Edward Gibbon, belongs to historical rather than to literary studies. It is time to turn to poetry.

There orthodox classicism still held sway; the manner and metre of Pope or Thomson ruled the roost of singing fowl. In the main it had done its work, and the bulk of fresh things conceived in it were dull and imitative, even though occasionally, as in the poems of Johnson himself and of Goldsmith, an author arose who was able to infuse sincerity and emotion into a now moribund convention. The classic manner—now more that of Thomson than of Pope—persisted till it overlapped romanticism; Cowper and Crabbe each owe a doubtful allegiance, leaning by their formal metre and level monotony of thought to the one and by their realism to the other. In the meantime its popularity and its assured position were beginning to be assailed in the coteries by the work of two new poets.

The output of Thomas Gray and William Collins is small; you might almost read the complete poetical works of either in an evening. But for all that they mark a period; they are the first definite break with the classic convention which had been triumphant for upwards of seventy years when their prime came. It is a break, however, in style rather than in essentials, and a reader who seeks in them the inspiriting freshness which came later with Wordsworth and Coleridge will be disappointed. Their carefully drawn still wine tastes insipidly after the 'beaded bubbles winking at the brim' of romance. They are fastidious and academic; they lack the authentic fire; their poetry is 'made' poetry like Tennyson's and Matthew Arnold's. On the comparative merits a deal of critical ink has been spilt. Arnold's characterization of Gray is well known —'he never spoke out'. Sterility fell upon him because he lived in an age of prose just as it fell upon Arnold himself because he lived too much immersed in business and routine. But in what he wrote he had the genuine poetic gift—the gift of insight and feeling. Against this, Swinburne with characteristic vehemence raised the standard of Collins, the latchet of whose shoe Gray, as a lyric poet, was not worthy to unloose. 'The muse gave birth to Collins, she did but give suck to Gray.' It is more to our point to observe that neither, though their work abounds in felicities and in touches of a geniune poetic sense, was fitted to raise the standard of revolt. Revolution is for another and braver kind of genius than theirs. Romanticism had to wait for Burns and Blake.

In every country at any one time there are in all probability not one but several literatures flourishing. The main stream flowing through the publishers and booksellers, conned by critics and coteries, recognized as the national literature, is commonly only the largest of several channels of thought. There are besides the national literature local literatures—books, that is, are published which enjoy popularity and critical esteem in their own county or parish and are utterly unknown outside; there may even be (indeed, there are in several parts of the country) distinct local schools of writing and dynasties of local authors. These localized literatures rarely become known to the outside world; the national literature takes little account of them, though their existence and probably some special knowledge of one or other of them is within the experience of most of us. But every now and again some one of their authors transcends his local importance, gives evidence of a genius which is not to be denied even by those who normally have not the knowledge to appreciate the particular flavour of locality which his writings impart, and becomes a national figure. While he lives and works the national and his local stream turn and flow together.

This was the case of Robert Burns. All his life long he was the singer of a parish—the last of a long line of 'forbears' who had used the Scottish lowland vernacular to rhyme in about their neighbours and their scandals, their loves and their church. Himself at the confluence of the two streams, the national and the local, he pays his tribute to two sets of originals, talks with equal reverence of names known to us like Pope and Gray and Shenstone and names unknown which belonged to local 'bards', as he would have called them, who wrote their poems for an Ayrshire public. If he came upon England as an innovator it was simply because he brought with him the highly individualized style of Scottish local vernacular verse; to his own people he was no innovator but a fulfilment. As W. E. Henley[1] said, he brought nothing to the literature he became a part of but himself. His daring and splendid genius made the local universal, raised out of rough and cynical satirizing a style as rich and humorous and astringent as that of Rabelais, lent inevitableness and pathos and romance to lyric and song. But he was content to better the work of other men. He made hardly anything new.

Stevenson in his essay on Burns remarks his readiness to use up the work of others or take a large hint

[1] *Essay on Burns.*

from it 'as if he had some difficulty in commencing'. He omits to observe that the very same trait applies to other great artists. There seem to be two orders of creative writers. On the one hand are the innovators, the new men like Blake, Wordsworth, Byron and Shelley, and later Browning. These men owe little to their predecessors; they work on their own devices and construct their medium afresh for themselves. Commonly their fame and acceptance is slow, for they speak in an unfamiliar tongue and they have to educate a generation to understand their work. The other order of artists have to be shown the way. They have little fertility in construction or invention. You have to say to them 'Here is something that you could do too; go and do it better', or 'Here is a story to work on, or a refrain of a song; take it and give it your subtlety, your music'. The villainy you teach them they will use and it will go hard with them if they do not better the invention; but they do not invent for themselves. To this order of artists Burns—like Shakespeare, and among the lesser men Tennyson—belongs. In all his plays Shakespeare is known to have invented only one plot; in many he is using not only the structure but in many places the words devised by an older author; his mode of treatment depends on the conventions common in his day, on the tragedy of blood and madness and revenge, on the comedy of intrigue and disguises, on the romance with its strange happenings and its reuniting of long parted friends. Burns goes the same way to work; scarcely a page of his but shows traces of some original in the Scottish vernacular school. The elegy, the verse epistle, the satirical form of *Holy Willie's Prayer*, the song and recitative of *The Jolly Beggars*, are all to be found in his predecessors, in Fergusson, Ramsay, and the local poets of the south-west of Scotland. In the songs often whole verses, nearly always the refrains, are from older folk poetry. What he did was to pour into these forms the incomparable richness of a personality whose fire and brilliance and humour transcended all locality and all tradition, a personality which strode like a colossus over the formalism and correctness of his time. His use of familiar forms explains, more than anything else, his immediate fame. His countrymen were ready for him; they could hail him on the instant (just as an Elizabethan audience could hail Shakespeare) as something familiar and at the same time more splendid than anything they knew. He spoke in a tongue they could understand.

It is impossible to judge Burns from his purely English verse; though he did it as well as any of the minor followers of the school of Pope he did it no better. Only the weakest side of his character—his sentimentalism—finds expression in it; he had not the sense of tradition nor the intimate knowledge necessary to use English to the highest poetic effect; it was indeed a foreign tongue to him. In the vernacular he wrote the language he spoke, a language whose natural force and colour had become enriched by three centuries of literary use, which was capable, too, of effects of humour and realism impossible in any tongue spoken out of reach of the soil. It held within it an unmatched faculty for pathos, a capacity for expressing a lambent and kindly humour, a power of pungency in satire and a descriptive vividness that English could not give. How express in the language of Pope or even of Wordsworth an effect like this:—

> They reel'd, they set, they cross'd, they cleekit.
> Till ilka carlin swat and reekit,
> And coost her duddies to the wark,
> And linkit at it in her sark!

or this—

> Yestreen, when to the trembling string
>   The dance gaed thro' the lighted ha',
> To thee my fancy took its wing—
>   I sat, but neither heard nor saw:
> Tho' this was fair, and that was braw,
>   And yon the toast of a' the town,
> I sigh'd, and said amang them a',
>   'Ye are na Mary Morison.'

It may be objected that in all this there is only one word, and but two or three forms of words, that are not English. But the accent, the rhythm, the air of it are all Scots, and it was a Burns thinking in his native tongue who wrote it, not the Burns of

> Anticipation forward points the view;

or

> pleasures are like poppies spread—
> You seize the flow'r, its bloom is shed,

or any other of the exercises in the school of Thomson and Pope.

It is easy to see that though Burns admired unaffectedly the 'classic' writers, his native realism and his melody made him a potent agent in the cause of naturalism and romance. In his ideas, even more than in his style, he belongs to the oncoming school. The French Revolution, which broke upon Europe when he was at the height of his career, found him already converted to its principles. As a peasant, particularly a Scotch peasant, he believed passionately in the native worth of man as man and gave ringing expression to it in his verse. In his youth his liberal-mindedness made him a Jacobite out of mere antagonism to the existing régime; the Revolution only discovered for him the more logical Republican creed. As the leader of a loose-living, hard drinking set, such as was to be found in every parish, he was a determined and free-spoken enemy of the kirk, whose tyranny he several times encountered. In his writing he is as vehement an anti-clerical as Shelley and much more practical. The political side of romanticism, in fact, which in England had to wait for Byron and Shelley, is already full-grown in his work. He anticipates and gives complete expression to one half of the Romantic movement.

What Burns did for the idea of liberty, Blake did for that and every other idea current among Words-worth and his successors. There is nothing stranger in the history of English literature than the miracle by which this poet and artist, working in obscurity, utterly unknown to the literary world that existed out-side him, summed up in himself all the thoughts and tendencies which were the fruit of anxious discussion and propaganda on the part of the authors—Words-worth, Coleridge, Lamb—who believed themselves to be the discoverers of fresh truth unknown to their generation. The contemporary and independent dis-covery by Wallace and Darwin of the principle of natural selection furnishes, perhaps, a rough parallel, but the fact serves to show how impalpable and universal is the spread of ideas, how impossible it is to settle literary indebtedness or construct literary genealogy with any hope of accuracy. Blake, by himself, held and ex-pressed quite calmly that condemnation of the 'classic' school that Wordsworth and Coleridge proclaimed against the opposition of a deriding world. As was his habit he compressed it into a rude epigram.

Great things are done when men and mountains meet;
This is not done by jostling in the street.

The case for nature against urbanity could not be more tersely nor better put. The German metaphysical doctrine which was the deepest part of the teaching of Wordsworth and Coleridge and their main discovery, he expresses as curtly and off-handedly,

> The sun's light, when he unfolds it,
> Depends on the organ that beholds it.

In the realm of childhood and innocence, which Wordsworth entered fearfully and pathetically as an alien traveller, he moves with the simple and assured ease of one native. He knows the mystical wonder and horror that Coleridge set forth in *The Ancient Mariner*. As for the beliefs of Shelley, they are already fully developed in his poems. 'The king and the priest are types of the oppressor; humanity is crippled by "mind-forg'd manacles"; love is enslaved to the moral law, which is broken by the Saviour of mankind; and, even more subtly than by Shelley, life is pictured by Blake as a deceit and a disguise veiling from us the beams of the Eternal.'[1]

In truth, Blake, despite the imputation of insanity which was his contemporaries' and some of his later commentators' refuge from assenting to his conclusions, is as bold a thinker in his own way as Neitzsche and as consistent. An absolute unity of belief inspires all his utterances, cryptic and plain. That he never succeeded in founding a school nor gathering followers must be put down in the first place to the form in which his work was issued (it never reached the public of his own day) and the dark and mysterious mythology in which the prophetic books which are the full and extended statement of his philosophy, are couched, and in the second place to the inherent difficulty of the philosophy itself. As he himself says, where we read black, he reads white. For the common distinction between good and

[1] Sir Walter A. Raleigh.

evil, Blake substitutes the distinction between imagination and reason; and reason, the rationalizing, measuring, comparing faculty by which we come to impute praise or blame is the only evil in his eyes. 'There is nothing either good or bad but thinking makes it so'; to rid the world of thinking, to substitute for reason, imagination, and for thought, vision, was the object of all that he wrote or drew. The implications of this philosophy carry far, and Blake was not afraid to follow where they led him. Fortunately for those who hesitate to embark on that dark and adventurous journey, his work contains delightful and simpler things. He wrote lyrics of extraordinary freshness and delicacy and spontaneity; he could speak in a child's voice of innocent joys and sorrows and the simple elemental things. His odes to 'Spring' and 'Autumn' are the harbingers of Keats. Not since Shakespeare and Campion died could English show songs like his

> My silks and fine array

and the others which carry the Elizabethan accent. He could write these things as well as the Elizabethans. In others he was unique.

> Tiger! Tiger! burning bright
> In the forests of the night,
> What immortal hand or eye
> Could frame thy fearful symmetry.

In all the English lyric there is no voice so clear, so separate or distinctive as his.

CHAPTER VII

THE ROMANTIC REVIVAL

(1)

THERE are two ways of approaching the periods of change and new birth in literature. The commonest and, for all the study which it entails, the easiest, is that summed up in the phrase, literature begets literature. Following it, you discover and weigh literary influences, the influence of poet on poet, and book on book. You find one man harking back to earlier models in his own tongue, which an intervening age misunderstood or despised; another, turning to the contemporary literatures of neighbouring countries; another, perhaps, to the splendour and exoticism of the east. In the matter of form and style, such a study carries you far. You can trace types of poetry and metres back to curious and unsuspected originals, find the well-known verse of Burns's epistles turning up in Provençal; Tennyson's *In Memoriam* stanza in use by Ben Jonson; the metre of *Christabel* in minor Elizabethan poetry; the peculiar form of Fitzgerald's translation of *Omar Khayyam* followed by so many imitators since, itself to be the actual reflection of the rough metrical scheme of his Persian original. But such a study, though it is profitable and interesting, can never lead to the whole truth. As we saw in the beginning of this book, in the matter of the Renaissance, every age of discovery and re-birth has its double aspect. It is a revolution in style and language, an age of literary experiment and achievement, but its experiments are dictated by the excitement of a new subject-matter, and that subject-matter is so much in the air, so impalpable and universal that it eludes analysis. Yet we can be sure that it is this weltering contagion of new ideas and new thought—the 'Zeitgeist', the spirit of the age, or whatever it may be called —that is the essential and controlling force. Literary loans and imports give the forms into which it can be moulded, but without them it would still exist, and they are only the means by which a spirit which is in life itself, and which expresses itself in action, and in concrete human achievement, gets itself into the written word. The romantic revival numbers Napoleon amongst its leaders as well as Byron; Wellington, Pitt and Wilberforce, as well as Keats and Wordsworth. Only the literary manifestations of the time concern us here, but it is important to remember that the passion for simplification and for a return to nature as a refuge from the artificial complexities of society, which inspired the *Lyrical Ballads*, inspired no less the course of the Revolution in France and, later, the destruction by Napoleon of the smaller feudal states of Germany which made possible German nationality and a national spirit.

In this romantic revival, however, the revolution in form and style matters more than in most. The classicism of the previous age had been so fixed and immutable; it had been enthroned in high places, enjoyed the esteem of society, arrogated to itself the acceptance which good breeding and good manners demanded. Dryden had been a Court poet, careful to change his allegiance with the changing monarchy. Pope had been the equal and intimate of the great people of his day, and his followers, if they did not enjoy the equality, enjoyed at any rate the patronage of many noble lords. The effect of this was to give the prestige of social usage to the verse in which they wrote

and the language they used. 'There was,' said Dr.
Johnson, 'before the time of Dryden no poetical diction,
no system of words at once refined from the grossness
of domestic use, and free from the harshness of terms
appropriated to particular arts. Words too familiar
or too remote to defeat the purpose of a poet.' This
poetic diction, refined from the grossness of domestic
use, was the standard poetic speech of the eighteenth
century. The heroic couplet in which it was cast was
the standard metre. So that the first object of the
revolt of the romantics was the purely literary object
of getting rid of the vice of an unreal and artificial
manner of writing. They desired simplicity of style.

When the *Lyrical Ballads* of Wordsworth and
Coleridge were published in 1798, the preface which
Wordsworth wrote as their manifesto hardly touched
at all on the poetic imagination or the attitude of the
poet to life and nature. The only question is that of
diction. 'The majority of the following poems,' he
writes, 'are to be considered as experiments. They
were written chiefly with a view to ascertain how far
the language of conversation in the middle and lower
classes of society is adapted to the purposes of poetic
pleasure.' And in the longer preface to the second
edition, in which the theories of the new school on the
nature and methods of the poetic imagination are set
forth at length, he returns to the same point. 'The
language too, of these men (that is those in humble
and rustic life) has been adopted . . . because such men
hourly communicate with the best objects from which
the best part of language is originally derived, and
because from their rank in society, and the sameness
and narrow circle of their intercourse, being less under
the influence of social vanity, they convey their feelings
and notions in simple unelaborated expressions.' Social

vanity—the armour which we wear to conceal our deepest thoughts and feelings—that was what Wordsworth wished to be rid of, and he chose the language of the common people, not because it fitted, as an earlier school of poets who used the common speech had asserted, the utterance of habitual feeling and common sense, but because it is the most sincere expression of the deepest and rarest passion. His object was the object attained by Shakespeare in some of his supremest moments; the bare intolerable force of the speeches after the murder of Macbeth, or of King Lear's

> Do not laugh at me;
> For, as I am a man, I think this lady
> To be my child Cordelia.

Here, then, was one avenue of revolt from the tyranny of artificiality, the getting back of common speech into poetry. But there was another, earlier and more potent in its effect. The eighteenth century, weary of its own good sense and sanity, turned to the Middle Ages for picturesqueness and relief. Romance of course, had not been dead in all these years, when Pope and Addison made wit and good sense the fashionable temper for writing. There was a strong romantic tradition in the eighteenth century, though it does not give its character to the writing of the time. Dr. Johnson was fond of old romances. When he was in Skye he amused himself by thinking of his Scottish tour as the journey of a knight-errant. 'These fictions of the Gothic romances,' he said, 'are not so remote from credibility as is commonly supposed.' It is a mistake to suppose that the passion for mediævalism began with either Coleridge or Scott. Horace Walpole was as enthusiastic as either of them; good eighteenth-century prelates like Hurd and Percy found in what

K

they called the Gothic an inexhaustible source of delight. As was natural, what attracted them in the Middle Ages was not their resemblances to the time they lived in, but the points in which the two differed. None of them had knowledge enough, or insight enough, to conceive or sympathize with the humanity of the thirteenth century, to shudder at its cruelties and hardnesses and persecutions, or to comprehend the spiritual elevation and insight of its rarest minds. 'It was art,' said William Morris, 'art in which all men shared, that made life romantic as people called it in those days. That and not robber barons, and inaccessible kings, with their hierarchy of serving nobles, and other rubbish.' Morris belonged to a time which knew its Middle Ages better. To the eighteenth century the robber-barons and the 'other rubbish' were the essence of romance. For Percy and his followers, mediævalism was a collection of what actors call 'properties', gargoyles, and odds and ends of armour, and castle keeps with secret passages, banners and gay colours, and gay shimmering obsolete words. Mistaking for rudeness and quaintness what was on its surface at any rate a subtle and complex civilization, they seemed to themselves to pass back into a freer air, where any extravagance was possible, and good breeding and mere circumspection and restraint vanished like the wind.

A similar longing to be rid of the precision and order of everyday life drove them to the mountains, and to the literature of Wales and the Highlands, to Celtic, or pseudo-Celtic romance. To the fashion of the time mountains were still frowning and horrid steeps; in Gray's Journal of his tour in the Lakes, a new understanding and appreciation of nature is only struggling through; and when mountains became fashionable it was at first, and remained in part at least till the time of Byron, for those very theatrical qualities which had hitherto put them in abhorrence. Wordsworth, in his *Lines written above Tintern Abbey*, in which he sets forth the succeeding stages of his mental development, refers to this love of the mountains for their spectacular qualities as the first step in the progress of his mind to poetic maturity:

> The sounding cataract
> Haunted me like a passion; the tall rock,
> The mountain, and the deep and gloomy wood,
> Their colours and their forms, were then to me
> An appetite.

This same passion for the 'sounding cataract' and the 'tall rock', this appetite for the deep and gloomy wood, gave its vogue in Wordsworth's boyhood to Macpherson's *Ossian*, a book which, whether it be completely fraudulent or not, was of capital importance in the beginnings of the romantic movement.

The love of mediæval quaintness and obsolete words led, however, to a more important literary event —the publication of Bishop Percy's edition of the ballads in the Percy folio—the *Reliques of Ancient Poetry*. Percy to his own mind knew the Middle Ages better than they knew themselves, and he took care to dress to advantage the rudeness and plainness of his originals. Perhaps we should not blame him. Sir Walter Scott did the same with better tact and skill in his Border minstrelsy, and how many distinguished editors there are who have tamed and smoothed down the natural wildness and irregularity of Blake. But it is more important to observe that when Percy's reliques came to have their influence on writing his additions were imitated as much as the poems on which he grafted them. Chatterton's *Rowley Poems*, which in many places seem almost inconceivably banal and artificial to us to-day, caught their accent from the episcopal editor as much as from the ballads themselves. None the less, whatever its faults, Percy's collection gave its impetus to one half of the romantic movement; it was eagerly read in Germany, and when it came to influence Scott and Coleridge it did so not only directly, but through Burger's imitation of it; it began the modern study and love of the ballad which produced *Sister Helen*, *The White Ship*, and *The Lady of Shalott*.

But the romantic revival goes deeper than any change, however momentous, of fashion or style. It meant certain fundamental changes in human outlook. In the first place, one notices in the authors of the time an extraordinary development of imaginative sensibility; the mind at its countless points of contact with the sensuous world and the world of thought seems to become more alive and alert. It is more sensitive to fine impressions, to finely graded shades of difference. Outward objects and philosophical ideas seem to increase in their content and their meaning, and acquire a new power to enrich the intensest life of the human spirit. Mountains and lakes, the dignity of the peasant, the terror of the supernatural, scenes of history, mediæval architecture and armour, mediæval thought and poetry, the arts and mythology of Greece—all became springs of poetic inspiration and poetic joy. The impressions of all these things were unfamiliar and ministered to a sense of wonder, and by that very fact they were classed as romantic, as modes of escape from a settled way of life. But they were also in a sense familiar too. The mountains made their appeal to a deep implanted feeling in man, to his native sense of his own worth and dignity and splendour as a part of nature, and his recognition of natural scenery as necessary (and in its fullest meaning as sufficient) for his spiritual needs. They called him back from the artificiality and complexity of the cities he had built for himself, and the society he had weaved round him, to the natural world in which Providence had planted him of old, and which was full of significance for his soul. The greatest poets of the romantic revival strove to capture and convey the influence of nature on the mind and of the mind on nature interpenetrating one another. They were none the less artists because they approached nature in a state of passive receptivity They believed in the autocracy of the individual imagination none the less because their mission was to divine nature and to understand her, rather than to correct her profusions in the name of art.

In the second place the romantic revival meant a development of the historical sense. Thinkers like Burke and Montesquieu helped students of politics to acquire perspective; to conceive modern institutions not as things separate, and separately created, but as conditioned by, and evolved from, the institutions of an earlier day. Even the revolutionary spirit of the time looked both before and after, and took history as well as the human perfectibility imagined by philosophers into its purview. In France the reformers appealed in the first instance for a States General—a mediæval institution—as the corrective of their wrongs, and later when they could not, like their neighbours in Belgium, demand reform by way of the restoration of their historical rights, they were driven to go a step still further back, beyond history to what they conceived to be primitive society, and demand the rights of man. This development of the historical sense, which had such a widespread influence on politics, got itself into literature in the creation of the historical novel. Scott and Chateaubriand revived the old romance in which by a peculiar ingenuity of form the adventures of a typical hero of fiction are cast in a historical setting and set about with portraits of real personages. The historical sense affected, too, novels dealing with contemporary life. Scott's best work, his novels of Scottish character, catch more than half their excellence from the richness of colour and proportion which the portraiture of the living people acquires when it is aided by historical knowledge and imagination.

Lastly, besides this awakened historical sense, and this quickening of imaginative sensibility to the message of nature, the romantic revival brought to literature a revival of the sense of the connexion between the visible world and another world which is unseen. The supernatural which in all but the crudest of mechanisms had been out of English literature since *Macbeth*, took hold on the imagination of authors, and brought with it a new subtlety and a new and nameless horror and fascination. There is nothing in earlier English literature to set beside the strange and terrible indefiniteness of *The Ancient Mariner*, and though much in this kind has been written since, we have not got far beyond the skill and imagination with which Coleridge and Scott worked on the instinctive fears that lie buried in the human mind.

Of all these aspects of the revival, however, the new sensitiveness and accessibility to the influences of external nature was the most pervasive and the most important. Wordsworth speaks for the love that is in homes where poor men lie, the daily teaching that is in

> woods and rills;
> The silence that is in the starry sky,
> The sleep that is among the lonely hills.

Shelley for the wildness of the west wind, and the

ubiquitous spiritual emotion which speaks equally in the song of a skylark or a political revolution. Byron for the swing and roar of the sea. Keats for verdurous glooms and winding mossy ways. Scott and Coleridge, though like Byron they are less with nature than with romance, share the same communion.

This imaginative sensibility of the romantics not only deepened their communion with nature, it brought them into a truer relation with what had before been created in literature and art. The romantic revival is the Golden Age of English criticism; all the poets were critics of one sort or another—either formally in essays and prefaces, or in passing and desultory flashes of illumination in their correspondence. Wordsworth, in his prefaces, in his letter to a friend of Burns which contains such a breadth and clarity of wisdom on things that seem alien to his sympathies, even in some of his poems; Coleridge, in his *Biographia Literaria*, in his notes on Shakespeare, in those rhapsodies at Highgate which were the basis for his recorded table talk; Keats in his letters; Shelley in his *Defence of Poetry*; Byron in his satires and journals; Scott in those lives of the novelists which contain so much truth and insight into the works of fellow craftsmen—they are all to be found turning the new acuteness of impression which was in the air they breathed to the study of literature as well as to the study of nature. Alongside of them were two authors, Lamb and Hazlitt, whose bent was rather critical than creative, and the best part of whose intelligence and sympathy was spent on the sensitive and loving divination of our earlier literature. With these two men began the criticism of acting and of pictorial art that have developed since into two of the main kinds of modern critical writing.

Romantic criticism, both in its end and its method, differs widely from that of Dr. Johnson and his school. Wordsworth and Coleridge were concerned with deep-seated qualities and temperamental differences. Their critical work revolved round their conception of the fancy and the imagination, the one dealing with nature on the surface and decorating it with imagery, the other penetrating to its deeper significances. Hazlitt and Lamb applied in the same fashion their analogous conception of wit as a lower quality than humour. Dr. Johnson looked on the other hand for correctness of form, for the subordination of the parts to the whole, for the self-restraint and good sense which common manners would demand in society and wisdom in practical life. His school cared more for large general outlines than for truth in detail. They would not permit the idiosyncrasy of a personal or individual point of view; hence they were incapable of understanding lyricism, and they preferred those forms of writing which set themselves to express the ideas and feelings that most men may be supposed to have in common. Dr. Johnson thought a bombastic and rhetorical passage in Congreve's *Mourning Bride* better than the famous description of Dover cliff in *King Lear*. 'The crows, sir,' he said of the latter, 'impede your fall.' Their town breeding, and possibly, as we saw in the case of Dr. Johnson, an actual physical disability, made them distrust any clear and sympathetic rendering of the sense impressions which nature creates. One cannot imagine Dr. Johnson caring much for the minute observations of Tennyson's nature poems, or delighting in the verdurous and mossy alleys of Keats. His test in such a case would be simple; he would not have liked to be in such places, nor reluctantly compelled to go there would he in all likelihood have had much to say about them beyond that they were damp. For the poetry—such as Shelley's—which worked by means of impalpable and indefinite suggestion, he would, one may conceive, have cared even less. New modes of poetry asked of critics new sympathies and a new way of approach.

But it is time to turn to the authors themselves.

(2)

The case of Wordsworth is peculiar. In his own day he was vilified and misunderstood; poets like Byron, whom most of us would now regard simply as depending from the school he created, sneered at him. Shelley and Keats failed to understand him or his motives; he was suspected of apostasy, and when he became Poet Laureate he was written off as a turncoat who had played false to the ideals of his youth. Now, common opinion regards him as a poet above all the others of his age and amongst all the English poets standing beside Milton, but a step below Shakespeare himself— and we know more about him, more about the processes by which his soul moved from doubts to certainties, from troubles to triumph, than we do about any other author we have. This knowledge we have from the poem called *The Prelude*, which was published after his death. It was designed to be only the opening and explanatory section of a philosophical poem, which was never completed. Had it been published earlier it would have saved Wordsworth from the coldness and neglect he suffered at the hands of younger men like Shelley; it might even have made their work different from what it is. It has made Wordsworth very clear to us now.

Wordsworth is that rarest thing amongst poets, a complete innovator. He looked at things in a new way.

He found his subjects in new places; and he put them into a new poetic form. At the turning point of his life, in his early manhood, he made one great discovery, had one great vision. By the light of that vision and to communicate that discovery he wrote his greatest work. By and by the vision faded, the world fell back into the light of common day, his philosophy passed from discovery to acceptance, and all unknown to him his pen fell into a common way of writing. The faculty of reading which has added fuel to the fire of so many waning inspirations was denied him. He was much too self-centred to lose himself in the works of others. Only the shock of a change of environment—a tour in Scotland, or abroad—shook him into his old thrill of imagination, so that a few fine things fitfully illumine the enormous and dreary bulk of his later work. If we lost all but the *Lyrical Ballads*, the poems of 1804, and *The Prelude*, and *The Excursion*, Wordsworth's position as a poet would be no lower than it is now, and he would be more readily accepted by those who still find themselves uncertain about him.

The determining factor in his career was the French Revolution—that great movement which, besides remaking France and Europe, made our very modes of thinking anew. While an undergraduate in Cambridge Wordsworth made several vacation visits to France. The first peaceful phase of the Revolution was at its height; France and the assembly were dominated by the little group of revolutionary orators who took their name from the south-western province from which most of them came, and with this group—the Girondists—Wordsworth threw in his lot. Had he remained he would probably have gone with them to the guillotine. As it was, the commands of his guardian brought him back to England, and he was forced to contemplate from a distance the struggle in which he burned to take an active part. One is accustomed to think of Wordsworth as a mild old man, but such a picture if it is thrown back as a presentment of the Wordsworth of the nineties is far from the truth. This darkly passionate man tortured himself with his longings and his horror. War came and the prayers for victory in churches found him in his heart praying for defeat; then came the execution of the king; then the plot which slew the Gironde. Before all this Wordsworth trembled as Hamlet did when he learned the ghost's story. His faith in the world was shaken. First his own country had taken up arms against what he believed to be the cause of liberty. Then faction had destroyed his friends whom he believed to be its standard-bearers. What was in the world, in religion, in morality that such things could be? In the face of this tremendous problem, Wordsworth, unlike Hamlet, was resolute and determined. It was, perhaps, characteristic of him that in his desire to get his feet on firm rock again he fled for a time to the exactest of sciences —to mathematics. But though he got certainties there, they must have been, one judges, certainties too arid for his thirsting mind. Then he made his great discovery—helped to it, perhaps, by his sister Dorothy and his friend Coleridge—he found nature, and in nature, peace.

Not a very wonderful discovery, we might say; but though the cleansing and healing force of natural surroundings on the mind is a familiar enough idea now, that is only because Wordsworth found it. When he gave his message to the world it was a new message. It is worth while remembering that it is still an unaccepted one. Most of his critics still consider it only Wordsworth's fun when he wrote:

> One impulse from a vernal wood
>   May teach you more of man,
> Of moral evil and of good,
>   Than all the sages can.

Yet Wordsworth really believed that moral lessons and ideas were to be gathered from trees and stones. It was the main part of his teaching. He claimed that his own morality had been so furnished him, and he wrote his poetry to convince other people that what had been true for him could be true for them too.

For him life was a series of impressions, and the poet's duty was to recapture those impressions, to isolate them and brood over them, till gradually as a result of his contemplation emotion stirred again—an emotion akin to the authentic thrill that had excited him when the impression was first born in experience. Then poetry is made; this emotion 'recollected' as Wordsworth said (we may add, recreated) 'in tranquillity' passes into enduring verse. He treasured numberless experiences of this kind in his own life. Some of them are set forth in *The Prelude*, that for instance on which the poem *The Thorn* in the *Lyrical Ballads* is based; they were one or other of them the occasion of most of his poems; the best of them produced his finest work—such a poem for instance as *Resolution and Independence* or *Gipsies*, where some chance sight met with in one of the poet's walks is brooded over till it becomes charged with a tremendous significance for him and for all the world. If we ask how he differentiated his experiences, which had most value for him, we shall find something deficient. That is to say, things which were unique and precious to him do not always appear so to his readers. He counted as gold much that we regard as dross. But though we may differ from his judgements, the test which he applied

to his recollected impressions is clear. He attached
most value to those which brought with them the sense
of an indwelling spirit, transfusing and interpenetrating
all nature, transfiguring with its radiance rocks and
fields and trees and the men and women who lived
close enough to them to partake of their strength—the
sense, as he calls it in his *Lines above Tintern Abbey* of
something 'more deeply interfused' by which all
nature is made one. Sometimes, as in the hymn to
Duty, it is conceived as law. Duty before whom the
flowers laugh, is the daughter of the voice of God,
through whom the most ancient heavens are fresh and
strong. But in most of his poems its ends do not
trouble; it is omnipresent; it penetrates everything and
transfigures everything; it is God. It was Wordsworth's belief that the perception of this indwelling
spirit weakened as age grew. For a few precious and
glorious years he had the vision

> when meadow, grove, and stream,
> The earth, and every common sight,
> To me did seem
> Apparelled in celestial light,
> The glory and the freshness of a dream.

Then, as childhood—when 'these intimations of
immortality', this perception of the infinite are most
strong—passed further and further away, the vision
faded and he was left gazing in the light of common
day. He had his memories and that was all.

There is, of course, more in the matter than this,
and Wordsworth's beliefs were inextricably entangled
with the conception which Coleridge borrowed from
German philosophy.

> We receive but what we give,

wrote Coleridge to his friend,

> And in our life alone does nature live.

And Wordsworth came to know that the light he had imagined to be bestowed was a light reflected from his own mind. It is easy to pass from criticism to metaphysics where Coleridge leads, and wise not to follow.

If Wordsworth represents that side of the Romantic Revival which is best described as the return to Nature, Coleridge has justification for the phrase 'Renascence of Wonder'. He revived the supernatural as a literary force, emancipated it from the crude mechanism which had been applied to it by dilettantes like Horace Walpole and Mrs. Radcliffe, and invested it instead with that air of suggestion and indefiniteness which gives the highest potency to it in its effect on the imagination. But Coleridge is more noteworthy for what he suggested to others than for what he did in himself. His poetry is, even more than Wordsworth's, unequal; he is capable of large tracts of dreariness and flatness; he seldom finished what he began. *The Ancient Mariner*, indeed, which was the fruit of his close companionship with Wordsworth, is the only completed thing of the highest quality in the whole of his work. *Christabel* is a splendid fragment; for years the first part lay uncompleted and when the odd accident of an evening's intoxication led him to begin the second, the inspiration had fled. For the second part, by giving to the fairy atmosphere of the first a local habitation and a name, robbed it of its most precious quality; what it gave in exchange was something the public could get better from Scott. *Kubla Khan* went unfinished because the call of a friend broke the thread of the reverie in which it was composed. In the end came opium and oceans of talk at Highgate and fouled the springs of poetry. Coleridge never fulfilled the promise of his early days with Wordsworth. 'He never spoke out.' But it is on the lines laid down by his share in the pioneer work rather than on the lines of Wordsworth's that the second generation of Romantic poets—that of Shelley and Keats—developed.

The work of Wordsworth was conditioned by the French Revolution but it hardly embodied the revolutionary spirit. What he conceived to be its excesses revolted him, and though he sought and sang freedom, he found it rather in the later revolt of the nationalities against the Revolution as manifested in Napoleon himself. The spirit of the Revolution, as it was understood in France and in Europe, had to wait for Shelley for its complete expression. Freedom is the breath of his work—freedom not only from the tyranny of earthly powers, but from the tyranny of religion, expressing itself in republicanism, in atheism, and in complete emancipation from the current moral code both in conduct and in writing. The reaction which had followed the overthrow of Napoleon at Waterloo, sent a wave of absolutism and repression all over Europe. Italy returned under the heel of Austria; the Bourbons were restored in France; in England came the days of Castlereagh and Peterloo. The poetry of Shelley is the expression of what the children of the Revolution—men and women who were brought up in and believed the revolutionary gospel—thought about these things.

But it is more than that. Of no poet in English, nor perhaps in any other tongue, could it be said with more surety that the pursuit of the spirit of beauty dominates all his work. For Shelley it interfused all nature and to possess it was the goal of all endeavour. The visible world and the world of thought mingle themselves inextricably in his contemplation of it. For him there is no boundary-line between the two, the one is as real and actual as the other. In his hands that old trick of the poets, the simile, takes on a new and surprising form. He does not enforce the creations of his imagination by the analogy of natural appearances; his instinct is just the opposite—to describe and illumine nature by a reference to the creatures of thought. Other poets, Keats for instance, or Tennyson, or the older poets like Dante and Homer, might compare ghosts flying from an enchanter like leaves flying before the wind. They might describe a poet wrapped up in his dreams as being like a bird singing invisible in the brightness of the sky. But Shelley can write of the west wind as

> Thou, from whose unseen presence the leaves dead
>> Are driven, like ghosts from an enchanter fleeing.

and he can describe a skylark in the heavens as

>> Like a Poet hidden
>> In the light of thought.

Of all English poets he is the most completely lyrical. Nothing that he wrote but is wrought out of the anguish or joy of his own heart.

>> Most wretched men,

he writes

>> Are cradled into poetry by wrong:
>> They learn in suffering what they teach in song.

Perhaps his work is too impalpable and moves in an air too rarefied. It sometimes lacks strength. It fails to take grip enough of life. Had he lived he might have given it these things; there are signs in his last poems that he would have given it. But he could hardly have bettered the sheer and triumphant lyricism of *The Skylark*, of some of his choruses, of the *Ode to Dejection* and of the *Lines written amongst the Euganean hills*.

If the Romantic sense of the one-ness of nature

found its highest exponent in Shelley, the Romantic sensibility to outward impressions reached its climax in Keats. For him life is a series of sensations, felt with almost febrile acuteness. Records of sight and touch and smell crowd every line of his work; the scenery of a garden in Hampstead becomes like a landscape in the tropics, so extraordinarily vivid and detailed is his apprehension and enjoyment of what it has to give him. The luxuriance of his sensations is matched by the luxuriance of his powers of expression. Adjectives heavily charged with messages for the senses crowd every line of his work, and in his earlier poems overlay so heavily the thought they are meant to convey that all sense of sequence and structure is apt to be smothered under their weight. Not that consecutive thought claims a place in his conception of poetry. His ideal was passive contemplation rather than active mental exertion. 'O for a life of sensations rather than of thoughts,' he exclaimed in one of his letters: and in another, 'It is more noble to sit like Jove than to fly like Mercury.' His work has one message and one only, the lastingness of beauty and its supreme truth. It is stated in *Endymion* in lines that are worn bare with quotation. It is stated again, at the height of his work in his greatest ode,

> 'Beauty is truth, truth beauty,'—that is all
> Ye know on earth, and all ye need to know.

His work has its defects; he died at twenty-six, so it would be a miracle if it were not so. He lacks taste and measure; he offends by an over-luxuriousness and sensuousness; he fails when he is concerned with flesh and blood; he is apt, as Robert Bridges has said, 'to class women with roses and sweetmeats'. But in his short life he attained with surprising rapidity and

L

completeness to poetic maturity, and perhaps from no other poet would we find things to match his greatest—*Hyperion*, *Isabella*, *The Eve of St. Agnes*, and the *Odes*.

There remains a poet over whom opinion is more sharply divided than it is about any other writer in English. In his day Lord Byron was the idol, not only of his countrymen, but of Europe. Of all the poets of the time he was, if we except Scott, whose vogue he eclipsed, the only one whose work was universally known and popular. Everybody read him; he was admired not only by the multitude and by his equals, but by at least one who was his superior, the German poet Goethe, who did not hesitate to say of him that he was the greatest talent of the century. Though this exalted opinion still persists on the Continent, hardly anyone could be found in England to subscribe to it now. Without insularity, we may claim to be better judges of authors in our own tongue than foreign critics are, however distinguished and comprehending. How then shall be explained Lord Byron's instant popularity and the position he won? What were the qualities which gave him the power he enjoyed?

In the first place he appealed by virtue of his subject-matter—the desultory wanderings of *Childe Harold* traversed ground every mile of which was memorable to men who had watched the struggle which had been going on in Europe with scarcely a pause for twenty years. Descriptive journalism was then and for nearly half a century afterwards unknown, and the poem by its descriptiveness, by its appeal to the curiosity of its readers, made the same kind of success that vividly written special correspondence would to-day; and it had the charm of metre super-added. Lord Byron gave his readers something more, too, than mere description. He added to it the charm

of a personality, and when that personality was enforced by a title, when it proclaimed its sorrows as the
age's sorrows, endowed itself with an air of symbolism
and set itself up as a kind of scapegoat for the nation's
sins, its triumph was complete. Most men have from
time to time to resist the temptation to pose to themselves; many do not even resist it. For all those who
chose to believe themselves blighted by pessimism,
and for all the others who would have loved to believe
it, Byron and his poetry came as an echo of themselves.
Shallow called to shallow. Men found in him, as their
sons found more reputably in Tennyson, a picture of
what they conceived to be the state of their own minds.

But he was not altogether a man of pretence. He
really and passionately loved freedom; no one can
question his sincerity in that. He could be a fine and
scathing satirist; and though he was careless, he had
great poetic gifts.

(3)

The age of the Romantic Revival was one of poetry
rather than of prose; it was in poetry that the best
minds of the time found their means of expression.
But it produced prose of rare quality too, and there is
delightful reading in the works of its essayists and
occasional writers. In its form the periodical essay had
changed little since it was first made popular by
Addison and Steele. It remained, primarily, a vehicle
for the expression of a personality, and it continued to
seek the interests of its readers by creating or suggest-
ing an individuality strong enough to carry off any
desultory adventure by the mere force of its own
attractiveness. Yet there is all the difference in the
world between Hazlitt and Addison, or Lamb and
Steele. The *Tatler* and the *Spectator* leave you with

a sense of artifice; Hazlitt and Lamb leave us with a grip of a real personality—in the one case very vigorous and combative, in the other set about with a rare plaintiveness and gentleness, but in both absolutely sincere. Addison is gay and witty and delightful but he only plays at being human; Lamb's essays—the translation into print of a heap of idiosyncrasies and oddities, and likes and dislikes, and strange humours —come straight and lovably from a human soul.

The prose writers of the romantic movement brought back two things into writing which had been out of it since the seventeenth century. They brought back egotism and they brought back enthusiasm. They had the confidence that their own tastes and experiences were enough to interest their readers; they mastered the gift of putting themselves on paper. But there is one wide difference between them and their predecessors. Robert Burton was an egotist but he was an unconscious one; the same is, perhaps, true— though much less certainly—of Sir Thomas Browne. In Lamb and Hazlitt and De Quincey egotism was deliberate, consciously assumed, the result of a compelling and shaping art. If one reads Lamb's earlier essays and prose pieces one can see the process at work—watch him consciously imitating Fuller, or Burton, or Browne, mirroring their idiosyncrasies, making their quaintnesses and graces his own. By the time he came to write the *Essays of Elia* he had mastered the personal style so completely that his essays seem simply the overflow of talk. They are so desultory; they move from one subject to another so waywardly —such an essay as *A Chapter on Ears*, for instance, passing with the easy inconsequence of conversation from anatomy through organ music to beer—when they quote, as they do constantly, it is incorrectly, as in the random reminiscences of talk. Here one would say is the cream risen to the surface of a full mind and skimmed at one taking. How far all this is from the truth we know—know, too, how for months he polished and rewrote these magazine articles, rubbing away roughnesses and corners, taking off the traces of logical sequences and argument, till in the finished work of art he mimicked inconsequence so perfectly that his friends might have been deceived. And the personality he put on paper was partly an artistic creation, too. In life Lamb was a nervous, easily excitable and emotional man; his years were worn with the memory of a great tragedy and the constantly impending fear of a repetition of it. One must assume him in his way to have been a good man of business— he was a clerk in the East India House, then a throbbing centre of trade, and the largest commercial concern in England, and when he retired his employers gave him a very handsome pension. In the early portrait by Hazlitt there is a dark and gleaming look of fire and decision. But you would never guess it from his books. There he is the gentle recluse, dreaming over old books, old furniture, old prints, old plays and play-bills; living always in the past, loving in the town secluded byways like the Temple, or the libraries of Oxford colleges, and in the country quiet and shaded lanes, none of the age's enthusiasm for mountains in his soul. When he turned critic it was not to discern and praise the power and beauty in the works of his contemporaries but to rediscover and interpret the Elizabethan and Jacobean romantic plays.

This quality of egotism Lamb shares with other writers of the time, with De Quincey, for instance, who left buried in work which is extensive and unequal much that lives by virtue of the singular elaborateness and loftiness of the style which he could on occasion command. For the revival of enthusiasm one must turn to Hazlitt, who brought his passionate and combative disposition to the service of criticism, and produced a series of studies remarkable for their earnestness and their vigour, and for the essential justness which they display despite the prejudice on which each of them was confessedly based.

CHAPTER VIII

THE VICTORIAN AGE

(1)

HAD it not been that with two exceptions all the poets of the Romantic Revival died early, it might be more difficult than it is to draw a line between their school and that of their successors. As it happened, the only poet who survived and wrote was Wordsworth, the oldest of them all. For long before his death he did nothing that had one touch of the fire and beauty of his earlier work. The respect he began to receive in the years immediately before his death, after a lifetime of neglect, was paid not to the conservative Laureate of 1848, but to the revolutionary in art and politics of fifty years before. He had lived on long after his work was done

> To hear the world applaud the hollow ghost
> Which blamed the living man.

All the others, Keats, Shelley, Byron, were dead before 1830, and the problem which might have confronted us had they lived, of adult work running counter to the tendencies and ideals of youth, does not exist. Keats or Shelley might have lived as long as Carlyle, with whom they were almost exactly contemporary; had they done so, the age of the Romantic Revival and the Victorian Age would have been united in the lives of authors who were working in both. We should conceive, that is, the whole period as one, just as we conceive of the Renaissance in England, from Surrey to Shirley, as one. As it is, we have accustomed ourselves to a strongly marked line of division. A man must be on either one side or the other: Wordsworth, though he wrote on till 1850, is on the further side; Carlyle, though he was born in the same year as Keats, on the hither side. Still, the accident of length of days must not blind us to the fact that the Victorian period, though in many respects its ideals and modes of thinking differed from those of the period which preceded it, is essentially an extension of the Romantic Revival and not a fresh start. The coherent inspiration of romanticism disintegrated into separate lines of development, just as in the seventeenth century the single inspiration of the Renaissance broke into different schools. Along these separate lines represented by such men as Browning, the Pre-Raphaelites, Arnold, and Meredith, literature enriched and elaborated itself into fresh forms. None the less, every author in each of these lines of literary activity invites his readers to understand his direct relation to the romantic movement. Rossetti touches it through his original, Keats; Arnold through Goethe and Byron; Browning first through Shelley and then in item after item of his varied subject-matter.

In one direction the Victorian Age achieved a salient and momentous advance. The Romantic Revival had been interested in nature, in the past, and in a lesser degree in art, but it had not been interested in men and women. To Wordsworth the dalesmen of the lakes were part of the scenery they moved in; he saw men as trees walking, and when he writes about them as in such great poems as *Resolution and Independence*, *The Brothers*, or *Michael*, it is as natural objects he treats them, invested with the lonely remoteness that separates them from the complexities and passions of life as it is lived. They are there, we feel, to teach the same lesson as the landscape teaches in which they are set.

The passing of the old Cumberland beggar through villages and past farmsteads, brings to those who see him the same kind of consolation as the impulses from a vernal wood that Wordsworth celebrated in his purely nature poetry. Compare Browning with Wordsworth, and note the fundamental change in the attitude of the poet that his work reveals. *Pippa Passes* is a poem on exactly the same scheme as *The Old Cumberland Beggar*, but in treatment no two things could be further apart. The intervention of Pippa is dramatic, and though her song is in the same key as the wordless message of Wordsworth's beggar she is a world apart from him, because she is something not out of natural history, but out of life. The Victorian Age extended to the complexities of human life the imaginative sensibility which its predecessor had brought to bear on nature and history. It searched for individuality in character, studied it with a loving minuteness, and built up out of its discoveries amongst men and women a body of literature which in its very mode of conception was more closely related to life, and thus the object of greater interest and excitement to its readers, than anything which had been written in the previous ages. It is the direct result of this extension of romanticism that the novel became the characteristic means of literary expression of the time, and that Browning, the poet who more than all others represents the essential spirit of his age, should have been, as it were, a novelist in verse. Only one other literary form, indeed, could have ministered adequately to this awakened interest; but by some luck not easy to understand, the drama, which might have done with greater economy and directness the work the novel had to do, remained outside the main stream of literary activity. To the drama it seemed later that we were returning, and it may be that in the future the direct representation of the clash of human life which was for long in the hands of the novelists may come back to its own domain.

The Victorian Age, then, added humanity to nature and art as the subject-matter of literature. But it went further than that. For the first time since the Renaissance came an era which was conscious of itself as an epoch in the history of mankind, and confident of its mission. The fifteenth and sixteenth centuries revolutionized cosmography and altered the face of the physical world. The nineteenth century, by the discoveries of its men of science and by the remarkable and rapid succession of inventions which revolutionized the outward face of life, made hardly less alteration in accepted ways of thinking. The evolutionary theory, which had been in the air since Goethe, and to which Darwin was able to give an incontrovertible basis of scientific fact, profoundly influenced man's attitude to nature and to religion. Physical as apart from natural science made scarcely less advance, and instead of a world created in some fixed moment of time, on which had been placed by some outward agency all the forms and shapes of nature that we know, came the conception of a planet congealing out of a nebula, and of some lower, simpler and primeval form of life multiplying and diversifying itself through suceeding stages of development to form both the animal and the vegetable world. This conception not only enormously excited and stimulated thought, but it gave thinkers a strange sense of confidence and certainty not possessed by the age before. Everything seemed plain to them; they were heirs of all the ages. Their doubts were as certain as their faith.

> There lives more faith in honest doubt,
> Believe me, than in half the creeds

said Tennyson; 'honest doubt', hugged with all the certainty of a revelation, is the creed of most of his philosophical poetry, and, what is more to the point, was the creed of the masses that were beginning to think for themselves, to whose awakening interest his work so strongly appealed. There were, no doubt, literary side-currents. Disraeli survived to show that there were still young men who thought Byronically. Rossetti and his school held themselves proudly aloof from the rationalistic and scientific tendencies of the time, and found in the Middle Ages, better understood than they had been either by Coleridge or Scott, a refuge from a time of factories and fact. The Oxford Movement ministered to the same tendencies in religion and philosophy; but it is the scientific spirit, and all that the scientific spirit implied, its certain doubt, its care for minuteness and truth of observation, its growing interest in social processes and the conditions under which life is lived, that is the central fact in Victorian literature.

Tennyson represents more fully than any other poet this essential spirit of the age. If it be true, as has been often asserted, that the spirit of an age is to be found best in the work of lesser men, his complete identity with the thought of his time is in itself evidence of his inferiority to his contemporary, Browning. Comparisons between the two men seem inevitable; they were made by readers when *In Memoriam* and *Men and Women* came hot from the press, and they have been made ever since. There could, of course, scarcely be two men more dissimilar, Tennyson elaborating and decorating the obvious; Browning delving into the esoteric and the obscure and bringing up strange and unfamiliar finds; Tennyson in faultless verse registering current newly accepted ways of thought; Browning in

advance thinking afresh for himself, occupied cease-
lessly in the arduous labour of creating an audience fit
to judge him. The age justified the accuracy with
which Tennyson mirrored it by accepting him and
rejecting Browning. It is this very accuracy that almost
forces us at this time to minimize and disparise
Tennyson's work. We have passed from Victorian
certainties, and when he writes in the mood of *Locksley
Hall* and the rest he is apt to appear to us a little
shallow, a little empty, and a little pretentious.

His earlier poetry, before he took upon himself the
burden of the age, is his best work, and it bears strongly
marked upon it the influence of Keats. Such a poem
for instance as *Œnone* shows an extraordinarily fine
sense of language and melody, and the capacity caught
from Keats of conveying a rich and highly coloured
pictorial effect. No other poet save Keats has had a
sense of colour so highly developed as Tennyson's.
From his boyhood he was an exceedingly close and
sympathetic observer of the outward forms of nature,
and he makes a splendid use of what his eyes had taught
him in these earlier poems. Later his interest in insects
and birds and flowers outran the legitimate opportunity
he possessed of using it in poetry. It was his habit, his
son tells us, to keep notebooks of things he had
observed in his garden or in his walks, and to work
them up afterwards into similes for *The Princess* and
the *Idylls of the King*. Read in the books written by
admirers, in which they have been studied and collected
(there are several of them), these similes are pleasing
enough; in the text where they stand they are apt to
have the air of impertinences, beautiful and extravagant
impertinences no doubt, but alien to their setting. In
one of the *Idylls of the King* the fall of a drunken knight
from his horse is compared to the fall of a jutting edge

of cliff and with it a lance-like fir-tree, which Tennyson had observed near his home, and one cannot resist the feeling that the comparison is a thought too great for the thing it was meant to illustrate. So, too, in *The Princess* when he describes a handwriting,

> In such a hand as when a field of corn
> Bows all its ears before the roaring East,

he is using up a sight noted in his walks and transmuted into poetry on a trivial and frivolous occasion. You do not feel, in fact, that the handwriting visualized spontaneously called up the comparison; you are as good as certain that the simile existed waiting for use before the handwriting was thought of.

The accuracy of his observation of nature, his love of birds and larvæ, is matched by the carefulness with which he embodies, as soon as ever they were made, the discoveries of natural and physical science. Nowadays, possibly because these things have become commonplace to us, we may find him a little schoolboy-like in his pride of knowledge. He knows that

> This world was once a fluid haze of light,
> Till toward the centre set the starry tides,
> And eddied into suns, that wheeling cast
> The planets,

just as he knows what the catkins on the willows are like, or the names of the butterflies; but he is capable, on occasion, of 'dragging it in', as in

> the nebulous star we call the Sun,
> If that hypothesis of theirs be sound,

from the mere pride in his familiarity with the last new thing. His dealings with science, that is, like his dealings with nature, are wanting in that inevitableness, that spontaneous appropriateness, that we feel we have a right to ask from great poetry.

Had Edgar Allan Poe wanted an example for his theory of the impossibility of writing, in modern times, a long poem, he might have found it in Tennyson. His strength is in his shorter pieces; even where, as in *In Memoriam*, he has conceived and written something at once extended and beautiful, the beauty lies rather in the separate parts; the thing is more in the nature of a sonnet sequence than a continuous poem. Of his other larger works, *The Princess*, a scarcely happy blend between burlesque in the manner of *The Rape of the Lock* and a serious apostleship of the liberation of women, is solely redeemed by these lyrics. In writing it Tennyson's innate conservatism hardly squared with the liberalizing tendencies he caught from the more advanced thought of his age. Something of the same kind is true of *Maud*, which is a novel told in dramatically varied verse. The hero is morbid, his social satire peevish, and a story which could have been completely redeemed by the ending (the death of the hero) which artistic fitness demands, is of value for us now through its three amazing songs, in which the lyric genius of Tennyson reached its finest flower. It cannot be denied, either, that he failed—though magnificently—in the *Idylls of the King*. The odds were heavily against him in the choice of a subject. Arthur is at once too legendary and too shadowy for an epic hero, and nothing but the treatment that Milton gave to Satan (i.e. flat substitution of the legendary person by a newly created character) could fit him for the place. Even if Arthur had been more promising than he is, Tennyson's sympathies were fundamentally alien from the moral and religious atmosphere of Arthurian romance. His robust Protestantism left no room for mysticism; he could neither appreciate nor render the mystical fervour and exultation which is in the old history of the Holy Grail. Nor could he comprehend the morality of a society where courage, sympathy for the oppressed, loyalty and courtesy were the only essential virtues, and love took the way of freedom and the heart rather than the way of law. In his heart Tennyson's attitude to the ideals of chivalry and the old stories in which they are embodied differed probably very little from that of Roger Ascham or any other Protestant Englishman; when he endeavoured to make an epic of them and to fasten to it an allegory in which Arthur should typify the war of soul against sense, what happened was only what might have been expected. The heroic enterprise failed, and left us with a series of mid-Victorian novels in verse in which the knights figure as heroes of the generic mid-Victorian type.

But if he failed in his larger poems, he had a genius little short of perfect in his handling of shorter forms. The Arthurian story which produced only middling moralizing in the *Idylls*, gave us as well the supremely written Homeric episode of the *Morte d'Arthur*, and the sharp and defined beauty of *Sir Galahad* and *The Lady of Shalott*. Tennyson had a touch of the Pre-Raphaelite faculty of minute painting in words, and the writing of these poems is as clear and naïve as in the best things of Rossetti. He had also what neither Rossetti nor any of his contemporaries in verse, except Browning, had, a fine gift of understanding humanity. The peasants of his English idylls are conceived with as much breadth of sympathy and richness of humour, as purely and as surely, as the peasants of Chaucer or Burns. A note of passionate humanity is indeed in all his work. It makes vivid and intense his scholarly handling of Greek myth; always the unchanging human aspect of it attracts him most, in Œnone's grief, in the

indomitableness of Ulysses, in the weariness and disillusionment in Tithonus. It has been the cause of the
comfort he has brought to sorrow; none of his generation takes such a human attitude to death. Shelley
could yearn for the infinite, Browning treat it as the
last and greatest adventure, Arnold meet it clear-eyed
and resigned; to Wordsworth it is the mere return of
man the transient to Nature the eternal:

> No motion has she now, no force;
> She neither hears nor sees;
> Rolled round in earth's diurnal course,
> With rocks, and stones, and trees.

To Tennyson it brings the fundamental human home-
sickness for familiar things.

> Ah, sad and strange as in dark summer dawns
> The earliest pipe of half-awaken'd birds
> To dying ears, when unto dying eyes
> The casement slowly grows a glimmering square.

It is an accent which wakes an echo in a thousand
hearts.

(2)

While Tennyson, in his own special way and, so to
speak, in collaboration with the spirit of the age, was
carrying on the work of Romanticism on its normal
lines, Browning was finding a new style and a new
subject matter. In his youth he had begun as an
imitator of Shelley, and *Pauline* and *Paracelsus* remain
to show what the influence of the 'sun-treader' was on
his poetry. But as early as his second publication, *Bells
and Pomegranates*, he had begun to speak for himself,
and with *Men and Women*, a series of poems of amazing
variety and brilliance, he placed himself unassailably
in the first rank. Like Tennyson's, his genius continued

high and undimmed while life was left him. *Men and Women* was followed by an extraordinary narrative poem, *The Ring and the Book*, and it by several volumes scarcely less brilliant, the last of which appeared on the very day of his death.

Of the two classes into which, as we saw when we were studying Burns, creative artists can be divided, Browning belongs to that one which makes everything new for itself, and has in consequence to educate the readers by whom its work can alone be judged. He was an innovator in nearly everything he did; he thought for himself; he wrote for himself, and in his own way. And because he refused to follow ordinary modes of writing, he was and is still widely credited with being tortured and obscure.[1] The charge of obscurity is unfortunate because it tends to shut off from him a large class of readers for whom he has a sane and special and splendid message.

His most important innovation in form was his device of the dramatic lyric. What interested him in life was men and women, and in them, not their actions but the motives which governed their actions. To lay bare fully the working of motive in a narrative form with himself as narrator was obviously impossible; the strict dramatic form, though he attained some success in it, does not seem to have attracted him, probably because in it the ultimate stress must be on the thing done rather than the thing thought; there remained

[1] The deeper causes of Browning's obscurity have been detailed in Chapter IV of this book. It may be added for the benefit of the reader who fights shy on the report of it, that in nine cases out of ten it arises simply from his colloquial method; we go to him expecting the smoothness and completeness of Tennyson; we find in him the irregularities, the suppressions, the quick changes of talk—the clipped, clever talk of much-idea'd people who hurry breathlessly from one aspect of a subject to another.

M

therefore, of the ancient forms of poetry, the lyric. The lyric had of course been used before to express emotions imagined and not real to the poet himself; Browning was the first to project it to express imagined emotions of men and women, whether typical or individual, whom he himself had created. Alongside this perversion of the lyric, he created a looser and freer form, the dramatic monologue, in which most of his famous poems, *Cleon*, *Sludge the Medium*, *Bishop Blougram's Apology*, etc., are cast. In the convention which Browning established in it, all kinds of people are endowed with a miraculous articulation, a new gift of tongues; they explain themselves, their motives, the springs of those motives (for in Browning's view every thought and act of a man's life is part of an interdependent whole), and their author's peculiar and robust philosophy of life. Out of the dramatic monologues he devised the scheme of *The Ring and the Book*, a narrative poem in which the episodes, and not the plot, are the basis of the structure, and the story of a trifling and sordid crime is set forth as it appeared to the minds of the chief actors in succession. To these new forms he added the originality of an extraordinary realism in style. Few poets have the power by a word, a phrase, a flash of observation in detail to make us see the event as Browning makes us.

Many books have been written on the philosophy of Browning's poetry. Stated briefly its message is that of an optimism which depends on a recognition of the strenuousness of life. The basis of his creed, as of Carlyle's, is the gospel of labour; he believes in the supreme moral worth of effort. Life is a 'training school' for a future existence, and our place in it depends on the courage and strenuousness with which we have laboured here. Evil is in the world only as an instrument in the process of development; by conquering it we exercise our spiritual faculties the more. Only torpor is the supreme sin, even as in *The Statue and the Bust* where effort would have been to a criminal end.

> The counter our lovers staked was lost
> As surely as if it were lawful coin:
> And the sin I impute to each frustrate ghost
> Is—the unlit lamp and the ungirt loin,
> Though the end in sight was a vice, I say.

All the other main ideas of his poetry fit with perfect consistency on to his scheme. Love, the manifestation of a man's or a woman's nature, is the highest and most intimate relationship possible, for it is an opportunity —the highest opportunity—for spiritual growth. It can reach this end though an actual and earthly union is impossible.

> She has lost me, I have gained her;
> Her soul's mine: and thus, grown perfect,
> I shall pass my life's remainder.
> Life will just hold out the proving
> Both our powers, alone and blended:
> And then, come next life quickly!
> This world's use will have been ended.

It follows that the reward of effort is the promise of immortality, and that for each man, just because his thoughts and motives taken together count, and not one alone, there is infinite hope.

The contemporaries of Tennyson and Browning in poetry divide themselves into three separate schools. Nearest to them in temper is the school of Matthew Arnold and Arthur Hugh Clough; they have the same quick sensitiveness to the intellectual tendencies of the age, but their foothold in a time of shifting and dissolving creeds is a stoical resignation very different from the buoyant optimism of Browning, or Tennyson's mixture of science and doubt and faith. Very remote from them on the other hand is the backward-gazing mediævalism of Rossetti and his circle, who revived (Rossetti from Italian sources, Morris from Norman) a Middle Age which neither Scott nor Coleridge had more than partially and brokenly understood. The last school, that to which Swinburne and Meredith with all their differences unite in belonging, gave up Christianity with scarcely so much as a regret,

We have said to the dream that caressed and the dread that smote us
Goodnight and goodbye,

and turned with a new hope and exultation to the worship of our immemorial mother the earth. In both of them, the note of enthusiasm for political liberty which had been lost in Wordsworth after 1815, and was too early extinguished with Shelley, was revived in splendour and fire by the Italian Revolution.

(3)

As one gets nearer one's own time, a certain change comes insensibly over one's literary studies. Literature comes more and more to mean imaginative literature or writing about imaginative literature. The mass of writing comes to be taken not as literature, but as argument or information; we consider it purely from the point of view of its subject matter. A comparison will at once make this clear. When a man reads Bacon he commonly regards himself as engaged in the study of English literature; when he reads Darwin he is occupied in the study of natural science. A reader in Bacon's time would have looked on him as the Victorians looked on Darwin.

The distinction is obviously illogical, but a writer

on English literature within brief limits is forced to bow to it if he wishes his book to avoid the dreariness of a summary, and he can plead in extenuation the increased literary output of the later age and the incompleteness with which time has so far done its work in sifting the memorable from the forgettable, the ephemeral from what is going to last. The main body of imaginative prose literature—the novel—is treated in the next chapter and no attempt will be made here to deal with any but the admittedly greatest names. Nothing can be said, for instance, of that fluent journalist and biased historian Macaulay, nor of the mellifluousness of Newman, nor of the vigour of Kingsley or F. D. Maurice; nor of the writings, admirable in their literary qualities of purity and terseness, of Darwin or Huxley; nor of the culture and apostleship of Matthew Arnold. These authors, one and all, interpose no barrier, so to speak, between their subject-matter and their readers; you are not when you read them conscious of a literary intention, but of some utilitarian one, and as an essay on English literature is by no means a handbook to serious reading they will be no more mentioned here.

In the case of one nineteenth-century writer in prose, this method of exclusion cannot apply. Both Carlyle and Ruskin were professional men of letters; both in the voluminous compass of their works touched on a large variety of subjects; both wrote highly individual and peculiar styles; and both without being either professional philosophers or professional preachers were—as every good man of letters, whether he denies it or not, is and must be—lay moralists and prophets. Of the two Ruskin is plain and easily read, and he derives his message; Carlyle, his original, is apt to be tortured and obscure. Inside the body of Ruskin's work the student of nineteenth-century literature is probably in need of some guidance; outside so far as prose is concerned he can fend for himself.

As we saw, Carlyle was the oldest of the Victorians; he was over forty when the Queen came to the throne. Already his years of preparation in Scotland, in town and country, were over, and he had settled in that famous little house in Chelsea which for nearly half a century to come was to be one of the central hearths of literary London. More than that, he had already fully formed his mode of thought and his peculiar style. *Sartor Resartus* was written and published serially before the Queen came to the throne; *The French Revolution* came in the year of her accession at the very time that Carlyle's lectures were making him a fashionable sensation; most of his miscellaneous essays had already appeared in the reviews. But with the strict Victorian era, as if to justify the usually arbitrary division of literary history by dynastic periods, there came a new spirit into his work. For the first time he applied his peculiar system of ideas to contemporary politics. *Chartism* appeared in 1839; *Past and Present*, which does the same thing as *Chartism* in an artistic form, three years later. They were followed by one other book—*Latter Day Pamphlets*—addressed particularly to contemporary conditions, and by two remarkable and voluminous historical works. Then came the death of his wife, and for the last fifteen years of his life silence broken only briefly and at rare intervals.

The reader who comes to Carlyle with preconceived notions based on what he has heard of the subject-matter of his books is certain to be surprised by what he finds. There are histories in the canon of his works and pamphlets on contemporary problems, but they are composed on a plan that no other historian and no other social reformer would own. A reader will find in them no argument, next to no reasoning, and little practical judgement. Carlyle was not a great 'thinker' in the strictest sense of that term. He was under the control, not of his reason, but of his emotions; deep feeling, a volcanic intensity of temperament flaming into the light and heat of prophecy, invective, derision, or a simple splendour of eloquence, is the characteristic of his work. Against coldblooded argument his passionate nature rose in fierce rebellion; he had no patience with the formalist or the doctrinaire. Nor had he the faculty of analysis; his historical works are a series of pictures or tableaux, splendidly and vividly conceived, and with enormous colour and a fine illusion of reality, but onesided as regards the truth. In his essays on hero-worship he contents himself with a noisy reiteration of the general predicate of heroism; there is very little except their names and the titles to differentiate one sort of hero from another. His picture of contemporary conditions is not so much a reasoned indictment as a wild and fantastic orgy of epithets: 'dark simmering pit of Tophet', 'bottomless universal hypocrisies', and all the rest. In it all he left no practical scheme. His works are fundamentally not about politics or history or literature, but about himself. They are the exposition of a splendid egotism, fiercely enthusiastic about one or two deeply held convictions; their strength does not lie in their matter of fact.

This is, perhaps, a condemnation of him in the minds of those people who ask of a social reformer an actuarially accurate scheme for the abolition of poverty, or from a prophet a correct forecast of the result of the next general election. Carlyle has little help for these and no message save the disconcerting one of their own futility. His message is at once larger and simpler, for though his form was prose, his soul was a poet's soul, and what he has to say is a poet's word. In a way, it is partly Wordsworth's own. The chief end of life, his message is, is the performance of duty, chiefly the duty of work. 'Do thy little stroke of work; this is Nature's voice, and the sum of all the commandments, to each man.' All true work is religion, all true work is worship; to labour is to pray. And after work, obedience the best discipline for governing, so he says in *Past and Present*, and 'our universal duty and destiny; wherein whoso will not bend must break'. Carlyle asked of every man, action and obedience and to bow to duty; he also required of him sincerity and veracity, the duty of being a real and not a sham, a strenuous warfare against cant. The historical facts with which he had to deal he grouped under these embracing categories, and in *The French Revolution*, which is as much a treasure-house of his philosophy as a history, there is hardly a page on which they do no appear. 'Quack-ridden,' he says, 'in that one word lies all misery whatsoever.'

These bare elemental precepts he clothes in a garment of amazing and bizarre richness. There is nothing else in English faintly resembling the astonishing eccentricity and individuality of his style. Gifted with an extraordinarily excitable and vivid imagination; seeing things with sudden and tremendous vividness, as in a searchlight or a lightning flash, he contrived to convey to his readers his impressions full charged with the original emotion that produced them, and thus with the highest poetic effect. There is nothing in all descriptive writing to match the vividness of some of the scenes in *The French Revolution* or in the narrative part of *Cromwell's Letters and Speeches*, or—more perhaps than in any of his books, because in it he was setting down deep-seated impressions of his boyhood rather than those got from brooding over documents—in *Sartor Resartus*. Alongside this unmatched pictorial vividness and a quite amazing richness and rhythm of language, more surprising and original than anything out of Shakespeare, there are of course, striking defects —a wearisome reiteration of emphasis, a clumsiness of construction, a saddening fondness for solecisms and hybrid inventions of his own. The reader who is interested in these (and everyone who reads him is forced to become so) will find them faithfully dealt with in John Sterling's remarkable letter (quoted in Carlyle's *Life of Sterling*) on *Sartor Resartus*. But gross as they are, and frequently as they provide matter for serious offence, these eccentricities of language link themselves up in a strange indissoluble way with Carlyle's individuality and his power as an artist. They are not to be imitated, but he would be much less than he is without them, and they act by their very strength and pungency as a preservative of his work. That of all the political pamphlets which the new era of reform occasioned, his, which were the least in sympathy with it and are the furthest off the main stream of our political thinking, alone continue to be read, must be laid down not only to the prophetic fervour and fire of their inspiration but to the dark and violent magic of their style.

CHAPTER IX

THE NOVEL

(1)

THE faculty for telling stories is the oldest artistic faculty in the world, and the deepest implanted in the heart of man. Before the rudest cave-pictures were scratched on the stone, the story-teller, it is not unreasonable to suppose, was plying his trade. All early poetry is simply story-telling in verse. Stories are the first literary interest of the awakening mind of a child. As that is so, it is strange that the novel, which of all literary ways of story-telling seems closest to the unstudied tale-spinning of talk, should be the late discovery that it is. Of all the main forms into which the literary impulse moulds the stuff of imagination, the novel was the last to be devised. The drama dates from prehistoric times, so do the epic, the ballad and the lyric. The novel, as we know it, dates practically speaking from 1740. What is the reason it is so late in appearing?

The answer is simply that there seemed no room for good drama and good fiction at the same time in literature; drama and novels could not exist side by side, and the novel had to wait for the decadence of the drama before it could appear and triumph. If one were to make a table of succession for the various kinds of literature as they have been used naturally and spontaneously (not academically), the order would be: epic, drama, novel; and it would be obvious at once that the order stood for something more than chronological succession, and that literature in its function as a representation and criticism of life passed from form to form in the search for greater freedom, greater subtlety, and greater power. At present we seem to be at the climax of the third stage in this development; there are signs that the fourth is on the way, and that it will be a return to drama, not to the old, formal, ordered kind, but, something new and freer, ready to gather up and interpret what there is of newness and freedom in the spirit of man and the society in which he lives.

The novel, then, had to wait for the drama's decline, but there was literary story-telling long before that. There were mediæval romances in prose and verse; Renaissance pastoral tales, and stories of adventure; collections, plenty of them, of short stories like Boccaccio's, and those in Painter's *Palace of Pleasure*. But none of these, not even romances which deal in moral and sententious advice like *Euphues*, approach the essence of the novel as we know it. They are all simple and objective (except *Euphues*, which is simply a framework of travel for a book of aphorisms) they set forth incidents or series of incidents; long or short they are anecdotes only—they take no account of character. It was impossible we should have the novel as distinct from the tale till stories acquired a subjective interest for us; till we began to think about character and to look at actions not only outwardly, but within at their springs.

As has been stated early in this book, it was in the seventeenth century that this interest in character was first wakened. Shakespeare had brought to the drama, which before him was concerned with actions viewed outwardly, a psychological interest; he had taught that 'character is destiny', and that men's actions and fates spring not from outward agencies, but from within in their own souls. The age began to take a deep and curious interest in men's lives; biography was written for the first time, and autobiography; it is the great period of memoir-writing both in England and France; authors like Robert Burton came, whose delight it was to dig down into human nature in search for oddities and individualities of disposition; humanity as the great subject of inquiry for all men, came to its own. All this has a direct bearing on the birth of the novel. One transient form of literature in the seventeenth century—the Character—is an ancestor in the direct line. The collections of them—Earle's *Microcosmography* is the best—are not very exciting reading, and they never perhaps quite succeeded in naturalizing a form borrowed from the later age of Greece, but their importance in the history of the novel to come is clear. Take them and add them to the story of adventure— i.e. introduce each fresh person in your plot with a description in the character form, and the step you have made towards the novel is enormous; you have given the added interest of character to plot which was already there.

That, however, was not quite the way the thing worked in actual fact. At the heels of the Character came the periodical essay of Addison and Steele. Their interest in contemporary types was of the same quality as Earle's or Hall's, but they went a different way to work. Where these compressed and cultivated a style which was staccato and epigrammatic, huddling all the traits of their subject in short sharp sentences that follow each other with all the brevity and curtness of items in a prescription, Addison and Steele observed a more artistic plan. They made up the prescription, as it were, adding one ingredient after another slowly as the mixture dissolved. You are introduced to Sir Roger de Coverley, and to a number of other typical people, and then in a series of essays which if they were disengaged from their setting would be to all intents a novel, and a fine one, we are made aware one by one of different traits in his character and those of his friends, each trait generally enshrined in an incident which illustrates it; we get to know them, that is, gradually, as we should in real life, and not all in a breath, in a series of compressed statements, as is the way of the Character writers. With the Coverley essays in the *Spectator*, the novel in one of its forms—that in which an invisible and all knowing narrator tells a story in which someone else whose character he lays bare for us is the hero—is as good as achieved.

Another manner of fiction—the autobiographical— had already been invented. It grew directly out of the public interest in autobiography, and particularly in the tales of their voyages which the discoverers wrote and published on their return from their adventures. Its establishment in literature was the work of two authors, Bunyan and Defoe. The books of Bunyan, whether they are told in the first person or not, are and were meant to be autobiographical; their interest is a subjective interest. Here is a man who endeavours to interest you, not in the character of some other person he has imagined or observed, but in himself. His treatment of it is characteristic of the awakening talent for fiction in his time. *The Pilgrim's Progress* is begun as an allegory, and so continues for a little space till the story takes hold of the author. When it does, whether he knew it or not, allegory goes to the winds. But the autobiographical form of fiction in its highest art is the creation of Defoe. He told stories of adventure, incidents modelled on real life, as many tellers of tales had done before him, but to the form as he found it he super-added a psychological interest—the interest of the character of the narrator. He contrived to observe in his writing a scrupulous and realistic fidelity and appropriateness to the conditions in which the story was to be told. For instance, we learn about Crusoe's island gradually, just as Crusoe learns about it himself; though the author is careful, by taking his narrator up to a high point of vantage the day after his arrival, that we shall learn the essentials of it, as long as verisimilitude is not sacrificed, as soon as possible. It is the paradox of the English novel that these our earliest efforts in fiction were meant, unlike the romances which preceded them, to pass for truth. Defoe's *Journal of the Plague Year* was widely taken as literal fact, and it is still occasionally quoted as such by rash though reputable historians. So that in England the novel began with realism, as it has culminated, and across two centuries Defoe and the 'naturalists' join hands. Defoe, it is proper also in this place to notice, fixed the peculiar form of the historical novel. In his *Memoirs of a Cavalier*, the narrative of an imaginary person's adventures in a historical setting, is interspersed with the entrance of actual historical personages, exactly the method of historical romancing which was brought to perfection by Sir Walter Scott.

(2)

In the eighteenth century came the decline of the drama for which the novel had been waiting. By 1660 the romantic drama of Elizabeth's time was dead; the comedy of the Restoration which followed, witty and brilliant though it was, reflected a society too licentious and artificial to secure it permanence; by the time of Addison playwriting had fallen to journey-work, and the theatre to openly expressed contempt. When

Richardson and Fielding published their novels there was nothing to compete with fiction in the popular taste. It would seem as though the novel had been waiting for this favourable circumstance. In a sudden burst of prolific inventiveness, which can be paralleled in all letters only by the period of Marlowe and Shakespeare, masterpiece after masterpiece poured from the press. Within two generations, besides Richardson and Fielding came Sterne and Goldsmith and Smollett and Fanny Burney in naturalism, and Horace Walpole and Mrs. Radcliffe in the new way of romance. Novels by minor authors were published in thousands as well. The novel, in fact, besides being the occasion of literature of the highest class, attracted by its lucrativeness that undercurrent of journey-work authorship which had hitherto busied itself in poetry or plays. Fiction has been its chief occupation ever since.

Anything like a detailed criticism or even a bare narrative of this voluminous literature is plainly impossible within the limits of a single chapter. Readers must go for it to books on the subject. It is possible here merely to draw attention to those authors to whom the English novel as a more or less fixed form is indebted for its peculiar characteristics. Foremost amongst these are Richardson and Fielding; after them there is Walter Scott. After him, in the nineteenth century, Dickens and Meredith and Hardy; last of all the French realists and the new school of romance. To one or other of these originals all the great authors in the long list of English novelists owe their method and their choice of subject-matter.

With Defoe fiction gained verisimilitude, it ceased to deal with the incredible; it aimed at exhibiting, though in strange and memorable circumstances, the workings of the ordinary mind. It is Richardson's main claim to fame that he contrived a form of novel which exhibited an ordinary mind working in normal circumstances, and that he did this with a minuteness which till then had never been thought of and has not since been surpassed. His talent is very exactly a microscopical talent; under it the common stuff of life separated from its surroundings and magnified beyond previous knowledge, yields strange and new and deeply interesting sights. He carried into the study of character, which had begun in Addison with an eye to externals and eccentricities, a minute faculty of inspection which watched and recorded unconscious mental and emotional processes.

To do this he employed a method which was, in effect, a compromise between that of the autobiography and that of the tale told by an invisible narrator. The weakness of the autobiography is that it can write only of events within the knowledge of the supposed speaker, and that consequently the presentation of all but one of the characters of the book is an external presentation. We know, that is, of Man Friday only what Crusoe could, according to realistic appropriateness, tell us about him. We do not know what he thought or felt within himself. On the other hand the method of invisible narration had not at his time acquired the faculty which it possesses now of doing Friday's thinking aloud or exposing fully the workings of his mind. So that Richardson, whose interests were psychological, whose strength and talent lay in the presentation of the states of mind appropriate to situations of passion or intrigue, had to look about him for a new form, and that form he found in the novel of letters. In a way, if the end of a novel be the presentation not of action, but of the springs of action; if the external event in it is always of less importance than the emotions which conditioned it, and the emotions which it set working, the novel of letters is the supreme manner of fiction. Consider the possibilities of it; there is a series of events in which A, B, and C are concerned. Not only can the outward events be narrated as they appeared to all three separately by means of letters from each to another, or to a fourth party, but the motives of each and the emotions which each experiences as a result of the actions of the others or them all, can be laid bare. No other method can wind itself so completely into the psychological intricacies and recesses which lie behind every event. Yet the form, as everybody knows, has not been popular; even an expert novel-reader could hardly name off-hand more than two or three examples of it since Richardson's day. Why is this? Well, chiefly it is because the mass of novelists have not had Richardson's knowledge of, or interest in, the psychological underside of life, and those who have—as, amongst the moderns, Henry James—have devised out of the convention of the invisible narrator a method by which they can with greater economy attain in practice fairly good results. For the mere narration of action in which the study of character plays a subsidiary part, it was, of course, from the beginning impossible. Scott turned aside at the height of his power to try it in *Redgauntlet*; he never made a second attempt.

For Richardson's purpose, it answered admirably, and he used it with supreme effect. Particularly he excelled in that side of the novelist's craft which has ever since (whether because he started it or not) proved the subtlest and most attractive, the presentation of women. Richardson was one of those men who are not at their ease in other men's society, and whom other

N

men, to put it plainly, are apt to regard as coxcombs and fools. But he had a genius for the friendship and confidence of women. In his youth he wrote love-letters for them. His first novel grew out of a plan to exhibit in a series of letters the quality of feminine virtue, and in its essence (though with a ludicrous, and so to speak 'kitchen-maidish' misunderstanding of his own sex) adheres to the plan. His third and last novel, which designs to set up a model man against the monster of iniquity in *Pamela*, is successful only so far as it exhibits the thoughts and feelings of the heroine whom he ultimately marries. His second novel, *Clarissa Harlowe*, is a masterpiece of sympathetic divination into the feminine mind. Clarissa is, as has been well said, the 'Eve of fiction, the prototype of the modern heroine'; feminine psychology, as good as unknown before (Shakespeare's women being the 'Fridays' of a highly intelligent Crusoe), has hardly been brought further since. But Clarissa is more than mere psychology; whether she represents a contemporary tendency or whether Richardson made her so, she starts a new epoch. 'This', says Henley, 'is perhaps her finest virtue as it is certainly her greatest charm; that until she set the example, woman in literature as a self-suffering individuality, as an existence endowed with equal rights to independence—of choice, volition, action—with man had not begun to be.' She had not begun to be in life either.

What Richardson did for the subtlest part of a novelist's business, his dealings with psychology, Fielding did for the most necessary part of it, the telling of the story. Before him hardly any story had been told well; even if it had been plain and clear as in Bunyan and Defoe it had lacked the emphasis, the light and shade of skilful grouping. On the 'picaresque' (so the wandering roguish type of autobiographical novel was called abroad) convention of a journey he grafted a structure based in its outline on the form of the ancient epic. It proved extraordinarily suitable for his purpose. Not only did it make it easy for him to lighten his narrative with excursions in a heightened style, burlesquing his origins, but it gave him at once the right attitude to his material. He told his story as one who knew everything; could tell conversations and incidents as he conceived them happening, with no violation of credibility, nor any strain on his reader's imagination, and without impropriety could interpose in his own person, pointing to the reader things which might have escaped his attention, pointing at parallels he might have missed, laying bare the irony or humour beneath a situation. He allowed himself digressions and episodes, told separate tales in the middle of the action, introduced, as in Partridge's visit to the theatre, the added piquancy of topical allusion; in fact he did anything he chose. And he laid down that free form of the novel which is characteristically English, and from which, in its essence, no one till the modern realists has made a serious departure.

In the matter of his novels, he excels by reason of a Shakespearean sense of character and by the richness and rightness of his faculty of humour. He had a quick eye for contemporary types, and an amazing power of building out of them men and women whose individuality is full and rounded. You do not feel as you do with Richardson that his fabric is spun silkworm-wise out of himself; on the contrary you know it to be the fruit of a gentle and observant nature and a stock of fundamental human sympathy. His gallery of portraits, Joseph Andrews, Parson Adams, Parson Trulliber, Jones, Blifil, Partridge, Sophia and her father and all the rest are each of them minute studies of separate people; they live and move according to their proper natures; they are conceived not from without but from within. Both Richardson and Fielding were conscious of a moral intention; but where Richardson is sentimental, vulgar, and moral only so far as it is moral (as in *Pamela*) to inculcate selling at the highest price or (as in *Grandison*) to avoid temptations which never come in your way, Fielding's morality is fresh and healthy, and (though not quite free from the sentimentality of scoundrelism) at bottom sane and true. His knowledge of the world kept him right. His acquaintance with life is wide, and his insight is keen and deep. His taste is almost as catholic as Shakespeare's own, and the life he knew, and which other men knew, he handles for the first time with the freedom and imagination of an artist.

Each of the two—Fielding and Richardson—had his host of followers. Abroad Richardson won immediate recognition; in France Diderot went so far as to compare him with Homer and Moses! He gave the first impulse to modern French fiction. At home, less happily, he set going the sentimental school, and it was only when that had passed away that—in the delicate and subtle character studies of Jane Austen—his influence comes to its own. Miss Austen carried a step further, and with an observation which was first-hand and seconded by intuitive knowledge, Richardson's analysis of the feminine mind, adding to it a delicate and finely humorous feeling for character in both sexes which was all her own. Fielding's imitators (they number, each in his own way and with his own graces or talent added, his rival Smollett, Sterne, and Goldsmith) kept the way which leads to Thackeray and Dickens—the main road of the English Novel.

That road was widened two ways by Sir Walter Scott. The historical novel, which had been before his day either an essay in anachronism with nothing historical in it but the date, or a laborious and un-inspired compilation of antiquarian research, took form and life under his hands. His wide reading, stored as it was in a marvellous retentive memory, gave him all the background he needed to achieve a historical setting, and allowed him to concentrate his attention on the actual telling of his story; to which his genial and sympathetic humanity and his quick eye for character gave a humorous depth and richness that was all his own. It is not surprising that he gave the historical novel a literary vogue all over Europe. In the second place, he began in his novels of Scottish character a sympathetic study of nationality. He is not, perhaps, a fair guide to contemporary conditions; his interests were too romantic and too much in the past to catch the rattle of the looms that caught the ear of Galt, and if we want a picture of the great fact of modern Scotland, its industrialization, it is to Galt we must go. But in his comprehension of the essential character of the people he had no rival; in it his his-torical sense seconded his observation, and the two mingling gave us the pictures whose depth of colour and truth make his Scottish novels, *Old Mortality*, *The Antiquary*, *Redgauntlet*, the greatest things of their kind in literature.

(3)

The peculiarly national style of fiction founded by Fielding and carried on by his followers reached its culminating point in *Vanity Fair*. In it the reader does not seem to be present simply at the unfolding of a plot the end of which is constantly present to the mind of the author and to which he is always consciously working, every incident having a bearing on the course of the action; rather he feels himself to be the spectator of a piece of life which is too large and complex to be under the control of a creator, which moves to its close not under the impulsion of a directing hand, but independently impelled by causes evolved in the course of its happening. With this added complexity goes a more frequent interposition of the author in his own person—one of the conventions, as we have seen, of this national style. Thackeray is present to his readers, indeed, not as the manager who pulls the strings and sets the puppets in motion, but as an interpreter who directs the reader's attention to the events on which he lays stress, and makes them a starting-point for his own moralizing. This persistent moralizing—sham cynical, real sentimental—this thumping of death-bed pillows as in the dreadful case of Miss Crawley, makes Thackeray's use of the personal interposition almost less effective than that of any other novelist. Already while he was doing it, Dickens had conquered the public; and the English novel was making its second fresh start.

Dickens is an innovator in more ways than one. In the first place he is the earliest novelist to practise a conscious artistry of plot. *The Mystery of Edwin Drood* remains mysterious, but those who essay to conjecture the end of that unfinished story have at least the surety that its end, full worked out in all its details, had been in its author's mind before he set pen to paper. His imagination was as diligent and as disciplined as his pen. Dickens's practice in this matter could not be better put than in his own words, when he describes himself as 'in the first stage of a new book, which consists in going round and round the idea, as you see a bird in his cage go about and about his sugar before he touches it'. That his plots are always highly elaborated is the fruit of this preliminary disciplined exercise of thought. The method is familiar to many novelists now; Dickens was the first to put it into practice. In the second place he made a new departure by his frankly admitted didacticism and by the skill with which in all but two or three of his books—*Bleak House*, perhaps, and *Little Dorrit*—he squared his purpose with his art. Lastly came the discovery which has made him immortal. In him for the first time the English novel produced an author who dug down into the masses of the people for his subjects; apprehended them in all their inexhaustible character and humour and pathos, and reproduced them with a lively and loving artistic skill.

Dickens has, of course, serious faults. In particular, readers emancipated by lapse of time from the enslavement of their first enthusiasm have quarrelled with the mawkishness and sentimentality of his pathos, and with the exaggeration of his studies of character. It has been said of him, as of Thackeray, that he could not draw a 'good' woman and that Agnes Copperfield, like Amelia Sedley, is a very doll-like type of person. To critics of this kind it may be retorted that though 'good' and 'bad' are categories relevant to melodrama, they apply very ill to serious fiction, and that, indeed, to the characters of any of the novelists—the Brontës, Mrs. Gaskell or the like—who lay bare character with fullness and intimacy, they could not well be applied at all. The faultiness of them in Dickens is less than in Thackeray, for in Dickens they are only incident to the scheme, which lies in the hero (his heroes are excellent) and in the grotesque characters, whereas in his rival they are in the theme itself. For his pathos, not even his warmest admirer could perhaps offer a satisfactory case. The charge of exaggeration, however, is another matter. To the person who complains that he has never met Dick Swiveller or Micawber or Mrs. Gamp the answer is simply Turner's to the sceptical critic of his sunset, 'Don't you wish you could!' To the other, who objects more plausibly to Dickens's habit of attaching to each of his characters some label which is either so much flaunted all through that we cannot see the character at all or else mysteriously and unaccountably disappears when the story begins to grip the author, Dickens has himself offered an amusing and convincing defence. In the preface to *Pickwick* he answers those who criticized the novel on the ground that Pickwick began by being purely ludicrous and developed into a serious and sympathetic individuality, by pointing to the analogous process which commonly takes place in actual human relationships. We begin a new acquaintanceship with perhaps not very charitable prepossessions; these are removed later by a deeper and better knowledge, and where we have before seen an idiosyncrasy we come to love a character. It is ingenious and it helps to explain Mrs. Nickleby, the Pecksniff daughters, and many another. Whether it is true or not (and it does not explain the faultiness of such pictures as Carker and his kind) there can be no doubt that this trick in Dickens of beginning with a salient impression and working outwards to a fuller conception of character is part at least of the reason of his enormous hold upon his readers. No man leads us into the mazes of his invention so easily and with such a persuasive hand.

The great novelists who were writing contemporarily with him—the Brontës, Mrs. Gaskell, George Eliot— it is impossible to deal with here, except to say that the

last is indisputably, because of her inability to fuse
completely art and ethics, inferior to Mrs. Gaskell or to
either of the Brontë sisters. Nor of the later Victorians
who added fresh variety to the national style can the
greatest, Meredith, be more than mentioned for the
exquisiteness of his comic spirit and the brave gallery
of English men and women he has given us in what is,
perhaps, fundamentally the most English thing in
fiction since Fielding wrote. For our purpose Thomas
Hardy, though a less brilliant artist, is more to the
point. His novels brought into England the contemporary pessimism of Schopenhauer and the Russians,
and found a home for it among the English peasantry.
Convinced that in the upper classes character could be
studied and portrayed only subjectively because of the
artificiality of a society which prevented its outlet in
action, he turned to the peasantry because with them
conduct is the direct expression of the inner life.
Character could be shown working, therefore, not
subjectively but in the act, if a peasant subject were
chosen. His philosophy, expressed in this medium, is
sombre. In his novels you can trace a gradual realization of the defects of natural laws and the quandary men
are put to by their operation. Chance, an irritating and
trifling series of coincidences, plays the part of fate.
Nature seems to enter with the hopelessness of man's
mood. Finally the novelist turns against life itself.
'Birth', he says, speaking of Tess, 'seemed to her an
ordeal of degrading personal compulsion whose
gratuitousness nothing in the result seemed to justify
and at best could only palliate.' It is strange to find
pessimism in a romantic setting; strange, too, to find
a paganism which is so little capable of light or joy.

(4)

The characteristic form of English fiction—that in which the requisite illusion of the complexity and variety of life is rendered by discursiveness, by an author's licence to digress, to double back on himself, to start maybe in the middle of a story and work subsequently to the beginning and the end; in short by his power to do whatever is most expressive of his individuality—found a rival in the last twenty years of the nineteenth century in the French Naturalistic or Realist school, in which the illusion of life is got by a studied and sober veracity of statement, and by the minute accumulation of detail. To the French Naturalists a novel approached in importance the work of a man of science, and they believed it ought to be based on documentary evidence, as a scientific work would be. Above all it ought not to allow itself to be coloured by the least gloss of imagination or idealism; it ought never to shrink from a confrontation of the naked fact. On the contrary it was its business to carry it to the dissecting table and there minutely examine everything that lay beneath its surface.

The school first became an English possession in the early translations of the work of Zola; its methods were transplanted into English fiction by George Moore. From his early novels, both in passages of direct statement and in the light of his practice, it is possible to gather together the materials of a manifesto of the English Naturalistic school. The naturalists complained that English fiction lacked construction in the strictest sense; they found in the English novel a remarkable absence of organic wholeness; it did not fulfil their first and broadest canon of subject-matter—by which a novel has to deal in the first place with a single and rhythmical series of events; it was too discursive. They made this charge against English fiction; they also retorted the charge (brought by native writers and their readers against the French) of foulness, sordidness and pessimism in their view of life. 'We do not,' says a novelist in one of George Moore's books, 'we do not always choose what you call unpleasant subjects, but we do try to get to the roots of things; and the basis of life being material and not spiritual, the analyst sooner or later finds himself invariably handling what this sentimental age calls coarse.' 'The novel,' says the same character, 'if it be anything, is contemporary history, an exact and complete reproduction of the social surroundings of the age we live in.' That succinctly was the naturalistic theory of the novel as a work of science—that as the history of a nation lies hidden often in social wrongs and in domestic grief as much as in the movements of parties or dynasties, the novelist must do for the former what the historian does for the latter. It is his business in the scheme of knowledge of his time.

But the naturalists believed quite as profoundly in the novel as a work of art. They claimed for their careful pictures of the grey and sad and sordid an artistic worth, varying in proportion to the intensity of the emotion in which the picture was composed and according to the picture's truth, but in its essence just as real and permanent as the artistic worth of romance. 'Seen from afar,' said George Moore, 'all things in nature are of equal worth; and the meanest things, when viewed with the eyes of God, are raised to heights of tragic awe which conventionality would limit to the deaths of kings and patriots.' On such a lofty theory they built their treatment and their style. It is a mistake to suppose that the realist school deliberately cultivates the sordid or shocking. Examine in this connexion George Moore's *Mummer's Wife*, our greatest English realist novel and for the matter of that one of the supreme things in English fiction, and it will be seen that the scrupulous fidelity of the author's method, though it denies him those concessions to a sentimentalist or romantic view of life which are the common implements of fiction, denies him no less the extremities of horror or loathesomeness. The heroine sinks into the miserable squalor of a dipsomaniac and dies from a drunkard's disease, but her end is shown as the ineluctable consequence of her life, its early greyness and monotony, the sudden shock of a new and strange environment, and the resultant weakness of will which a morbid excitability inevitably brought about. The novel, that is to say, deals with a 'rhythmical series of events and follows them to their conclusion'; it gets at the roots of things; it tells us of something which we know to be true in life whether we care to read it in fiction or not. There is nothing in it of sordidness for sordidness' sake, nor have the realists any philosophy of an unhappy ending. In this case the ending is unhappy because the sequence of events admitted of no other solution; in others the ending is happy or merely neutral as the preceding story decides. If what one may call neutral endings predominate, it is because they also—notoriously—predominate in life. But the question of unhappiness or its opposite has nothing whatever to do with the larger matter of beauty; it is the triumph of the realists that at their best they discovered a new beauty of things, the loveliness that lies in obscure places, the splendour of sordidness, humility, and pain. They have taught us that beauty, like the Spirit, blows where it lists, and we know from them that the antithesis between realism and idealism is only on their lower levels; at their summits they unite and are one. No true realist but is an idealist too.

Most of the best English novels of the next two or three decades were occasioned by their work; Gissing and Arnold Bennett may be mentioned as two authors who were fundamentally realist in their conception of the art of the novel, and the realist ideal operated in a greater or less degree in the work of nearly all their eminent contemporaries. But realism is not and cannot be interesting to the great public; it portrays people as they are, not as they would like to be, and where they are, not where they would like to be. It gives no background for day-dreaming. Now literature (to repeat what has been stated more than once earlier in this book) is a way of escape from life as well as an echo or mirror of it, and the novel, as the form of literature which more than any other men read for pleasure, is the main avenue for this escape. So that alongside this invasion of realism it is not strange that there grew a revival of romance.

The main agent of it, Robert Louis Stevenson, had the romantic strain in him intensified by the conditions under which he worked; a weak and anæmic man, he loved bloodshed as a cripple loves athletics—passionately and with the intimate enthusiasm of make-believe which an imaginative man can bring to bear on the contemplation of what can never be his. His natural attraction for 'redness and juice' in life was seconded by a delightful and fantastic sense of the boundless possibilities of romance in everyday things. To a realist a hansom-cab driver is a man who makes twenty-five shillings a week, lives in a back street in Pimlico, has a wife who drinks and children who grow up with an alcoholic taint; the realist will compare his lot with that of other cab-drivers, and find what part

of his life is the product of the cab-driving environment, and on that basis he will write his book. To
Stevenson and to the romanticists generally, a hansom-
cab driver is a mystery behind whose apparent commonplaceness lie magic possibilities beyond all telling;
not one but may be the agent of the Prince of Bohemia,
ready to drive you off to some mad and magic adventure
in a street which is just as commonplace to the outward
eye as the cab-driver himself, but which implicates by
its very deceitful commonness whole volumes of
romance. The novel-reader to whom Gissing's *Demos*
was a repetition of what he had seen and known and
had planted sickness in his soul, found the *New
Arabian Nights* a refreshing miracle. Stevenson discovered that modern London had its possibilities
of romance. To these two elements of his romantic
equipment must be added a third—travel. Defoe
never left England, and other early romanticists less
gifted with invention than he wrote from the mind's
eye and from books. To Stevenson, to Rudyard
Kipling, whose 'discovery' of India was one of the
salient features of modern English letters, and to
Joseph Conrad belong the credit of teaching novelists
to draw on experience for the scenes they seek to
present. A fourth element in the equipment of modern
romanticism—that which draws its effects from the
'miracles' of modern science—was added by H. G.
Wells, in whose best work the realistic and romantic
schools seemed to unite.

CHAPTER X

THE TWENTIETH CENTURY

WE have carried our study down to the death of
Ruskin and included it in authors like Swinburne and
Meredith who survived till 1909; and in discussing the
novel we have included such men as Rudyard Kipling
and Thomas Hardy. It would be possible and perhaps
safer to stop there and make no attempt to bring
writers later than these into our survey. To do so is to
court an easily and quickly stated objection. One is
anticipating the verdict of posterity. How can we who
are contemporaries tell whether an author's work is
permanent or not?

Of course, in a sense the point of view expressed by
these questions is true enough. It is always idle to
anticipate the verdict of posterity. Remember Matthew
Arnold's prophecy that at the end of the nineteenth
century Wordsworth and Byron would be the two great
names in English Romantic poetry. We are many years
past that date now, and so far as Byron is concerned,
at any rate, there is no sign that Arnold's prediction
will come true. But the obvious fact that we cannot do
our grandchildren's thinking for them, is no reason why
we should refuse to think for ourselves. No notion is so
destructive to the formation of a sound literary taste
as the notion that books become literature only when
their authors are dead. Round us men and women are
putting into plays and poetry and novels the best that
they can or know. They are writing not for a dim and
uncertain future, but for us, and on our recognition
and welcome they depend, sometimes for their livelihood, always for the courage which carries them on to

fresh endeavour. Literature is an ever-living and continuous thing, and we do it less than its due service if
we are so occupied reading Shakespeare and Milton
and Scott that we have no time to read W. B. Yeats,
Shaw, or H. G. Wells. Students of literature must
remember that classics are being manufactured daily
under their eyes, and that on their sympathy and
comprehension depends whether an author receives
the success he merits when he is alive to enjoy it.

The purpose of this chapter, then, is to draw a rough
picture of some of the lines or schools of contemporary
writing—of the writings mainly, though not altogether,
of living authors. It is intended to indicate some
characteristics of the general trend or drift of literary
effort as a whole. The most remarkable feature of the
nineteen-hundreds, as far as writing is concerned, was
without doubt its inattention to poetry. Tennyson was
a popular author; his books sold in thousands; his
lines passed into that common conversational currency
of unconscious quotation which is the surest testimony
to the permeation of a poet's influence. Even Browning, though his popularity came late, found himself
carried into all the nooks and corners of the reading
world. His robust and masculine morality, understood at last, or expounded by a semi-priestly class of
interpreters, made him popular with those readers—
and they are the majority—who love their reading to
convey a moral lesson, just as Tennyson's reflection of
his time's distraction between science and religion
endeared him to those who found in him an answer (or
at least an echo) to their own perplexities. A work
widely different from either of these, Fitzgerald's
Rubáiyát of Omar Khayyám, shared and has probably
exceeded their popularity for similar reasons. Its easy
pessimism and cult of pleasure, its delightful freedom

from any demand for continuous thought from its readers, its appeal to the indolence and moral flaccidity which is implicit in all men, all contributed to its immense vogue; and among people who perhaps did not fully understand it but were merely lulled by its sonorousness, a knowledge of it once passed for the insignia of a love of literature and the possession of literary taste. But after Fitzgerald—who? What poet then commanded the ear of the reading public or even a fraction of it? Not Swinburne certainly, partly because of his undoubted difficulty, partly because of the suspicion held of his moral and religious tenets, largely from material reasons quite unconnected with the quality of his work; not Morris, nor his followers; none of the so-called minor poets whom we shall notice presently—poets who discovered the moods that nourished much of their work from the decadents of France. Probably the only writer of verse who was at the same time a poet and had acquired a large popularity and public influence was Kipling. His work as a novelist we mentioned in the last chapter. It remains to say something of his achievements in verse.

Let us grant at once his faults. He could be violent, and over-rhetorical; he belaboured us with sense impressions, and with the polysyllabic rhetoric he learned from Swinburne—and (though this is not the place for a discussion of political ideas) he could offend by the sentimental brutalism which too often passed for patriotism in his poetry. Not that this last represents the total impression of his attitude as an Englishman. His later work in poetry and prose, devoted to the reconstruction of English history, is remarkable for the justness and saneness of its temper. There are other faults—a lack of sureness in taste is one—that could be mentioned, but they do not affect the main greatness

O

of his work. He is great because he discovered a new subject-matter, and because of the white heat of imagination which in his best things he brought to bear on it and by which he transposed it into poetry. It was Kipling's special distinction that the apparatus of modern civilization—steam engines, and steamships, and telegraph lines, and the art of flight—took on in his hands a poetic quality as authentic and inspiring as any that ever was cast over the implements of other and what the mass of men believe to have been more picturesque days. Romance is in the present, so he maintained, not in the past, and we do it wrong to leave it only the territory we have ourselves discarded in the advance of the race. That and the great discovery of India—an India misunderstood for his own purposes no doubt, but still the first presentment of an essential fact in our modern history as a people—gave him the hold that he had, and rightly, over the minds of his readers.

It is in a territory poles apart from Kipling's that the main stream of romantic poetry flows. Apart from the gravely delicate and scholarly work of Robert Bridges, and the poetry of some others who worked separately away from their fellows, English romantic poetry at the turn of the century concentrated itself into one chief school—the school of the 'Celtic Revival' of which the leader was W. B. Yeats. Two sources went to its making. In its inception, it arose out of a group of young poets who worked in conscious imitation of the methods of the French decadents: chiefly of Baudelaire and Verlaine. As a whole their work was merely imitative and not very profound, but each of them— Ernest Dowson, Lionel Johnson, and others—produced enough to show that they had at their command a vein of poetry that might have deepened and proved more rich had they gone on working it. W. B. Yeats, by his birth and his reading in Irish legend and folklore, became possessed of a subject-matter denied to his fellows, and it is from the combination of the mood of the decadents with the dreaminess and mystery of Celtic tradition and romance—a combination which came to pass in his poetry—that the Celtic school sprang. In a sense it added to the territory explored by Coleridge and Scott and Morris a new province. Only nothing could be further from the objectivity of these men than the way in which the Celtic school approached its material. Its stories were clear to itself, it may be, but not to its readers. Deirdre and Conchubar and Angus and Maeve and Dectora and all the shadowy figures in them scarcely become embodied. Their lives and deaths and loves and hates are only a scheme on which they weave a delicate and dim embroidery of pure poetry—of love and death and old age and the passing of beauty and all the sorrows that have been since the world began and will be till the world ends. If Kipling is of the earth earthy, if the clangour and rush of the world is in everything he wrote, the early Yeats and his school lived consciously sequestered and withdrawn, and the world never broke in on their ghostly troubles or their peace.[1] Poetry never fails to relate itself to its age; if it is not with it, it is against it; it is never merely indifferent. The poetry of these men was the denial, passionately made, of everything the world prized. Where such a denial is sincere, as in the best of them, then the verses they

[1] The later poems of Yeats show more awareness of the contemporary world, and some have a definite political content. A remarkable feature of the older Yeats was the way in which he kept abreast of changing literary and political tendencies. He was still in the vanguard when he died at seventy-four.—A. C. W.

made are true and fine. But when it is assumed, as in some of their imitators, then the work is not true poetry.

But the literary characteristic of the early years of this century—the one which differentiated it from its predecessor—is the revival of the drama. When we left it before the Commonwealth the great English literary school of playwriting—the romantic drama— was already dead. It has had since no second birth. There followed after it the heroic tragedy of Dryden and Shadwell—a turgid, declamatory form of art—and two brilliant comic periods, the earlier and greater that of Congreve and Wycherley, the later more sentimental with less art and vivacity, that of Goldsmith and Sheridan. After Sheridan the drama as a literary force died a second time. It was not born again until more than a hundred years had passed. It is, of course, unnecessary to point out that the writing of plays did not cease in the interval; it never does cease. The production of dramatic journey-work has been continuous since the re-opening of the theatres in 1660, and it is carried on as plentifully as ever. Only side by side with it there grew up in the 1900's and after a new literary drama, and gradually the main stream of artistic endeavour which for nearly a century preoccupied itself with the novel almost to the exclusion of other forms of art, turned back to the stage as its channel to articulation and an audience. An influence from abroad set it in motion. The plays of Ibsen— produced, the best of them, in the eighties of the last century—came to England in the nineties. In a way, perhaps, they were misunderstood by their worshippers hardly less than by their enemies; but, all excrescences of enthusiasm apart, they taught men a new and freer approach to moral questions, and a new and freer dramatic technique. Where plays had been constructed on a journeyman plan evolved by Labiche and Sardou —mid-nineteenth century writers in France—a plan delighting in symmetry, close-jointedness, false correspondences, an impossible use of coincidence, and a quite unreal complexity and elaboration, they become bolder and less artificial, more close to the likelihoods of real life. The gravity of the problems with which they set themselves to deal heightened their influence. In England men began to ask themselves whether the theatre here too could not be made an avenue towards the discussion of living difficulties, and then arose the new school of dramatists—of whom the first and most remarkable is George Bernard Shaw. In his earlier plays he set himself boldly to attack established conventions, and to ask his audiences to think for themselves. *Arms and the Man* dealt a blow at the cheap romanticism with which a peace-loving public invested the profession of arms; *The Devil's Disciple* was a shrewd criticism of the preposterous self-sacrifice of which melodrama, the most popular non-literary form of playwriting, is commonly based; *Mrs. Warren's Profession* made a brave and plain-spoken attempt to drag the public face to face with the nauseous realities of prostitution; *Widowers' Houses* laid bare the sordidness of a Society which bases itself on the exploitation of the poor for the luxuries of the rich. It took Shaw close on ten years to persuade even the moderate number of men and women who make up a theatre audience that his plays were worth listening to. But before success came he had attained a substantial popularity with the public which read. Possibly his early failure on the stage—mainly due to the obstinacy of playgoers immersed in a stock tradition—was partly due also to his failure in constructive power. He is an adept at tying knots and impatient of unravelling them; his third acts are apt either to evaporate in talk or to find some unreal and unsatisfactory solution for the complexity he has created. But constructive weakness apart, his amazing brilliance and fecundity of dialogue ought to have given him an immediate and lasting grip of the stage. There has probably never been a dramatist who could invest conversation with the same vivacity and point, the same combination of surprise and inevitableness that distinguishes his best work.

Alongside Shaw, more immediately successful and not traceable to any obvious influence, English or foreign, came the comedies of Oscar Wilde. For a parallel to their pure delight and high spirits, and to the exquisite wit and artifice with which they were constructed, one would have to go back to the dramatists of the Restoration. To Congreve and his school, indeed, Wilde belongs rather than to any later period. With his own age he had little in common; he was without interest in its social and moral problems; when he approved of socialism it was because in a socialist state the artist might be absolved from the necessity of carrying a living, and be free to follow his art undisturbed. He loved to think of himself as symbolic, but all he symbolized was a fantasy of his own creating; his attitude to his age was decorative and withdrawn rather than representative. He was the licensed jester to society, and in that capacity he gave us his plays. Shaw may be said to have founded a school; at any rate he gave a start to John Galsworthy and some lesser dramatists. Wilde founded nothing, and his works remain as complete and separate as those of the earlier artificial dramatists of two centuries before.

There was another school of drama, homogeneous and quite apart from the rest. We have seen how the

'Celtic Revival', as the Irish literary movement was called by its admirers, gave us a new kind of romantic poetry. As an offshoot from it there came into being an Irish school of drama, drawing its inspiration from two sources—the body of the old Irish legends and the highly individualized and richly-coloured life of the Irish peasants in the mountains of Wicklow and of the West, a life, so the dramatists believed, still unspoiled by the deepening influences of a false system of education and the wear and tear of civilization whose values are commercial and not spiritual or artistic. The school founded its own theatre, trained its own actors, fashioned its own modes of speech (the chief of which was a frank restoration of rhythm in the speaking of verse and of cadence in prose), and having all these things it produced a series of plays all directed to its special ends, and all composed and written with a special fidelity to country life as it has been preserved, or to what it conceived to be the spirit of Irish folk-legend. It reached its zenith quickly, and as far as the production of plays is concerned seemed soon to be in its decline. That is to say, what in the beginning was a fresh and vivid inspiration caught direct from life became a pattern whose colours and shape can be repeated or varied by lesser writers who take their teaching from the original discoverers. But in the course of its brief and striking course it produced one great dramatist—a writer whom his contemporaries instinctively classed with the masters of his art.

J. M. Synge, in the earlier years of his manhood, lived entirely abroad, leading the life of a wandering scholar from city to city and country to country till he was persuaded to give up the Continent and the criticism and imitation of French literature, to return to England, and then to go and live on the Aran

Islands. From that time till his death—some ten years —he spent a large part of each year among the peasantry of the desolate Atlantic coast and wrote the plays by which his name is known. His literary output was not large, but he supplied the Irish dramatic movement with exactly what it needed—a vivid contact with the realities of life. Not that he was a mere student or transcriber of manners. His wandering life among many peoples and his study of classical French and German literature had equipped him, as perhaps no other modern dramatist has been equipped, with an imaginative insight and reach of perception which enabled him to give universality and depth to his portrayal of the peasant types around him. He got down to the great elemental forces which throb and pulse beneath the common crises of everyday life and laid them bare, not as ugly and horrible, but with a sense of their terror, their beauty and their strength. His earliest play, *The Well of the Saints*, treats of a sorrow that is as old as Helen of the vanishing of beauty and the irony of fulfilled desire. The great realities of death pass through *Riders to the Sea*, till the language takes on a kind of simplicity as of written words shrivelling up in a flame. *The Playboy of the Western World* is a study of character, terrible in its clarity, but never losing the savour of imagination and of the astringency and saltness that was characteristic of his temper. He had at his command an instrument of incomparable fineness and range in the language which he fashioned out of the speech of the common people amongst whom he lived. In his dramatic writings this language took on a kind of rhythm which had the effect of producing a certain remoteness of the highest possible artistic value. The people of his imagination appear a little disembodied. They talk with that straightforward and simple kind of innocency which makes strange and impressive the dialogue of Maeterlinck's earlier plays. Through it, as W. B. Yeats said, he saw the subject-matter of his art 'with wise, clearseeing, unreflecting eyes—and he preserved the innocence of good art in an age of reasons and purposes'. He had no theory except of his art; no 'ideas' and no 'problems'; he did not wish to change anything or to reform anything; but he saw all his people pass by as before a window, and he heard their words. This resolute refusal to be interested in or to take account of current modes of thought has been considered by some to detract from his eminence. Certainly if by 'ideas' we mean current views on society or morality, he is deficient in them; only his very deficiency brings him nearer to the great masters of drama—to Ben Jonson, to Cervantes, to Molière—even to Shakespeare himself. Probably in no single case amongst our contemporaries could a high and permanent place in literature be prophesied with more confidence than in his.

In the past it has seemed impossible for fiction and the drama, i.e. serious drama of high literary quality, to flourish side by side. It seems as though the best creative minds in any age could find strength for only one of these two great outlets for the activity of the creative imagination. In the reign of Elizabeth the drama outshone fiction; in the reign of Victoria the novel crowded out the drama. There are signs that a literary era is commencing in which the drama will regain to the full its position as a literature. More and more the bigger creative artists will turn to a form which by its economy of means to ends, and the chance it gives not merely of observing but of creating and displaying character in action, has a more vigorous principle of life in it than its rival.

CHAPTER XI

THE TWENTIETH CENTURY (II)

THE expectation, voiced in the preceding chapter, of a major revival in English drama was frustrated by the war of 1914–18, which stimulated the preference for light entertainment. By the end of the war most of the central London playhouses were controlled by men whose interest in the stage was mainly financial, and theatre rents soared until it was almost impossible for writers of plays with an intellectual bias, and therefore appealing to a numerically limited audience, to get a hearing for their work. In the immediate post-war years, even so well established a writer as Bernard Shaw found the United States and other countries abroad readier to produce his new plays than England was. In such conditions the drama wilted again, though a few serious plays with a contemporary bearing were successful (e.g. Galsworthy's *The Skin Game*). One or two adventurous producers slipped through the financial stranglehold by taking over old theatres in districts away from the fashionable theatreland of Shaftesbury Avenue, Piccadilly Circus, and the Strand; the most notable of such enterprises in the early 1920s being the migration of Nigel Playfair, a successful West-end actor, to Hammersmith, where (at the Lyric Theatre) he produced Shakespeare, seventeenth- and eighteenth-century comedy, ballad opera, and some modern pieces including John Drinkwater's *Abraham Lincoln*, which ran for many performances. By adroit team-work which enlisted the enthusiasms of young artists, designers, musicians, authors, and actors, he attracted a loyal audience from many directions, and for several years his theatre was the liveliest in London. The peak of his success was the sophisticated stylized revival of John Gay's *The Beggar's Opera*, with settings and costumes by Claud Lovat Fraser, played 1,463 times. Though it cannot be said that Playfair did a great deal directly for contemporary drama his Lyric season acted as a reviving cordial to the moribund metropolitan theatre and encouraged local ventures elsewhere. Another outstanding success was Lilian Baylis's tenancy of the Old Vic in Waterloo Bridge Road, where within a few years the complete canon of Shakespeare's plays was performed to the most varied audiences drawn into any one theatre since Shakespeare's own day. In the provinces Miss Horniman's pre-war Manchester Repertory Company ended its valuable work after having staged plays by Stanley Houghton, Allan Monkhouse, Harold Brighouse, and other local writers, as well as many standard works. The disbanding of this Company was compensated by the good work of the Birmingham Repertory Company, under Barry Jackson, who afterwards founded the annual Malvern Festival, devoted mainly at first to Bernard Shaw's plays.

As the nineteen-twenties drew on, the British public ceased to look upon Bernard Shaw as the *enfant terrible* of the English stage and adopted him as its Grand Old Man. His new status was due chiefly to the vigorous popular success of *Saint Joan*, produced after he had been written off as exhausted by the critics who were themselves exhausted by the five nights of his 'metabiological pentateuch' *Back to Methuselah*. At eighty Shaw was as active, mentally and physically, as many half his age, and his technical vagaries in the late nineteen-twenties and in the nineteen-thirties were the tricks of a virtuoso grown impatient of the limitations of his familiar instrument. He continued to give faithful warnings that civilization would founder if men and women stubbornly ignored the universal law of the Life Force (a neologism for the Will of God[1]), but up to 1939 his warnings were more needed than heeded. His influence was limited by the intermittent flippancy which was his antidote to heavy solemnity, and when this habit grew upon him he alternated between the authority of a major prophet and the *gaucherie* of a schoolboy who cuts stupid capers lest he should be caught out in the performance of good works. Yet Shaw did not palter with the eternal verities; nor, as was often alleged, was he only a destructive critic. His triflings never obscured the basic truth to which all his work is adjusted: *God is not mocked*—which remains a basic truth even when rationalized as *Good is not mocked*. He was a destructive critic only if it is destructive to call one's generation in season and out of season to listen to the voice of God and to help God's work. Shaw attacked slum landlordism, the causes of sexual prostitution, war, joyless and inert religion, the rating of art above virtue, tyranny (whether political or parental, professional, pedagogic, or doctrinal). He stood by the principle that the total quality of human society is dependent upon the personal quality of its individual members and that the way of salvation does not lie primarily through the field of political and social reform. Yet the social and other abuses and shortcomings against which he crusaded could not be ignored when he had shewn them up, nor could the national conscience remain asleep.

[1] 'I believe in the Holy Ghost, the Catholic Church, the Communion of Saints, and the Life Everlasting.'—Bernard Shaw in the *New Statesman*, 3 July 1943.

No creative writer survives on ethical values alone, however. Shaw's place in literature will be decided by his quality as a writer of English in the line of Bunyan, Defoe, and Swift; by his incandescent wit; and by his power of making intellectual discussion on the stage so absorbing and exciting as to extend to the plane of ideas the interest and intensity that most previous dramatists had supposed to be reserved to physical action and emotional entanglements.

The stature of Bernard Shaw beside other dramatists of his period corresponds to that of Shakespeare beside his contemporaries. Marlowe would seem a greater figure if he stood alone in his time, and John Galsworthy would be a more impressive playwright if his almost unrelieved seriousness had not to bear comparison with the comic spirit of Shaw. Though Galsworthy had a sense of character and construction which, at its best, is superior to Shaw's, he was too often the victim of his own sympathies to hold a steady course amid the problems and perplexities that distressed him. In *Strife* and *The Skin Game* and a few other plays there is an admirable firmness of outline in character and situation, a commendable longing for justice, an engaging human warmth, an exemplary economy of means; but Galsworthy the tight-lipped Englishman had no such resilience or reserve of energy as was at the command of the Irishman, who could in a crisis guffaw his way back to an exhilarating view of the universe while Galsworthy stayed emotionally under the weather.

Granville Barker—essentially a man of the theatre as actor, producer, and playwright—was a dramatist of much promise until he turned to other interests after writing one of the best plays of his generation, *The Voysey Inheritance.*

J. M. Barrie, following a hard youth in Scotland, became a successful novelist in London and then a still more successful dramatist. His deep-seated pessimism took its revenge in the creation of a world of whimsy in which problems of the actual world were mooted but usually evaded, and in which hardly anyone was quite adult. His cold-shouldering of realities in a period when realities pressed painfully everywhere, stirred resentment against him among critics who judged him to be misleading his large public into a mood of facile and false optimism; but the fault probably lay as much in a mistaken critical approach as in any shortcomings of the work criticized. Barrie was not an intellectualist but an entertainer with feminine sensibilities: his *Quality Street* lies snugly on the skirts of Cranford. Destiny often caught him on the wrong foot and manœuvred him into ambiguous situations. He found life dark and difficult but he encouraged the illusion that it is bright and easy; he declared a preference for the company of the poor and simple, yet circumstance jockeyed him into friendship with the rich and sophisticated. His fondness for young people led to *Peter Pan, or The Boy Who Wouldn't Grow Up*, which for more than half a century delighted tens of thousands of children. Its first impact, as something entirely original, was tremendous, and it may be that its apparent encouragement of perpetual immaturity helped to foster the condition of lifelong adolescence, often thinly veiled by brittle sophistication, which became rife from the nineteen-twenties onward.

The most discussed younger dramatist between the World Wars was Noël Coward, who at times reflected and at other times seemed to initiate the moral mood of the moment. His work had little intellectual content, being concerned mainly with auto-parasitic types who feed upon their own nerves and desires. The wit is thin and febrile; the characters are bloodless and aimless creatures caught in a moral vacuum. It is a drama of disgust, more bitter in the mouth (but also more moral in intention) than the Restoration drama, where the playwrights were disgusting without being disgusted and gave no sign of being weighed down by the enormities of the small world scanned by them. That world was, indeed, a world of pure artifice, insusceptible to moral law. Noël Coward's plays are excellent 'theatre' even if poor literature; and in this connexion it must be acknowledged that inasmuch as it is the function of a playwright to fit his material to the requirements of stage entertainment, it is no fatal sign of inferiority if he comes short of meeting the sterner but duller demands of textual study.

The later plays of Somerset Maugham (e.g. *The Circle* and *Our Betters*), though superficially similar to Noël Coward's, have a dissimilar effect. Their author's attitude is more robust and almost entirely objective. The characters are more fully shaped, the wit is of a riper vintage, and the comedy unburdened by youth's crabbed sense of responsibility for the world's ills.

Since the eighteenth century England has grown used to finding its best dramatists among the Irish. Sean O'Casey's *Juno and the Paycock* and *The Plough and the Stars* showed that the Dublin Abbey Theatre group was still potent, and that the tragic poetry of life salted by rough comedy could be found among city tenements just as it had been found by Synge among the glens of Aran. But when O'Casey migrated to England, coterie influences diluted the natural richness of his talent, though the later plays were much praised by those who welcomed their indications of class-consciousness. In Scotland about the same time a young nationalist movement turned its attention to the possibilities of the stage for the furtherance of the nationalist cause. Though little political profit accrued from these efforts, in at least one instance literature benefited, for James Bridie was attracted to playwriting. His audacious exploratory mind, the astringent impudence of his humour, and his vigorously individual outlook made Bridie's plays the most notable of the nineteen-thirties. Even when innate capriciousness veiled his intentions there were nevertheless exciting hints of genius at play—a character searingly alive here, a mind-disturbing situation there, penetrating phrases, illuminating flashes of original thought, incoherence charged with significance (as in *A Sleeping Clergyman*). No difficulties arise, however, in *Tobias and the Angel*, his most *complete* success, though parts of the later *Mr. Bolfry* promised a developing profundity which his death in 1951 unhappily negated.

Looking back over the preceding quarter-century from the standpoint of 1939, a reader of contemporary fiction could find few major novelists who were not already well established by 1914. The general level of writing and the general standard of intelligence were almost certainly higher than in any previous generation, but this profusion of talent led to little more than a grading-up of mediocrity. A hundred twentieth-century writers worth attention in the next century might be selected, but not more than half a dozen are likely to be read then. The future is free to make its own discoveries among our neglected, but, though it is useless to attempt to forecast the tastes and interests of our descendants, there are certain human invariables which guarantee a maintenance of interest along particular well-marked lines. The great survive by reason of their unification of the commonplace and the exceptional: it is so with Chaucer, with Shakespeare, with Wordsworth, with Keats, with Dickens. This should be remembered in connexion with the writings of the middle decades of this century, when a thinly spreading intellectualism advertised the superiority of the abstruse and the abnormal. If such views were sound the highest place among the novelists of the time would have to be given (and by some critics has been given) to James Joyce. His disciples claim that Joyce's *Finnegans Wake* is a synthesis of all knowledge, a claim that has no relevance for literature and need not be discussed here. Literature, as a common possession, must have meaning for persons of average intelligence, who cannot and do not need to embrace all knowledge. Joyce's *Finnegans Wake*[1] (and parts of *Ulysses*) resemble Blake's prophetic books in refusing to yield their meaning to any but initiates. A proliferation of esoteric writings would set up a hieratic principle as inadmissible in literature as it is in politics—especially so by the English, to whom priestcraft and its corollaries are traditionally obnoxious. If creative writing is to be addressed only to exceptionally capacious minds, much hitherto accepted as good literature would have to be jettisoned. If, however, a more liberal view is justified, and if a wide popularity need not be taken as in itself evidence of the absence of merit, the then-living novelists who were outstanding in 1914 may still be regarded as foremost among their contemporaries.

---

[1] The language difficulties in *Finnegans Wake* while fully acknowledged by so sympathetic a critic as T. S. Eliot were attributed by him to Joyce's semi-blindness, which made him acutely (perhaps uniquely) sensitive to the aural affinities of words; and, it might be added, led him to attempt to impart a new dimension to language.

P

By 1914 (as can be seen in retrospect) H. G. Wells, John Galsworthy, Arnold Bennett, and Joseph Conrad had done their best work. H. G. Wells continued in abundant production for the next thirty years or more, but his interest had long since swung away from literature to statecraft and most of his writings after 1914 were severely didactic. Yet he was a more effective propagandist when, in the earlier novels and short stories, he was content to show the human hive in action, with its beauties and uglinesses, loves and hates, sense and nonsense, generosity and cupidity. *Tono-Bungay* and *The History of Mr. Polly* are better than any sermons he afterwards delivered, for the people in these novels are flesh of our flesh and the books are well shaped in orderly and pleasurable language. As Wells grew more self-consciously aware of a mission his style became diffuse and boneless, while his 'blue-prints' for a new world of universal peace, brotherhood, and justice promised everything except the atmosphere in which men and women could breathe. Though he was one of the most constructive critics of his time the apparent failure of his mission should have a moral for those who find no more than a destructive purpose in Bernard Shaw. Astute reformers draw upon the collective wisdom and experience of others for the practical planning and institution of reform, for whereas a single intelligence may detect and denounce wrong, a single intelligence is rarely qualified to determine what is both right and possible. Wells's ideas may, of course, have fertilized the modern mind in a degree beyond present computation, but it is more likely that the over-earnest second half of his career will bear little fruit.

John Galsworthy's novels, though they are the product of a sensitive social conscience, are concerned less with class conflict than with the friction between age-groups and changing ideals as one generation is displaced by the next. *The Forsyte Saga* (a collection of three novels and two shorter pieces) includes characteristic specimens of the best and worst of Galsworthy's prose and shows both the strength and weakness of his way of feeling and thinking—if these two activities can in his case be separated. Since his heart ruled his brain his sympathies were in a continuous state of emotional flux, as is shown by the central character of the *Saga*, Soames Forsyte, who begins as a near-villain and ends as a near-hero. This change is not brought about by inevitable development in Soames's nature, but by the fact that as the *Saga* progressed Galsworthy came to dislike other characters more than he had at first disliked Soames. Galsworthy was thirty-nine when the first novel of this group (*The Country House*) appeared and fifty-four when the *Saga* ended. Those fifteen years marked his own passage from a chivalrous romantic mood to a state of disillusioned regret for the passing of the old social order and its proprieties. He continued, however, to weave a bright aura about a particular type of young womanhood that engaged his affections, and throughout he clung to the view that where there was social disparity there was necessarily social injustice, though closer acquaintance with the evidence might have modified this opinion and deepened his disillusionment. The inconstancy of fashions in sentiment inspired excessive praise and some later excessive dispraise of *The Forsyte Saga*. It remains not only an exceptionally readable book but also a useful piece of social history throwing light upon domestic life among the upper middle classes during a phase which ended for ever with the Edwardian period.

While Wells and Galsworthy were caught up willingly in the circle of their own literary creation, Arnold Bennett aimed at an attitude of detachment, imperfectly modelled upon the practice of Balzac and Maupassant. Born in the pottery district (the 'Five Towns') of Staffordshire, he never fully succeeded in his efforts to become the complete cosmopolitan, notwithstanding much foreign travel and residence in France. He was surprised and delighted by his own success and by the attainment of prosperity which brought the material good things that were a source of almost unqualified pleasure to him. He took a special delight in the process of living, and in *process* itself discovered a peculiarly intense satisfaction: his last finished novel, *Imperial Palace*, is a sustained rhapsody on the process of running a luxury hotel. But though his pursuit of objectivity in fiction was hampered by a natural inability to conceal an immense appetite for life, which made complete separation from his characters impossible, his admirably controlled craftmanship enabled him to exercise a measure of discipline that might pass for detachment. As the best pure workman in English fiction since Trollope, like Trollope he trained himself in habits of solid industry. Also like Trollope he drew excellent pictures of provincial life, though he never matched Trollope's skill in making the commonplaces of daily life unflaggingly interesting within their own dull ambit. The drab passages in Bennett's books have always an artful thread of colour; the ordinary receives a dash of sensationalism cunningly administered (as in *The Old Wives' Tale*). His Five Towns people, though true to the local environment, have vestiges of universality; the prose of their lives is touched at moments by poetry and glory so that they walk for a while transfigured.

When Bennett turned away from the Five Towns his vitality seemed to be lost, but he made a striking recovery in the novel about Clerkenwell (a much faded part of London), *Riceyman Steps*, which ranks next to *The Old Wives' Tale* and *Clayhanger*.

The realistic movement in fiction which flourished in France in the nineteenth century made little headway in England. The influence of George Moore's *Esther Waters* was transitory and his later books followed a very different mode, for the painstaking and finely-chiselled prose of the *The Brook Kerith*, *Héloïse and Abélard*, and *Aphrodite in Aulis* makes them works of art (or at least of artifice) at a distant remove from nature. Somerset Maugham, who began with an intimate study of the London slums, *Liza of Lambeth*, was by temperament and training (he qualified in medicine) better fitted than either Moore or Bennett to practise in the school of literary realism. He had the doctor's knack of seeing life as 'a patient etherized upon a table' and of discussing it without personal emotion or moralistic bias. For the purposes of fiction, however, the scientific attitude is unproductive and at variance with a novelist's principal interest, human nature. Somerset Maugham found it harder to control his antipathies than to check his sympathies. Sympathy relaxes, antipathy braces: it therefore follows that Somerset Maugham's work is highly invigorating, particularly as an irritant to those who are antipathetic to his own antipathies. This feature of his work is most evident in the short stories and in *The Moon and Sixpence*. There is a fuller and rounder view of the world in the long novel *Of Human Bondage*; while in his masterpiece *Cakes and Ale* the adorable Rosie is enchantingly shaped in an embracing matrix of the author's antipathies.

Joseph Conrad's Polish birth and upbringing did not prevent his becoming a master of English but it did prevent his writing like an Englishman. Conrad's English has always an iridescent and luminous quality which an Englishman requiring the language for everyday use cannot suitably maintain. Consequently Conrad's novels have an exotic pomp and splendour which in those of a native writer would be affectation. His foreignness also accounts for the presence of an imperative Idea throughout his novels. This is at variance with English literary custom, which permits a tentative hinting at ideas in fiction but does not encourage its use as a vehicle for metaphysics. The one major exception to the rule among our own writers is Hardy, who consistently presents man as at war with the modern age, as the mite of Nature, and as the victim of supernatural malice or blind indifference. Conrad's novels and stories are constant to a belief in a semi-mystical bond between man and man, a bond of immutable fidelity (see *Lord Jim* and *The Secret Sharer*). The breaking of that bond is an unforgivable transgression which besets the culprit to the end. It is characteristic of Conrad as of Shakespeare that his heroes are subject to self-destroying faults even though they also possess noble qualities. In Conrad's universe outraged humanity is avenged by unappeasable furies which otherwise good men carry within themselves, working redemption only at the price of full personal retribution. The conviction of Necessity behind this ruling principle invests Conrad's tales with a sense of majesty found nowhere else in English fiction.

Among the younger novelists of whom, just before the First World War, much was expected, only D. H. Lawrence actually did work above the average level. There was an element of the ridiculous in his writings, inasmuch as his detestation of the common English queasiness about sex led him to a counterbalancing but excessively solemn over-emphasis on sexual experience, while his doctrine of 'the wisdom of the blood' appeared to place instinct above intelligence. His exceptional gifts as a writer were opposed and thwarted by circumstance, by the conflict raging within himself, and by the culpable stupidity of followers who elevated him to messiahship. So long as a large proportion of the British use 'sex' and 'sin' as interchangeable terms there could be no general benevolence towards him. The coming of a time when these words were no longer used synonymously might have been supposed to serve his basic purpose of moral freedom, but the supervening looseness of behaviour would undoubtedly have distressed him. The paradox of Lawrence was a truly English one, for though he wished to release his countrymen from their one remaining puritan obsession he was himself an inverted puritan, as averse to license as any fundamentalist. To the discipline of continence he opposed the regimen of intercourse, not as a source of delight but as a proper gymnastic.

Inverted puritanism went a stage further in Aldous Huxley's novels, where a mood of fascinated disgust prevails as the literary pathologist dissects his human specimens. During the years in which Huxley wrote *Point Counter Point* and *Brave New World* (which is as savagely satirical as anything by Swift) a morbid conviction of the approaching catastrophic end of civilization settled upon Europe, and the air of the whole continent was tainted by odours of putridity as organized slaughter became a mainspring of political action. Britain faced crisis upon crisis in the years between the World Wars—a general strike, financial collapse, chronic large-scale unemployment, the abdication of a king, the progressive deterioration of foreign relations. This was not the atmosphere in which a sane and healthy literature could flourish, and more and more writers felt it a duty to plunge into controversy and devote their talents to propagandist ends. Of the very few first-rate writers who remained resolutely outside the political cockpit Virginia Woolf was perhaps the chief. Her novels and essays gave her high distinction in contemporary literature, even though her fastidiously sensitive mind was not wide enough nor robust enough to harbour the varied knowledge of humanity and the familiarity with the rough-and-tumble of life which are part of the mini- mum equipment of a novelist. For the creation of character she relied upon subtle nuances too faint to register more than a delicate impression of the writer's own rare personality. Her people are differentiated by little more than their names; for the most part their voices are one voice. Virginia Woolf's novels are, in truth, poems dressed in prose, as she herself was fated to wear the clothes of an age in which she was in all essentials an exile. But if she made no real contribution to the main tradition of the English novel she never- theless invented a literary instrument more sensitive than any existing before, an instrument responsive to every vibration of the senses, however slight. In reading her, every perception is sharpened; one sees, hears, touches, tastes, and smells through the aroused sensibilities. If Virginia Woolf owed anything at all to contemporary work it was probably to E. M. Forster that she owed most. He had written all but one of his five novels before 1914. *A Passage to India*, which followed in 1924, was much praised as the only novel (and one of the few English books of any kind) that shows adequate comprehension of the modern Indian mind—an opinion impatiently dismissed by those who condemn it as mere tendentious fiction. Forster appeals more to other writers than to the ordinary reader, for the merit of his novels lies rather in their manner than in any story they have to tell. The clash between the inner life of thought and aspiration and the outer life of action and acquisition, and also the social tension set up by snobberies and domestic neuroses, play a leading part in them, but of greater importance are the sanity and balance of the author's mind and the cool assurance of his prose style, decorated only occasionally by fine writing when his enthusiasm is stirred, as it is, for example, by music and nature. Though literature has been enriched by the writings of Virginia Woolf and E. M. Forster, their work in fiction is nevertheless symptomatic of the inadequacy of the novel as a medium for reflective prose of the modern philosophical-critical-poetic kind. The story element in Forster's novels is a burden under which the narrative jerks and staggers, not an easy-running vehicle assisting progression. A task facing contemporary authors is the evolution of a literary form in which the humanist can conduct his exploration of man and society without, on the one hand, subjection to the grosser artificialities of fiction or, on the other hand, to the chilling impersonality of non-imaginative writing. The 'old novel', losing its nineteenth-century virility, has degenerated into a chattering bore. The 'new novel' has a different genealogy and requires another name to release it from bondage to plot and incident and the introduction of character-types outside the usual range of intellectual experience. E. M. Forster's *Howards End* can hardly be overpraised as a magnificent exercise of the mature adult intelligence moving among contemporary themes. In its essentials it is that rare thing, a completely civilized book; but in certain incidentals—in e.g. a clumsy use of coincidence and in the character of Leonard Bast (a piece of mere mental slumming)—it falls much below the requirements of its own high standard.

The numerous historical novels written in the present century belong to a genre that has been largely elbowed out by a new hybrid—the biographical novel and its illegitimate cousin, novelized biography. When this appears with an honest face as fiction introducing actual people and a modicum of fact no reasonable objection can be made: it is as legitimate a form as the historical novel. When on the contrary it is presented as biography, notwithstanding that the author has introduced pseudo-scientific speculation, conjecture and fancy, and in certain instances pure invention, it is pernicious fabrication. Such books are read mainly by the non-critical who have neither a fund of appropriate knowledge nor the sixth sense which instinctively sorts fiction from fact. Though a deplorable misconception of his purpose, novelized biography stemmed from the work of the most stimulating biographical essayist of his time, Lytton Strachey—a genius in miniature. His *Eminent Victorians* was designed as a counterblast to the customary expansive type of biography which builds up a conventionalized public figure instead of a true likeness. Strachey's interest was in flesh-and-blood-and-brain men and women, not in reputations. He held that truth in biography required that light should be available upon all aspects of character, and that distortion by suppression was indefensible. But because much had already been written about his eminent Victorians he did not intend to re-traverse well trodden ground;

only to explore territory neglected by other biographers and to throw an investigating beam from new angles. His exceptionally brilliant qualities as a writer brought him a host of readers, the uninformed among whom mistook these partial portraits for whole-length photographs, while another group accused him of malicious malversation. The fairest assessment of him is Max Beerbohm's *Lytton Strachey* (given as the Rede Lecture at Cambridge in 1943), a generous and just salute from one fine craftsman to another. The mis-representation of Strachey as a muckraker set many otherwise negligible writers working to what was soon discovered to be a money-making formula: take a prominent man or woman, choose a few well-known facts, add every discoverable blemish of character, season with a liberal dash of fiction, and serve as biography. It was a singularly unhappy sequel to a literary episode which should have started a brilliant revival in English biography, and a sad comment on contemporary taste and intelligence as compared with that of the eighteenth century. Excellent work was, of course, done along more orthodox lines by other biographers and historians, notably G. M. Trevelyan and Winston Churchill. The merits of the latter as an historian will not be submerged in his greater fame as a statesman.

Poetry was the only kind of creative writing in which there was a marked quickening of public interest during the First World War. It is less important in the first place to inquire into the quality of the remarkably large output of verse between 1914 and 1918 than to note that, for the first time in several generations, the reading and writing of poetry were again considered normal activities. The immense popularity of Tennyson was that of a national oracle, and at his death public attention strayed to other attractions. When Robert Bridges became Poet Laureate in 1913 the majority of British people heard his name for the first time, though he had been writing poetry for forty years, beginning long before Alfred Austin was preposterously chosen as Tennyson's successor in the laureateship. Bridges's lyrics and at least one of his longer poems (*Eros and Psyche*), to say nothing for the moment of his last important work, give him an assured position with the English poets. Interest in the forms and themes of classical poetry is displayed throughout his writings, and his classical temper was in part responsible for that rigid control of emotion which was labelled emasculation by critics warmly nourished on romanticism. This seems a complete misjudgement when tested by some of his love poems. Sixteen years after his appointment as Laureate he achieved, by one of those quirks of fortune no one can foresee or explain, a resounding popular success with *The Testament of Beauty*, a poem in four parts and over 4,000 lines, published in 1929 after long gestation. He adopted a metre—'loose alexandrines'—which left many readers wondering whether it should be read as free-and-easy blank verse or as prose in harness, perplexities somewhat aggravated by his invention of a highly individual system of spelling. Philosophical in style, the poem goes far beyond the scope of its title and encompasses the ranging meditations of a learned elderly scholar about the world of his time as (in Sir Thomas Browne's phrase) 'a small parenthesis in eternity'. In spite of the variety of obstacles dropped in the reader's path, *The Testament of Beauty* was immediately so popular that it was reprinted thirteen times in the first twelve months. Within a few years denigrating critics fell upon it, but by that time it had ceased to be a topic of general interest and no settled judgement has yet been reached. Re-read many years after it was published, the poem appeared less portentously 'deep' than at first. There is much that gives pleasure and stimulates interest in a variety of things, and there are quietly amusing passages in which the poet's shy and sly humour ruffles the surface. Among the many traces of influence that of *The Prelude* is least concealed, and echoes from Gerard Hopkins (whose collected poems Bridges first made public) are heard from time to time. In the future the philosophy and prosody of the poem are likely to give as little trouble as Browning's 'obscurity' does now and the poem will be read more for pleasure than for mental exercise. *The Testament of Beauty* was the darling child of a wise even if sometimes crotchety old man to whom life at eighty was still so full that his interest and curiosity remained undulled: if there were anxious problems to be pondered there were also satisfactions to be ruminated, and Bridges does not call us to the former without inviting us also to the latter.

When the first of Bridges's poems came out in 1873 Thomas Hardy was just beginning as a novelist. When that phase ended with *Jude the Obscure* in 1896 he openly resumed the interest in poetry which had been constantly implicit in his prose. Apart from a few country ballads and a handful of nature lyrics and lighter pieces, Hardy's hundreds of short poems are uniformly dour and weighted by his lifelong conviction that man is the helpless sport of destiny. This is a point of view that could hardly be expressed in melodious language and it is not surprising that more should be heard of the scrannel pipe than of tuneful instruments in Hardy's verse. His place in English poetry will be decided, however, by *The Dynasts*, his 'epic-drama of the war with Napoleon, in three parts, nineteen acts, and one hundred and thirty scenes'. Blank verse, rhymed verse, prose; dialogue, narrative; tragedy, comedy, philosophy, psychology; monarchs, statesmen, nobles, peasants; generals, field officers, common soldiers; townsfolk, rustics, supernatural presences; England, France, Italy, Spain, Austria, Germany, Russia, the Netherlands; land, sea, the over-world: all are incorporated in the grand structure of *The Dynasts*, one of the most impressively monumental creations conceived and executed by a single mind, though it is still relatively neglected even by a generation of English readers properly impressed by Tolstoy's *War and Peace*.

The contemporary popularity of A. E. Housman's poetry (*A Shropshire Lad* and other collections) is unlikely to be sustained in the future. A few lovely poems will undoubtedly survive but his verse as a whole is monotonously morbid and almost without humour.

As the second decade of the century began there were stirrings among a group of then little-known poets, and by 1914 the names of Rupert Brooke, Walter de la Mare, Ralph Hodgson, W. H. Davies, among others were beginning to be familiar. Rather earlier John Masefield (afterwards Poet Laureate) published the first of a series of lengthy narrative poems on violent themes treated in violent and simple language. Practical experience as a sailor gave a tone of authenticity to his sea poems and he helped to popularize modern poetry. In the early months of the First World War a small group of sonnets (*1914*) by Rupert Brooke was very widely read and quoted, and his early death in the Ægean while on war service made him something

of a national hero. Meanwhile many other soldiers—
some with no previous literary inclinations—were
finding in poetry the natural language of intensified
experience. It seems now that few of these were very
important poets, but they did excellent indirect service
by demonstrating that poetry is not an unmanly
exercise. Though some of the praise of poetry during
the war was no more than the spurious support given
to any passing fashion, poetry was at least lifted from
the negligible position it had occupied in England in
the nineteen-hundreds. The years from 1910 to 1920
can now be seen as the St. Martin's summer of romanticism, and before the decade closed anti-romanticism
was on the offensive. Edith Sitwell and her brothers
Osbert and Sacheverell took an aggressive part in the
new movement, though it is not clear that they were
anti-romantics, except in sharing the current distaste
for imprecision of language and imagery. Intelligent
reading of Edith Sitwell's earlier verse was sometimes
frustrated by idiosyncrasies of rhythm which called
for explication from those 'in the know'. To offset
such discouragements, however, there were attractive
stretches of brilliant colour, and strange objects and
creatures such as might be found in a child's world of
fairy tales and painted toys, or in a picture by Matisse.
As the European scene darkened, Edith Sitwell's verse
became monochromatic and more involved, and her
later work made an impressive addition to English
religious poetry.

About the middle of the nineteen-twenties certain
writers began to take up an attitude of studied contempt
towards the general reading public and to issue books
which (though offered for general sale) were sometimes
in the nature of private discussions among friends and
sometimes a bringing together of dissociated material

linked only by clues locked away in the author's mind. Simultaneously came a stronger revolt against the familiar content and verbal usages of romantic poetry: a revolt leading on the one side to the assumption of a new austerity derived partly from English seventeenth-century poetry and partly from Gerard Hopkins (a late nineteenth-century Jesuit poet whose religious intensity was nobly expressed in difficult metres of his own contriving); and on the other side to a modernistic cult based upon the theory that the machine age requires a poetry more closely associated with the cacophony of mechanistics and the material of industrialism than with melody and rural life. Rival political partisans also began to use verse for propagandist purposes and endeavoured to consolidate their invasion of this field by revaluing the literature of the past according to the degree of class-consciousness that could be discovered or read into it. An odd situation arose from the clash of these several cross-currents, for while the new poetry was growing less and less intelligible to ordinary minds the new poets were declaring their determination to write for 'the masses'. What the issue would have been cannot be known, for the Second World War crashed in.

By that time, however, T. S. Eliot, American by birth but naturalized in England, had established an almost unparalleled authority as poet and critic, though his output before 1939 was small. His place among contemporaries is discussed in the next chapter; but mention must be made here of a group of poets in whom the Hopkins-Eliot strain combined with a strong political impulse: W. H. Auden, Cecil Day Lewis, Stephen Spender, and (with a perhaps more independent bent) Louis MacNeice. Auden, besides much modern-toned verse, wrote verse plays in collaboration with Christopher Isherwood, one of which—*The Dog Beneath the Skin*—initiated a new approach to drama by employing a great deal of colloquial material and a consciously loose, non-literary structure. A new tradition of playwriting grew up, with past and present (and sometimes future) dissolved into a timeless simultaneity. A source-book for many writers struggling with the philosophical aspects of chronology was J. W. Dunne's *An Experiment with Time*.

Young writers in this period were much obfuscated by theory, and while the 'new learning' derived from Freud, Marx, and others has gone far towards re-shaping the world, imaginative literature has suffered greatly from the infusion of half-knowledge, and particularly of indigested Freud leading to an excessive preoccupation with morbid psychology and with the nature and behaviour of psychopathic characters.

CHAPTER XII

THE TWENTIETH CENTURY (III)

THE Second World War produced no such outpouring of intelligible and noble-spirited verse as had encouraged the belief a generation earlier that English poetry was experiencing a major revival during the 1914-18 war. In September 1939 the mood of Britain's reluctant warriors was that of men (and women) called to a task at once perilous and debasing, yet inescapable. There was a deadly job to be done, not an heroic adventure to embark upon, as the young men in August 1914 had believed. English romantics, then, were able to envisage war as a conflict between St. George and the dragon. In 1939, very differently, the war ahead appeared as an affair of political sanitation —the cleansing of the Augean stable of Hitler's monstrous realm.

Consequently nothing could be expected from poetry to match either the exaltation of Rupert Brooke's 'The Soldier' and Julian Grenfell's 'Into Battle', or the subsequent impassioned and defiant protest of Siegfried Sassoon's *Counter Attack*, or the tragic profundity of Wilfred Owen's 'Strange Meeting'. It was possible in 1920 for an anthologist, Jacqueline Trotter, to assemble (in *Valour and Vision*) poems of not inconsiderable worth by almost a hundred writers, some two-thirds of them 'soldier-poets'. No equivalent collection could be made after the later war, and apart from a few isolated lyrics the only notable poems by young men on active service were in Sidney Keyes's *Collected Poems* and Alun Lewis's *Ha! Ha! Among the Trumpets*, neither published until 1945, though Keyes died (aged 20) in North Africa in 1943 and Lewis (aged 28) in Burma in 1944.

In a Foreword to Lewis's volume Robert Graves (an outstanding poet since his own first volume appeared in 1916) wrote: 'The common people do not understand poetry, are shy of poetry. . . . This is why very little work by living poets has a wide circulation except what is comfortably third-hand and third-rate.' Yet he added, 'When [Lewis] died the people felt a sudden loss of power and a sorrow stole over them all, even over those who were incapable of understanding the meaning of his simplest poems.'

Any survey of the state of poetry—indeed, of literature as a whole—in the nineteen-forties and nineteen-fifties needs to include some inquiry into the causes which had opened a gulf between writers presumed to be first-rate and 'the common people'. While there is much among the great poetry of the past which then-contemporary common people—so far as they were 'literate' in the twentieth-century sense—may be supposed not to have understood, there is, nevertheless, no unbridgeable natural gulf between poetry and popularity. Elizabethan groundlings were not 'shy' of Shakespeare, even though he did not condescend to flatter them; and now that critical opinion has re-habilitated Tennyson, as an at least intermittently great poet, it is allowable to believe that common people were not only not shy of his poetry but that they possibly 'understood' more than a little of it; under-standing, perhaps, through immediate emotional sympathy rather than through laborious intellectual application.

Such observations are relevant to the much publi-cized 'crisis of poetry' which engaged the attention of poets, publishers, and others in the years following the end of the Second World War. The 'crisis' arose from the fact that the public were buying books of new poetry in numbers so inconsiderable that publishers lost money and poets made none. Publishers do not exist to lose money, although two or three poetry-loving ones were willing to do so within limits; nor do poets live on air in contented penury. The immediate need appeared to be the finding of means to keep poetry-publishing safe from bankruptcy and poets safe from starvation or from diversion into uncongenial and poetry-quelling employment.

The several expedients adopted—subsidies in various guises to poets, sales-promotion devices, cheaper publications, and so on—made only a faint impression. The very few living poets who achieved substantial sales in the period did so independently of these special efforts: e.g. Dylan Thomas, who, through a beguiling incantatory style in readings of his own poetry, and through his broadcast fantasia on a day's doings in a Welsh village, *Under Milk Wood*, fascinated radio and television audiences; John Betjeman, whose straightforward and mostly lighthearted verses were also helped into exceptional popularity by the wide favour he won as an engaging broadcaster on architectural topics; T. S. Eliot, already established as a force in contemporary poetry.

In the opinion of at least one academic critic, the publication of Eliot's *The Waste Land* in 1922 was as important in its influence on English poetry as the appearance of *Lyrical Ballads* in 1798. Whether the Romantic Revival would or would not have come about without the Wordsworth and Coleridge volume cannot be settled with dogmatic certainty. Equally, it may remain an unsettled question whether the twentieth-century anti-romantic or neo-classical movement would or would not have developed without T. S. Eliot.

Even if it be conceded that Eliot as poet, critic, and playwright deployed genius of rare quality, it can also be simultaneously held that his literary influence was disastrous, as disastrous as Shakespeare's. It took English poetic dramatists some three hundred years to work Shakespeare out of their system; it is impossible to foretell how long will be needed for the purgation of Eliot from poetry, criticism, and poetic drama. If those were right who suspected *The Waste Land* of being 'the greatest hoax of the century', Eliot's shadow will endure little longer than the span of his own life; but if, on the other hand, succeeding generations accept him as an intellectual giant, the outlook is bleak. Very rarely can a solitary superabundant genius be afforded in the lifetime of any nation. The great man, willy-nilly, entices a host into discipleship, and as imitators their situation resembles that spoken of by Rosencrantz to Hamlet: 'their endeavour keeps in the wonted pace; but there is, sir, an aery of children, little eyases, that cry out on the top of question, and are most tyrannically clapped for it'.

The irony of the Eliot revolution is that he released English poetic drama from the stranglehold of Shakespearean blank verse only to clamp upon it the stranglehold of Eliotonian free verse. Comment on Eliot's own plays must, however, be reserved until the general consequences of his non-dramatic verse have been considered.

In *Lyrical Ballads* Wordsworth and Coleridge's aim was to bring about a return to simplicity and to stimulate the sense of wonder. In Eliot's creative writings the trend is towards complexity and the imposition of intellectual austerity—the displacement of imagination by cerebration, of emotion by metaphysics.

In his major non-dramatic production after *The Waste
Land*—*Four Quartets* (1936, 1940, 1941, 1942)—
there is much traditional poetic material: cornstalk and
leaf, wild thyme and wild strawberry, children in the
apple tree, the dove descending and the kingfisher's
wing, as well as the *Stock Exchange Gazette*, the *Direct-
ory of Directors* and the 'underground train in the tube'
that 'stops too long between stations'; but there is as
little quickening of the pulse in contemplation of the
delights of nature as in the tedium of the stationary
tube train in which

> the conversation rises and slowly fades into silence
> And you see behind every face the mental emptiness
>   deepen
> Leaving only the growing terror of nothing to think about.

In extension of the metaphor of the Underground, it
might be said that Eliot's poetry runs round and round
a closed Inner Circle, taking on mentally conditioned
passengers at the several stations. In a burst of self-
revelation, he says in 'East Coker' (the second of the
Four Quartets):

> So here I am, in the middle way, having had twenty
>   years—
> Twenty years largely wasted, the years of *l'entre deux
>   guerres*—
> Trying to learn to use words, and every attempt
> Is a wholly new start, and a different kind of failure
> Because one has only learnt to get the better of words
> For the thing one no longer has to say, or the way in
>   which
> One is no longer disposed to say it. And so each venture
> Is a new beginning, a raid on the inarticulate
> With shabby equipment always deteriorating
> In the general mess of imprecision of feeling,
> Undisciplined squads of emotion.

If this is more than an access of dubious modesty, Eliot at the age of more than fifty was confessing that he was still *trying* to use words and at every attempt experiencing failure. The history of English poetry makes it plain that the great poets have mastered words (or have been mastered by them) in early life and that some measure of verbal spontaneity and certainty is prerequisite for the achievement of poetry of the greatest sort.

Yet if Eliot were only a poet *manqué* with crippling limitations, could it have come about that, without any proselytizing effort by himself, his writings would seep into the consciousness of a whole generation in all parts of the world? In book after book—by engineers and men of affairs as well as by scholars and littérateurs—quotations from Eliot habitually crop up: 'In my end is my beginning' (a reversal, perhaps unconscious, of Mary Queen of Scots' motto); 'a patient etherized upon a table'; 'the damp souls of housemaids'; 'I have seen the eternal Footman hold my coat and snicker'; 'I grow old . . . I shall wear the bottoms of my trousers rolled'; 'This is the way the world ends Not with a bang but a whimper'. To quote Eliot became, as it were, a ritual genuflexion to a world oracle. Something must of course be allowed to fashion, to which literature and thought are no more immune than women's clothes and faces are; more must be allowed to the spread of neo-scholasticism which, having abandoned the old folly that only past literature should be studied, plunged into the new folly that painstaking analysis (rather than plain enjoyment) of contemporary writings is also imperative. And since cerebration is more manageable in school and college than is the stimulation and directed use of imagination, hard nuts for the mind to crack tend to receive preference and to take on excessive importance.

But fashion and academicism apart, the disillusion in Eliot's earlier poems found such ready acceptance in 1917 and thereafter that he became the prophet of a new age. What remains to be determined by future inquiries is whether Eliot's waste land and hollow men were discoveries or inventions; whether they represented existing states of being in urgent need of spiritual reform, or metaphysical creations embraced as realities by a generation prone to imitative self-abasement and self-pity. Did Eliot prophesy a doomful condition created by his own prophecies? When it became evident as his work progressed that he was a Christian, not a despairing pagan, his religion appeared bleak enough to be condoned, or disregarded, even by unbelievers who had grown accustomed to call him Master.

Nor was this all. Among younger poets the attraction was a technical one, or, rather, an anti-technical one. Although he did not altogether forsake metre and rhyme, Eliot's characteristic medium was free verse, and free verse appears, superficially, to be absolutely *free*: free, that is, from the exacting discipline of metrical verse. That free verse does, in fact, demand a more exacting rhythmic discipline went largely unobserved or was slap-happily ignored. Indeed, Eliot was himself to adopt, later, a theory of non-poetic diction which veered of set purpose near to conversational prose.

The result, in summary effect, was a generation of poets who turned their backs upon, or felt no need to master, the *art* of poetry; who were able to mask feebleness of imagination and poverty of thought; and who were seduced by pseudo-scholarly writings into decorating the mask with a deliberated clustering of symbols and images. The function of symbolism in the past, before it became taken up by 'symbolists', was to serve as an illuminant, not as applied ornament; while images were an internal self-product of the poetic imagination, not a vagrant flock mentally pursued.

The new metaphysicals, as they might be called, can be found in any representative anthology of the period.[1] They need not be particularized here, since their unindividualized voices are for the most part indistinguishable and, with a very few exceptions, their names are less and less numerously remembered year by year. One of the few outstanding, Vernon Watkins, diagnosed by implication a serious weakness of contemporary verse:

> Who pulls tradition down and sets up fashion?
> Pretence is one thing, and another passion.
> In every smith whose work I come across
> Tradition is the ore, fashion the dross.

The 'crisis of poetry' arose from the poets' failure to establish communication with 'the common people', not from inborn antagonism in the people towards poetry. In truth, the people take to poetry almost from birth, through nursery rhymes and songs, secular and religious—all traditional and all simple.

Of the other poets who made their mark before 1940, Robert Graves increased his reputation and Cecil Day Lewis maintained his; both welded tradition and experiment into an harmonious whole. Edmund Blunden increased his intellectual stature while losing something of the lyrical limpidity which distinguished his earlier verse. Perhaps the only certain candidate

[1] e.g., *The Faber Book of Twentieth Century Verse, 1900-1950* (Faber, London, 1953).

for immortality that can be mentioned here is Walter de la Mare, a poet apart, who achieved, times without number, beauty and wisdom within simplicity.

In any search for works with an immediate subjective-contemporary reference, W. H. Auden's 'baroque eclogue' *The Age of Anxiety* will loom large, its purpose being to give a view of the unregenerate state of contemporary man refracted and fragmented through the thoughts and conversation of three men and a woman drinking in a bar and afterwards in the woman's apartment. Meanwhile, having reached a state of semi-intoxication in which they reveal 'capacities which are quite beyond them when they are sober', they experience in dream a pilgrimage of seven stages. When they resume consciousness after the dream they think 'of Man, of the torpor of his spirit, the indigent dryness of his soul, his bottomless credulity, his perverse preference for the meretricious or the insipid', and it seems impossible to them that there could be any survival for either Nature or Man 'had not some semi-divine stranger with superhuman powers . . . appeared from time to time to rescue both, for a brief bright instant, from their egregious destructive blunders'. Associating prose passages and verse in several styles—much of it alliterative in the manner of Anglo-Saxon poetry—*The Age of Anxiety* is a modernistic morality in often elusive language on the ageless theme of the world's need of a saviour. Meaning is seldom explicit in the lines, largely because of the wide range of their allusiveness, which stretches from myth and ancient history to sad and silly little tunes and 'hot numbers' from a juke box.

Auden's essentially introverted 'eclogue' is, in essence, a pilgrims' progress towards no heavenly city, and in that respect it is symptomatic of a common mood in the years around 1948 when it was published.

Born in 1907 and being therefore under twelve at the end of World War I, Auden was too young to be among those who proclaimed themselves after 1918 as part of 'the lost generation'. They were survivors from the vast company engulfed by the war, and it was their hope and intention to justify the claim that what the world had come through was indeed, as the politicians promised, 'a war to end war' and that the outcome in Britain would be the also-promised 'land fit for heroes'. But war, it soon appeared, was by no means ended; while millions of the 'heroes' found themselves workless and their families in want. Though faith in the League of Nations endured for some years, that faith, also, was falsified by the nineteen-thirties. The poets and other creative writers who felt themselves bound to engage in efforts to ensure peace and root out poverty, aligned themselves for the most part with the so-called Left Wing movements which encouraged belief in the possibility and utility of a 'proletarian literature'. Of all that chivalry of intention, however, little remains in evidence as writing effective for its purpose. The intellectuals were out of touch with their hoped-for audience, and the only piece of creative writing of that period with a genuine accent is *Love on the Dole*, a novel by Walter Greenwood, himself one of the working class: an insider, not a stranger peering in.

The lost generation had blamed 'the Old Men' for their plight, but by 1939 they had themselves become the next generation of Old Men and, in their turn, unable to avert war. The situation in Britain after 1945, however, was vastly different from what it had been after 1919. The measures for social levelling in the newly-established Welfare State, while by no means a panacea for all, averted mass unemployment and dire poverty, and a deal of credit for these more comfortable conditions belongs to John Maynard Keynes (later Lord Keynes) whose *General Theory of Employment, Interest and Money* was largely responsible for a fundamental change of thought and practice in economics.

As well as being an expert economist advocating revolutionary principles, Keynes was a man of exceptional culture and literary talent. It would be no great exaggeration to claim *The Economic Consequences of the Peace* (published in 1919 while the Versailles Conference was still in being) as, in the widest sense, the most influential book of the half-century. Keynes may have seasoned justice with far more than average common sense and generosity of spirit, but his literary skill was such that he was able to present a difficult economic—and humanitarian—argument in a form so readable as to be fascinatingly persuasive to lay minds. The danger inherent in Keynes's style was, indeed, its overpowering persuasiveness, so potent that it was not imperative to understand his argument before passionately approving it. Whether he was right or mistaken in his judgement on the Versailles proceedings is not a matter to be considered here, but only that *The Economic Consequences of the Peace*, directly or by repute, created a public mood which still endures.

Keynes was a man of consciously superior mind: he knew he was right, always! His pen portraits of Clemenceau and Woodrow Wilson[1] in *Economic Consequences* are masterpieces of illusion-free analysis.

---

[1] He withheld his characterization of Lloyd George as 'this syren, this goat-footed bard, this half-human visitor to our age from the hag-ridden magic and enchanted woods of Celtic antiquity' until 1933, when it appeared as one of Keynes's *Essays in Biography*.

No political reputation could withstand his irony. He was also an intimate among those writers—Virginia Woolf, Lytton Strachey, and others—who, between the wars, became known as the Bloomsbury Group and were frequently chided as intellectually arrogant. This was not a baseless charge, and Keynes's magnificent intellectual arrogance is demonstrated—and has been justified by subsequent history—in the preliminary pages of *Economic Consequences*: 'To the foundation of the general opinion of the future I dedicate this book.' He exhibited the statesmen of the world as—through ignorance or intrigue or subtlety or hatred—incompetent either to make or to preserve peace; and by stripping those great men morally and mentally naked he also stripped all who were or are in authority. Of Woodrow Wilson, at that time the hope of the world, he wrote: '. . . the President had thought out nothing; when it came to practice his ideas were nebulous and incomplete. He had no plan, no scheme, no constructive ideas whatever for clothing with the flesh of life the commandments which he had thundered from the White House. He could have preached a sermon on any one of them or have addressed a stately prayer to the Almighty for their fulfilment; but he could not frame their concrete application to the state of Europe.' More than Wilson's reputation is slain by that passage; it slays also all idealists whose golden words are unaccompanied by the capacity to translate goodwill into the hard currency of effective action.

Keynes's book helped to destroy faith and confidence all down the secular hierarchy. It gnawed at the foundations and weakened the superstructure. If statesmen had no valid claim to direct the nations, what competence had parents to direct a family? If a strictly Olympian view were possible, it might be seen that Keynes was, after all, merely an instrument of 'the spirit of the age', and that the decay of authority would have set in anyway.

But it was not only in connexion with economics and statecraft that Keynes's views are of account. As an undergraduate at Cambridge he was one of a brilliant group that came under the lifelong influence of *Principia Ethica* by G. E. Moore, then Professor of Philosophy in the University, though they dissented from Moore's principles in important particulars. In a paper read to friends many years later and published in 1949 in *Two Memoirs*, Keynes said:

We claimed the right to judge every individual case on its merits, and the wisdom, experience and self-control to do so successfully. This was a very important part of our faith, violently and aggressively held, and for the outer world it was our most obvious and dangerous characteristic. We repudiated entirely customary morals, conventions and traditional wisdom . . . we recognized no moral obligation on us, no inner sanction, to conform or to obey. Before heaven we claimed to be our own judge.

No scandal and no overt harm are known to have beset the group, for they possessed the wisdom and self-control, if not the experience, to hold potentially harmful opinions harmlessly to themselves; but while it may be safe for the wise and self-controlled to cut their own road to moral freedom, that road may be for others the highway into a moral swamp. Though this repudiation of customary morals did not get the publicity or condemnation provoked a generation earlier by Walter Pater's 'Conclusion' in *The Renaissance*, its long-term effect was more subtle and far-reaching, even though the means of its propagation were not in plain view.

What became clearly evident after 1945, in the early

years of the Welfare State, when respect for tradition and authority fell to a critically low ebb, was that the consequent assertion of personal freedom, even though then combined with a freer flow of money, produced, surprisingly, a sullenly discontented generation.

In literature this state of contemporary society gave birth to a perplexing human specimen, 'the angry young man'—whose prototype, however, bore little resemblance to the inheritors of the title. *Angry Young Man* by Leslie Paul, published in 1951, is for the most part a moderate-minded personal record by an East-end Londoner who progressed by way of Fleet Street and leadership in Youth movements to a prominent part in the General Strike of 1926 and to subsequent realization of the limitations of political extremism as a remedy for society's ills. Only during army service in World War II between 1939 and 1945 did he recognize that although through many pre-war years he had used with facility 'words like "the masses", "the proletariat", "the working classes" ' he had known almost nothing of them by direct personal contact. Now, however, 'my barrack-room mates were the masses: patient, hard-working, grumbling about authority yet obeying it, avoiding (in civvy street) public meetings like the plague, and holding only the most elementary views, their lives at home were bounded by desire for wives and sweethearts . . . and the tedium of their simple yet exacting jobs in farm and factory'.

Not until the production of *Look Back in Anger* by John Osborne, five years later, in 1956, did 'angry young men' become a catch phrase in the mass-circulation daily and weekly papers. The epithet was rarely appropriate, since what passed for anger was often nothing but spleen, which, paradoxically, tended to increase as success befell them. Whatever violent disturbance of feeling they experienced beforehand they shared with the majority of their generation, for the catastrophic beginning of the nuclear age at Hiroshima in August 1945 engendered almost universal dismay and rage. Though it is difficult to develop a philosophical attitude towards atom and hydrogen bombs, it is nevertheless certain that mankind has to learn to live with them equably, notwithstanding their ever-present contingent threat, even as those living in close proximity to Vesuvius must live equably with the volcano. Though there may be little direct reference to these weapons in contemporary imaginative writing, a mood of suppressed hysteria in much of the creative literature of the period can be regarded as the symptom of a 'chain reaction' originating from nerves abraded by fear.

The effects of fear upon young writers in the fifties were, however, incomparably less baleful than the harm done to them by hasty uncritical praise and premature and inflated publicity. To be butchered to make a Roman holiday was, spiritually, a less destructive fate than to be exploited to bolster a Fleet Street circulation. The young writer is now beset by traps attractively camouflaged: the personal publicity trap, the film trap, the radio and television traps, the cocktail-party trap. He lacks the experience to distinguish between notoriety and fame; and even if he is aware of the temptations all around, money is money and fame may be only a will-o'-the-wisp. But beyond any immediate harm done to the young writer by his precarious spell of adulation and easy money is the more important potential loss of mature works of literature, from the patient making of which he may be deflected by 'the bitch-goddess, Success'.

Though *Look Back in Anger* may in the long run be

no more than one of the ephemera of its generation, it furthered a tendency long in process and examined in *The Hero in Eclipse in Victorian Fiction* by Mario Praz (English edition 1956, translated by Angus Davidson) and *The Vanishing Hero: Studies in Novelists of the [Nineteen] Twenties* by Sean O'Faolain (1956). As part of the destructive mood greatly accelerated by the disillusions of the war periods and their post-war sequels, there had come a complete collapse of belief in the possibility of traditional heroic virtues—selfless courage, chivalry, generosity of spirit, gentility, courtesy and good manners. The hero did not so much vanish as become transmogrified into the no-hero, or the lout-as-hero, such as Jimmy Porter in John Osborne's play, where the graceless boor achieves his apotheosis.

Look Back in Anger was put on by the English Stage Company (formed to produce new plays by young writers) at the Royal Court Theatre, Sloane Square, which seemed likely to become again the nursery of genius it had been half a century earlier when the Vedrenne-Barker management fostered Bernard Shaw's fame there. In 1956, however, the audience to be won was totally different from that of 1906. Then it was an audience of eager, aspiring, hope-possessed minds; now it was an audience largely composed of the Chelsea Set, the down-at-heel successors of the super-elegant Bloomsbury Group.

The Chelsea Set became the imitative nucleus in England of the American 'Beat Generation', a dispersed assortment of young men and women who turned their backs on civilization and chose to live either wandering unrooted lives, or in urban nests of cultivated squalor where jazz music was the supreme delight. They were beat[en] by the effort required to maintain themselves

R

in the ranks of conventional society; and they found an anodyne for their oddly combined sense of personal inadequacy and group superiority in the frenzied beat of primitive rhythms.

Their British counterparts, in a more restricted geographical setting, found a centre of gravity in the coffee-bars which spread in profusion during the later nineteen-forties and throughout the next decade. The Chelsea Set was largely composed of young unsuccessful artists and make-believe artists and their hangers-on and copy-cats, who foregathered in garret-studios such as that here described:

There are no curtains, and no sheets on the bed; they are torn up and used as paint rags. The walls are bare, except for a Jugoslav string bag hanging from a nail. . . . There is no carpet and no lino. There is a bare wooden table covered with odds and ends—hairpins, razor-blades, broken cups without saucers, aspirins, a Russian primer, a paintbrush stuck in a milk bottle, some sagging chrysanthemums in a jam-jar.[1]

That apartment was occupied by a girl of seventeen, disowned by her middle-class parents, and living by odd jobs: she was one among many others of her kind who 'seem to achieve a sort of personal exaltation, not by producing works of art so much as by developing an artistic temperament'. The girl who lived in the room, 'as far as one could see, did not paint. Yet there were half a dozen tubes of oil paint on her table.'

Though possibly not more important individually

[1] This description is from an article on 'The Chelsea Set' by Atticus in *The Sunday Times*, 22 November 1959. But it should be pointed out that the 'set' was neither indigenous to Chelsea nor confined to it. The 'beat generation' cult was widespread—from California to Chelsea, from Oxford to Hoxton, from Mayfair to the Côte d'Azur.

than the inhabitants of Paris's Montmartre had been for generations past, they were nevertheless in the vanguard of an imitative army of the immature who popularized a cult of decrepitude. Whereas in the earlier years of the century an unkempt and neglected appearance was a genuine mark of poverty, now it became the badge of a false bohemianism. The young of both sexes, epicenely garbed, walked abroad uglified, tousled and sluttish, emancipated from cleanliness no less than from godliness, and ambitious to qualify as the devil's walking parody on all two-legged things— the line from G. K. Chesterton's 'The Donkey' lends itself here for appropriate adaptation.

This was the audience that responded to plays, novels, and poems which, far from crediting the principle that the function of art is to impose order upon chaos, stressed the chaotic and disorderly. In such writings they saw or imagined themselves reflected and felt themselves to be sharing an admirable anger as rebels, whereas few displayed more than the indulgent self-pity of wallowing misfits.

By an extraordinarily rapid reversal, the one-time European cultural domination of America turned in the nineteen-forties and nineteen-fifties into the subjugation of English literature by American. English novelists had already acknowledged the mastership of Henry James and English poets that of T. S. Eliot. Now, the plays of Arthur Miller and Tennessee Williams worked their ichor into the body of the 'newer' English drama, with consequences that encouraged the tendency to look downward into the cellars of life. The Pilgrim Fathers had returned—with a difference.

Ibsen's experience with his earliest critics warns us against the reactions of mere prejudice; but even though modern dramatists, following in the wake of Ibsen, make worthy efforts to bring social maladies into the light, they lack Ibsen's penetration and poetic insight. With him, but hardly ever with them, the sordid and the abnormal become transfigured. The spectacle of human degeneration *can* be made tragic; but in, for example, John Osborne's *The Entertainer* the degradation of the chief character fell far short of tragedy by being only repulsive, notwithstanding the masterly acting of Sir Laurence Olivier in the part.

An early practitioner of voluntarily contrived down-and-outery, George Orwell, turned his back upon an Eton upbringing and for a while shared the life of unfortunates in circumstances described in his *Down and Out in Paris and London*. Orwell's rise to general literary repute was long delayed and no doubt unexpectedly achieved with *Animal Farm*, a short political allegory which lost a great deal of its point after the death of Stalin, though its satire will not be entirely outmoded while totalitarian dictatorships remain. As a literary performance *Animal Farm* lacks subtlety though not pathos. Orwell's also immediately acclaimed novel, *1984*, supplements with additional touches of horror Aldous Huxley's *Brave New World* as a picture of a wholly mind-conditioned population.

The central problem of all works of literature which peer into the cellars is the problem of justification. Is the distastefulness of what is brought up justified by its serving as an aid to the betterment of life (for this, presumably, is the desire of the 'committed' or 'engaged' writer), or by its transmutation into a kind of beauty by the alchemy of art (which is a sufficient justification in terms of aesthetics)? This test if applied to one of the popular downward-looking plays of the nineteen-fifties, Shelagh Delaney's *A Taste of Honey*, produces only a negative answer on both counts. Though this play is a sincere attempt to depict life as lived by certain people in and about 'a comfortless flat' in a depressed part of Manchester, it remains an improbable, innocent-minded statement pressed into the contemporary formula which imposed concentration upon the affairs of those below the moral plimsoll-line. The success of the piece in the theatre (in so far as it was free from exceptional dependence upon the producer's artful aids, which included much co-operation by a jazz band) was no doubt due to the vicarious satisfaction produced in some by the illusion of contemplating 'a slice of life', and to the gratification which the more fortunate are prone to find in slumming-by-proxy—'seeing how the poor live' without direct approach to the poor.

This inclination on the part of theatre audiences to treat 'low-life' plays as a raree-show is the most crippling handicap facing an earnest dramatist of the people and the highest obstacle in the path of the theatre as an institution of reform. The most genuinely equipped people's-playwright of the nineteen-fifties, Arnold Wesker, says in his preliminary note to *Roots*: 'My people are not caricatures. . . . And though the picture I have drawn of them is a harsh one, yet still my tone is not of disgust. . . . I am at one with these people —it is only that I am annoyed with them and myself.' The source of the author's annoyance lies in the refusal of all but one of the characters (in *Roots* they are Norfolk farm-labourers) to endeavour actively 'to better themselves'. Beatie Bryant, who has become mentally energized through her lover in London, cries to her family at the end of the play, after he has discarded her:

Do you think we really count? . . . Do you think when the really talented people in the country get to work they get to work for us? . . . The writers don't write thinkin' we can understand, nor the painters don't paint expecting us to be interested—that they don't, nor don't the composers give out music thinking we can appreciate it. . . . they say 'the masses is too stupid for us to come down to them. . . . if they don't make no effort why should we bother?' So you know who come along? The slop singers and the pop writers and the film makers and women's magazines and the Sunday papers and the picture strip love stories—that's who come along, and you don't have to make no effort for them, it come easy. 'We know where the money lie,' they say, 'hell we do! The workers 've got it so let's give them what they want. If they want slop songs and film idols we'll give 'em that then. If they want words of one syllable, we'll give 'em that then. . . . Anything's good enough for them 'cos they don't ask for no more!' The whole stinkin' commercial world insults us and we don't care a damn. . . .

However pessimistic this declaration may seem, it represents in the play the beginning of hope: Beatie's soul has come alive. Arnold Wesker's greater effectiveness as a playwright of the people in comparison with others of similar intention is that he is upward-looking from the level of his own people, not downward-looking from another plane. *Roots* diagnoses truly the inertia of the majority who accept in art and life a commercialized set of values which in its turn debases literature and much else. The wave of financial prosperity after 1945 produced, among other and less fortunate effects, a vast increase in the spending capacity of adolescents, with the consequence that much of life became geared to adolescent demands, and immaturity approached self-deification through cynical commercialized flattery of the young.

In reaction against this tendency, 'serious' literature became more and more inclined to retreat into a private enclave, whence the occupants gazed uncomprehendingly and somewhat contemptuously upon those of normal intelligence outside; writing for themselves alone and despising simpler tastes. As the corollary of this, particular importance was frequently assumed to inhere in the abstruse, in ambiguity[1] and in ambivalence. A typical work of the kind is Samuel Beckett's *Waiting for Godot*, a play (or series of stage dialogues) which, though incomprehensible to the average mind, was found easy of esoteric interpretation. From its compound of patter in cross-talk comedians' mode, its clowning, its frightening cold brutality, its philosophizing, and its scriptural and other religious allusions, a sympathetic critic[2] deduced that *Waiting for Godot* is essentially 'a prolonged and sustained metaphor about the nature of human life' and that 'Godot himself stands for an anthropomorphic image of God', though he also speaks more than once of its ambiguity and, indeed, says of its longest speech that Beckett 'has never been more brilliantly unreadable'!

This play represents the culmination and possibly the collapse of the upsurge of religious drama which marked the nineteen-thirties to nineteen-fifties, beginning with T. S. Eliot's *Murder in the Cathedral*. To posterity, Eliot's plays may seem as lacking in dramatic energy as those of the nineteenth-century poets who experimented with stage plays, even though Eliot enjoyed so much immediate success and acclaim.

[1] William Empson's *Seven Types of Ambiguity* had an academic vogue.

[2] G. S. Fraser. His essay is included in *English Critical Essays, Twentieth Century*, 2nd series (World's Classics).

In view of this ready acceptance in both Britain and America, the opinion of a dissenting witness from outside is of perhaps sobering interest. Writing of a performance of Eliot's *The Family Reunion*, Erich Kästner, the German novelist, poet, and author of the children's classic, *Emil and the Detectives*, said:

As soon as the triviality looked like becoming so thick that you could cut it with a knife (which was continually happening) one of the characters would tell the other in an elegiac voice: 'You cannot understand me.' Or 'I cannot explain it to you.' Or 'Even if I did try to explain you wouldn't understand.' . . . And that always saved the situation for the time being. Because the audience then thought: This must be a most profound and significant play. Not even the actors know what it's about.[1]

Some essential triviality is also apparent in *The Cocktail Party*, where it seems that after a profound spiritual experience Edward and Lavinia Chamberlayne turn only, once again, to a life of cocktail parties—though, indeed, this may require symbolic interpretation.[2] What has been found more disturbing—for its taint of sadism—is the account in this play of the martyrdom of Celia Coplestone, who wanted 'to get into films' but, instead, joined a nursing order and went as a missionary nurse to Kinjanja, where she was captured during a native rebellion. The remains of her body were found and, says one of the characters,

> . . . from what we know of local practices
> It would seem that she must have been crucified
> Very near an ant-hill.

[1] Quoted in *The Times Literary Supplement*, 19 June 1959.

[2] Eliot has explained that *The Cocktail Party* projects into modern life the theme of Euripides' *Alcestis*. But the link is not evident, and is perhaps irrelevant.

But the wider contemporary significance of Eliot's plays lies in his theory of dramatic poetry, according to which, he says, 'we have to accustom our audiences to verse to the point at which they will cease to be conscious of it'. Of certain prose passages in his *Murder in the Cathedral* he remarks that if he had written them in the kind of verse used elsewhere in the play, 'the audience would have been uncomfortably aware that it was verse they were hearing'. The purport of his essay *Poetry and Drama* is that poetry written for the stage should not draw to itself the attention of the audience *as poetry*. This practice is followed in his own plays, where the distinction between verse and prose is frequently imperceptible, except possibly to the ear of faith. Yet the notion proved to be attractive, especially to actors, among whom it became a common practice to speak Shakespearean verse in the manner of plain prose.

It was therefore a welcome experience to very many when, in 1948, Christopher Fry, in *The Lady's Not For Burning*, used exuberantly undisguised verse of eloquence and beauty for dramatic-comedy purposes. More than a decade later, that play stood out still as a peak achievement, unchallenged in contemporary poetic drama, while the all-too-brief *A Phoenix Too Frequent* and the full-length *Venus Observ'd* rank only little below it. Later plays by Fry—*A Sleep of Prisoners* and *The Dark is Light Enough*—were more enthusiastically received by critics who had resented the restoration of uninhibited poetry to the stage, and it then seemed that Fry himself, too attentive to critical admonition, had withdrawn to a less exposed position.

Meanwhile, the theatre-going public in general continued to support what it enjoyed, whether or not the sources of its enjoyment were critically approved. Most of the outstandingly popular plays made no pretence of literary merit, though when current intellectual fashions have staled it is not impossible that some popular successes may find their way into the literary canon, as the best of Somerset Maugham's did in the preceding generation. Two at least of Terence Rattigan's plays, *The Winslow Boy* and *The Deep Blue Sea*, can claim a more than casual human significance.

Graham Greene, who had considerable success as playwright and novelist, divided his prose fiction into 'entertainments' and 'novels', and his plays could be similarly divided: the purpose of the entertainments is self-declared, and justified by the enjoyment they provide. The other part of Greene's work—to him no doubt the 'serious' part—is largely though not very effectually concerned with the dry-cleaning of soiled and shabby souls.

Though novels continue to proliferate, their value is of a diminishing order and in inverse proportion to their number. The only contemporary post-Conrad-Wells-Bennett-Galsworthy novelist for whom some degree of continuing wide fame can be forecast with confidence is Joyce Cary. His major gift consisted in the ability to project his imagination into protean forms, so that he *became* the characters of whom he wrote. Cary's most notable work is the trilogy comprising *Herself Surprised*, *To Be a Pilgrim*, and *The Horse's Mouth*, in which the central character, the rascal-painter Gully Jimson, is a Blakesque genius portrayed with absolute convincingness and astounding verve. Joyce Cary was little less successful, if less at all, in characterizing the cockney evacuee children in *Charley is My Darling* and the African men and women in *The African Witch* and *Mister Johnson*. His best novels are traditionally satisfying and experimentally exciting.

The curiously disquieting world of Ivy Compton-Burnett's novels is one in which human beings, particularly of the older generation—parents and their like—have all rags of pretence torn away until they stand shivering in spiritual nakedness. This ruthless operation is achieved by peculiarities of literary method which tend to generate extreme impatience and mental irritation in many readers. Her novels are very largely in dialogue, but as conversation pieces they lack differentiation of tone as between any one speaker and any other. In her choice of themes the author often resembles a gory medieval witch in the clothing of a mumchance Victorian aunt. Her originality, her uniqueness, is absolute. Whether from this will spring the waters of oblivion, or the fruit of immortality rests with the future.

Only passing mention can be made of C. P. Snow, who at the time of this present writing was still engaged on a long sequence of novels with a part-academic, part-scientific setting, both environments being familiar to the author. In the solidity of his style and the leisurely pace of his narrative Snow is a latter-day Trollope, but it is doubtful that his characters will for long be found of enough general interest to justify the length and weight of the narrative.

Angus Wilson's *The Wrong Set* and *Such Darling Dodos* introduced persons and themes 'all horrid', but such was the energy and drive of his style that these short stories were irresistible. When, as a novelist, he turned to larger canvases, his touch seemed less sure, though in *Anglo-Saxon Attitudes*, at least, there are passages of delicious satire. He was aware, as some of his contemporaries were not, that satire is the product of mental maturity and demands more than 'knowingness' and contempt vented in 'a loud barbaric yawp'.

The leap into prominence of Kingsley Amis with *Lucky Jim* was due to public readiness to accept as a richly comic character a 'hero' who exemplified the current admiration of bad manners. To despise one's elders, to burn holes in the bed clothing and sneak away when one is a guest, to go drunk to a public lecture—these exploits were accepted as delicious fun, all part of the gay adolescent adventure of thumbing the nose at one's elders and—unbearable thought—betters.

At the end of the nineteen-fifties the most acclaimed of the newer novelists was William Golding, whose first book *Lord of the Flies* was an exciting feat of creative imagination, though also a terrifying one. Through the story of a group of schoolboys marooned on a remote island, mankind's primitive and perpetual conflict between savagery and civilization is presented. But while *Lord of the Flies* is an allegory, it is not the less a novel, an enthralling piece of story-telling. In subsequent novels Golding was disposed to let allegory and symbolism and a determined pursuit of originality take precedence of story, and by 1959 his future development could only be indicated by a question mark. Similarly with Iris Murdoch, whose *Under the Net* was a novel of exceptional promise, not disproved, even if not wholly sustained, by the three following it.

A significant, much publicized product of the late nineteen-fifties, though of small intrinsic importance, was a volume of essays called *The Establishment*, by intention if not by demonstration a denigrating survey of the Civil Service, Parliament, the Army, the British Broadcasting Corporation, the City (in its control of finance), and the Public Schools. It assumed the existence of an over-riding hidden hand operating secretly behind these institutions and controlling the nation with power divorced from responsibility. The cure for this state of affairs—if it is not a myth—did not appear to be anything better than the setting up of an alternative 'establishment' more to the authors' liking. That, however, is a political matter, not a literary one, and the point of mentioning the book here is only that it includes a reference to the earliest use of the word 'Establishment' in this sense. One of the contributors is said to have 'first used the word in print in September 1955'. It did, however, appear in black and white as long before as 1723 (16 Feb.) when Alexander Pope wrote to a Secretary of State: 'I take myself to be the only Scribbler of my Time, of any degree of distinction, who never received any Places from the Establishment.'

．　　．　　．　　．　　．

Every generation has discovered in its midst 'enemies of books'; and for centuries the theatre has been 'dying'. Powerful enemies of literature and stage drama seemed to be rampant at the middle of the twentieth century, in the mass influence of television, the cinema, and papers with huge circulations but withered conscience. Despite the provision of more and more education it is these popular media of communication rather than the schools which affect public taste and, consequently, literature. If it should be considered extravagant to suggest that in our time credulity, triviality, and barbarism are rapidly broadening down from precedent to precedent, an answer can be given in Thomas Hardy's line:

If way to the Better there be, it exacts a full look at the worst.

That the worst is indeed in our midst appears in the assertion, within a few days of this writing, of a millionaire film magnate: 'My pictures make money— all of them. Horror pays off. The public wants horror, sex, brutality, violence. I give it to them.' This is not a negligible threat, and the current production of much horror and sex-crazed fiction evidences further the debauchery of public taste. Even superior minds— those of professors and bishops to wit—have become insensitive to crime through their appetite for 'thrillers'; while reviewers do nothing, collectively, to influence public opinion, since their standards of good and bad vary so widely from one reviewer to another that they cancel out and afford no guidance whatsoever. The danger is that Gresham's Law will at length operate in literature as in currency and the bad drive out the good.

A hope, perhaps forlorn and possibly final, rests in the genuinely instructed and experienced critic and scholar, who, says Helen Gardner, 'has a different function from that of the artist or original thinker. One of his uses is to help to preserve the creative thought of his own day from provincialism in time, by keeping alive and available to his own age what is neglected or disparaged by those absorbed in the preoccupations of the hour. *His humble task is to protect his betters from the corruption of fashions.*'[1] For 'his betters' let there be substituted 'all of us', and for 'humble' substitute 'vital'.

[1] *The Business of Criticism* (Oxford, 1959), p. 156. My italics.

BIBLIOGRAPHY

LIST OF AUTHORS AND WORKS

INDEX

BIBLIOGRAPHY

IT is best to study English literature one period, or even, in the case of the greatest, one author at a time. In every case the student should see to it that he knows the *text* of his authors; a knowledge of what critics have said about our poets is a poor substitute for a knowledge of what they have said themselves. Poetry ought to be read slowly and carefully, and the reader ought to pay his author the compliment of crediting him with ideas as important as and, on occasion, as abstruse as any in a work of philosophy or abstract science. When the meaning is mastered, the poem ought to be read a second time aloud to catch the magic of the language and the verse. The reading of prose presents less difficulty, but there again the rule is, never allow yourself to be lulled by sound. Reading is an intellectual and not an hypnotic exercise.

The following short bibliography is divided to correspond with the chapters in this book. For the subject as a whole, Chambers's *Cyclopædia of English Literature* (3 vols.), which contains biographical and critical articles on all authors, arranged chronologically and furnished very copiously with specimen passages, may be consulted.

* The books with an asterisk are suggested as those on which reading should be begun. The reader can then proceed to the others and after them to the many authors—great authors—who are not included in this short list.

CHAPTER I.—*More's *Utopia*; *Hakluyt's Voyages* (Ed. John Masefield, Everyman's Library, 8 vols). North's translation of *Plutarch's Lives*.

CHAPTER II.—Surrey's and Wyatt's Poems; *Spenser's Works; Sidney's Poems. A good idea of the atmosphere in which poetry was written can be obtained from Scott's *Kenilworth*, but it is full of inaccuracy in detail.

CHAPTER III.—*The dramatists in the Mermaid Series; *Everyman and other Plays*, ed. by A. W. Pollard (Everyman's Library).

CHAPTER IV.—*Bacon's Essays; Sir Thomas Browne's Works; *Milton's Works; *Poems and Sermons of John Donne; *Poems of Robert Herrick.

CHAPTER V.—*Poems of Dryden; *Poems of Pope; Poems of Thompson; *The Spectator* (Everyman's Library); *Swift's *Gulliver's Travels*; Defoe's Novels.

CHAPTER VI.—*Boswell's *Life of Johnson*; *Burke (in selections); *Sheridan's Plays; Goldsmith's Poems, Plays, and Essays; *Burns's Poetical Works; *Poems of Blake.

CHAPTER VII.—*Wordsworth (Golden Treasury Series); *Wordsworth's *Prelude*; Coleridge's Poems; *Keats's Poems; *Shelley's Poems; *Byron (Golden Treasury Series); *Lamb, *Essays of Elia*; Hazlitt (volumes of Essays in World's Classics series).

CHAPTER VIII.—*Tennyson's Works; *Browning's Works; Rossetti's Works; *Carlyle's *Sartor Resartus*, *Past and Present*, and *French Revolution*; Ruskin's *Unto this Last, Seven Lamps of Architecture*; Arnold's Poems; Swinburne (Selections).

CHAPTER IX.—*Fielding's *Tom Jones*; Smollett's *Roderick Random*; *Jane Austen's *Persuasion, Pride and Prejudice*, and *Northanger Abbey* (as a parody of the Radcliffe School); *Scott's *Heart of Midlothian, Waverley, Antiquary, Ivanhoe, Old Mortality, Bride of Lammermoor*. It seems hardly necessary to give a selection of later novels.

CHAPTER X.—W. B. Yeats's Poems; Wilde's *Importance of Being Earnest*; *Synge's Dramatic Works. And every new work of the best contemporary authors.

G. H. M.

CHAPTER XI.—Works mentioned in the text, and Shaw's complete plays and prefaces; Galsworthy's *The Silver Box, Strife, Justice*, and *Loyalties*; Barrie's *What Every Woman Knows* and *The Twelve-Pound Look*; Somerset Maugham's *The Circle*; Noel Coward's *Hay Fever*. Conrad's *Youth, Typhoon, The Nigger of the 'Narcissus', Chance, The Rescue*, and *The Mirror of the Sea*; D. H. Lawrence's *Sons and Lovers*; Virginia Woolf's *To the Lighthouse, The Waves, Orlando*, and *The Common Reader*. Rupert Brooke's *Selected Poems*; de la Mare's *Collected Poems*; Gerard Hopkins's *Collected Poems*; T. S. Eliot's *Collected Poems*; Winston Churchill's *The Second World War* (1-vol. edn.); G. M. Trevelyan's *English Social History*. Katherine Mansfield's *Collected Short Stories*.

CHAPTER XII.—Works mentioned in the text; and: *Collected Poems* of Walter de la Mare, Wilfred Owen, Edward Thomas, G. K. Chesterton, Hilaire Belloc, Robert Graves, Cecil Day Lewis, W. H. Auden, Dylan Thomas, Andrew Young, Edith Sitwell; Edmund Blunden's *Poems of Many Years*. Sir Osbert Sitwell's *Left Hand, Right Hand* (in 5 vols. with individual titles). Flora Thompson's *Lark Rise to Candleford*. Rose Macaulay's *Told by an Idiot, They Were Defeated, The World My Wilderness*. Sylvia Townsend Warner's *Lolly Willowes, The Corner That Held Them*. Ivy Compton-Burnett's *Elders and Betters*, etc.; C. P. Snow's *Strangers and Brothers*, etc.; William Golding's *The Inheritors, Pincher Martin, Free Fall*; Iris Murdoch's *The Flight from the Enchanter, The Sandcastle, The Bell*.

A. C. W.

LIST OF THE CHIEF AUTHORS AND
WORKS MENTIONED

The dates attached to the authors are those of birth and death; those with the books, of publication.

CHAPTER I

SIR THOMAS MORE, 1480–1535. *Utopia,* 1516 (in Latin).

WILLIAM TINDAL, 1484–1536. *Translation of the New Testament,* 1526.

SIR JOHN CHEKE, 1514–1557.

ROGER ASCHAM, 1515–1568. *Toxophilus,* 1545. *Schoolmaster,* 1570.

RICHARD HAKLUYT, 1553–1616. *Voyages of the English Nation,* 1598.

CHAPTER II

SIR THOMAS WYATT, 1503–1542.

THE EARL OF SURREY, 1517–1547. *Tottel's Miscellany* (containing their poems), 1557.

SIR PHILIP SIDNEY, 1554–1586. *Arcadia,* 1590. *Astrophel and Stella,* 1591.

EDMUND SPENSER, 1552–1599. *Shepheard's Calender,* 1579. *Fairie Queene,* 1589, 1596.

JOHN LYLY, 1554–1606. *Euphues,* 1579. *Euphues and his England,* 1580.

RICHARD HOOKER, 1553–1600. *Ecclesiastical Polity,* 1594.

CHAPTER III

CHRISTOPHER MARLOWE, 1564–1593. *Tamburlaine,* 1587 (date of performance). *Dr. Faustus,* 1588 (date of performance). *Edward II,* 1593.

THOMAS KYD, 1557 (?)–1595 (?). *The Spanish Tragedy,* 1594 (published).

JOHN WEBSTER, 1580 (?)–1625 (?). *The White Devil,*
1608 (date of performance). *Duchess of Malfi,* 1616
(date of performance).

BEN JONSON, 1573–1637. *Every Man in his Humour,*
1598. *Volpone,* 1605. *Poems,* 1616.

CHAPTER IV

JOHN DONNE, 1573–1631. *Poems,* 1633 (first published,
but known, like those of all Elizabethan poets, in
manuscript long before).

WILLIAM BROWNE, 1591–1643.

GEORGE HERBERT, 1593–1633.

ROBERT HERRICK, 1593–1674.

RICHARD CRASHAW, 1613–1649.

FRANCIS BACON, 1561–1626. *Advancement of Learning,*
1605. *Essays,* 1625.

THE BIBLE, *Authorised Version,* 1611.

ROBERT BURTON, 1577–1640. *Anatomy of Melancholy,*
1621.

SIR THOMAS BROWNE, 1605–1682. *Religio Medici,* 1642.

JOHN BUNYAN, 1628–1688. *Pilgrim's Progress,* 1678.

JOHN MILTON, 1608–1674. *Paradise Lost,* 1667. *Paradise Regained* and *Samson Agonistes,* 1671.

CHAPTER V

JOHN DRYDEN, 1631–1700. *Absolom and Achitophel* and
Religio Laici, 1682. *The Hind and the Panther,* 1687.

ALEXANDER POPE, 1688–1744. *Essay on Criticism,* 1711.
Rape of the Lock, 1714.

JAMES THOMSON, 1700–1748. *The Seasons,* 1730.

DANIEL DEFOE, 1661–1731. *Robinson Crusoe,* 1719.

JONATHAN SWIFT, 1667–1745. *The Tale of a Tub,* 1704.
Gulliver's Travels, 1726.

JOSEPH ADDISON, 1672–1719.

RICHARD STEELE, 1675–1729. *The Tatler,* 1709–1711.
The Spectator, 1711–1712.

CHAPTER VI

SAMUEL JOHNSON, 1709–1784.
EDMUND BURKE, 1728–1797.
OLIVER GOLDSMITH, 1728–1774.
THOMAS GRAY, 1716–1771.
WILLIAM COLLINS, 1721–1759.
ROBERT BURNS, 1759–1796. *Poems*, 1786.
WILLIAM BLAKE, 1757–1827. *Songs of Innocence*, 1789.

CHAPTER VII

WILLIAM WORDSWORTH, 1770–1850. *Lyrical Ballads*, 1798.
SAMUEL TAYLOR COLERIDGE, 1772–1834.
SIR WALTER SCOTT, 1771–1832.
LORD BYRON, 1788–1824. *Childe Harold's Pilgrimage*, 1812–1817.
PERCY BYSSHE SHELLEY, 1792–1822.
JOHN KEATS, 1795–1821.
CHARLES LAMB, 1775–1834. *Essays of Elia*, 1823.
WILLIAM HAZLITT, 1778–1830.
THOMAS DE QUINCEY, 1785–1859.

CHAPTER VIII

LORD TENNYSON, 1809–1892. *Poems*, 1842. *Idylls of the King*, 1859.
ROBERT BROWNING, 1812–1889. *Men and Women*, 1855. *The Ring and the Book*, 1868.
D. G. ROSSETTI, 1828–1882.
WILLIAM MORRIS, 1834–1896.
A. C. SWINBURNE, 1836–1909.
THOMAS CARLYLE, 1795–1880.
JOHN RUSKIN, 1819–1900.

CHAPTER IX

SAMUEL RICHARDSON, 1689–1761. *Pamela*, 1740. *Clarissa Harlowe*, 1750.

HENRY FIELDING, 1707–1754. *Joseph Andrews*, 1742. *Tom Jones*, 1749.

JANE AUSTEN, 1775–1817.

WILLIAM MAKEPEACE THACKERAY, 1811–1863.

CHARLES DICKENS, 1812–1870.

GEORGE MEREDITH, 1832–1909.

CHAPTER X

EDWARD FITZGERALD, 1809–1883. *The Rubáiyát of Omar Khayyám*, 1859.

OSCAR WILDE, 1854–1900.

GEORGE BERNARD SHAW, 1856–1950. *Plays Pleasant and Unpleasant*, 1898: *Widower's Houses*; *Mrs. Warren's Profession*; *Arms and the Man*.

RUDYARD KIPLING, 1865–1936.

WILLIAM BUTLER YEATS, 1865–1929.

JOHN MILLINGTON SYNGE, 1871–1909. *Riders to the Sea*, 1904. *The Well of the Saints*, 1905. *The Playboy of the Western World*, 1907.

G. H. M.

CHAPTER XI

THOMAS HARDY, 1840–1928. *The Dynasts*, 1904–8.

GERARD HOPKINS, 1844–89.

ROBERT BRIDGES, 1844–1930. *Eros and Psyche*, 1894. *The Testament of Beauty*, 1929.

GEORGE MOORE, 1852–1933. *Esther Waters*, 1894. *The Brook Kerith*, 1916. *Héloïse and Abélard*, 1921.

GEORGE BERNARD SHAW, 1856–1950. *Back to Methuselah*, 1921. *Saint Joan*, 1924.

JOSEPH CONRAD (Josef Konrad Korzeniowski), 1857–1924. *Lord Jim*, 1900. *The Secret Sharer* (in *'Twixt Land and Sea*, 1912).

ALFRED EDWARD HOUSMAN, 1859–1936. *A Shropshire Lad*, 1896.

SIR JAMES MATTHEW BARRIE, 1860–1937. *Quality Street*, 1901. *Peter Pan*, 1904.

HERBERT GEORGE WELLS, 1866–1946. *Tono-Bungay*, 1909. *The History of Mr. Polly*, 1910.

(ENOCH) ARNOLD BENNETT, 1867–1931. *The Old Wives' Tale*, 1908. *Riceyman Steps*, 1923. *Imperial Palace*, 1930.

JOHN GALSWORTHY, 1867–1933. *Strife*, 1909. *The Skin Game*, 1920. *The Forsyte Saga*, 1922.

SOMERSET MAUGHAM, 1874—. *Liza of Lambeth*, 1897. *Of Human Bondage*, 1915. *The Moon and Sixpence*, 1919. *The Circle*, 1921. *Our Betters*, 1923. *Cakes and Ale*, 1930.

EDWARD MORGAN FORSTER, 1879—. *Howards End*, 1910. *A Passage to India*, 1924.

(GILES) LYTTON STRACHEY, 1880–1932. *Eminent Victorians*, 1918.

JOHN DRINKWATER, 1882–1937. *Abraham Lincoln*, 1918.

VIRGINIA WOOLF, 1882–1941.

JAMES JOYCE, 1882–1941. *Ulysses*, 1922. *Finnegans Wake*, 1939.

SEAN O'CASEY, 1884—. *Juno and the Paycock*, 1925. *The Plough and the Stars*, 1926.

DAVID HERBERT LAWRENCE, 1885–1930.

RUPERT BROOKE, 1887–1915. *1914 and other Poems*, 1915.

EDITH SITWELL, 1887—.

THOMAS STEARNS ELIOT, 1888—. *The Waste Land*, 1922. *Four Quartets* (1936-42).

JAMES BRIDIE, 1888–1951. *Tobias and the Angel*, 1931. *A Sleeping Clergyman*, 1933. *Mr. Bolfry*, 1943.

ALDOUS HUXLEY, 1894—. *Point Counter Point*, 1928. *Brave New World*, 1932.

NOEL COWARD, 1899—.

CHAPTER XII

WALTER DE LA MARE (1873-1956).
JOHN MAYNARD KEYNES (LORD KEYNES) (1883-1946).
JOYCE CARY (1888-1957).
GEORGE ORWELL (1903-50).
W. H. AUDEN (1907-   ).
CHRISTOPHER FRY (1907-   ).
DYLAN THOMAS (1914-53).

A. C. W.

INDEX

Printed in Great Britain by
The Camelot Press Ltd., London and Southampton